CRITICAL DIALOGUES IN SOUTHEAST ASIAN STUDIES
Charles Keyes, Vicente Rafael, and Laurie J. Sears, Series Editors

†HE
NEW
WAY

PROTESTANTISM
and the HMONG
in VIETNAM

Tâm T. T. Ngô

UNIVERSITY OF WASHINGTON PRESS
Seattle and London

The New Way *was published with the assistance of grants from the Charles and Jane Keyes Endowment for Books on Southeast Asia, established through the generosity of Charles and Jane Keyes, and from the Southeast Asia Center in the Jackson School of International Studies at the University of Washington.*

UNIVERSITY OF WASHINGTON PRESS
www.washington.edu/uwpress

LIBRARY OF CONGRESS CATALOGING-IN-PUBLICATION DATA
Names: Ngo, Tam T. T., 1980– author.
Title: The new way : Protestantism and the Hmong in Vietnam / Tâm T.T. Ngô.
Description: Seattle : University of Washington Press, [2016] |
    Series: Critical dialogues in Southeast Asian studies |
    Includes bibliographical references and index.
Identifiers: LCCN 2016015368 | ISBN 9780295998275 (hardcover : alk. paper)
Subjects: LCSH: Protestantism—Vietnam. | Hmong (Asian people)—Vietnam—
    Religion. | Vietnam—Church history. | Ethnology—Vietnam.
Classification: LCC BR1187 .N46 2016 | DDC 305.6/804089959720597—dc23
LC record available at https://lccn.loc.gov/2016015368

For Peter, Linh, and Koos

CONTENTS

ACKNOWLEDGMENTS

This book is the result of a long research project during which I have accumulated a considerable debt to a number of institutions and people. This research project would not have been possible without the financial and institutional supports of The Department of Social and Cultural Anthropology at the Vrije Universiteit Amsterdam, The Netherlands Organization for Scientific Research (NWO), The Amsterdam Institute for International Development (AIID), The Southeast Asian Summer Study Institute (SEASSI) at the University of Madison, Wisconsin, Harvard Yenching Institute at Harvard University, and the Max Planck Institute for the Study of Ethnic and Religious Diversity, in Gottingen.

First among the people who have been most important to my research are my Hmong interlocutors, both Christian and non-Christian, both in Vietnam and in the United States. They opened their homes to me and shared with me their emotions and thoughts. They took considerable risks by engaging systematically with my inquiries into their past and present. I am grateful to them for accepting me and I have cherished the moments we shared. Unfortunately, for political reasons, I cannot give their names here but this book is first and foremost dedicated to them.

On my academic journey that leads to the publication of this book, I am indebted to a number of remarkable scholars. Adam Yuet Chau, Richard Madsen, Joel Robbins, and Louisa Schein have given precious feedback on different parts of the book. Peggy Lewitt, Patrick Eisenlohr, Peter Pels, (the late) Frans Hüsken, Peter Zinoman, Ken MacLean, Jacob Hickman, Justine Quijada, and Tavy Vorng all gave me important comments and criticism. I am thankful to Charles F. Keyes and Lorri Hagman at the University of Washington Press for believing in the value of my ethnography and for supporting the publication of this book.

My special appreciation goes to Oscar Salemink, Nguyễn Văn Huy and Birgit Meyer. In a graduate class at the University of Amsterdam twelve years ago, I stood up to challenge a guest lecturer about his critical view of the Vietnamese government regarding questions of religion and ethnicity. Although he jokingly accused me of being a "communist believer," the guest speaker since then has given me ample chance to deconvert; Oscar Salemink, my Thầy, has helped me to grow from a stubborn "communist believer" into an independent-minded scholar. His critical and insightful knowledge of Vietnam has been the source for my intellectual growth and I am most grateful for that. He also introduced me to Thầy Huy—Professor Nguyễn Văn Huy—then the director of Vietnam Museum of Ethnology (VME) in Hanoi who became my guardian. Not only has Thầy Huy shouldered considerable political inconveniency in order to provide me with the necessary permission for my fieldwork research in Vietnam, his perceptive advice and his kindness to me are so much appreciated. Finally, it was Birgit Meyer who gave a boost to my intellectual growth. Her expert knowledge and subtle insight in the study of religious conversion and media has made a lasting impact on my scholarship for which I am forever thankful.

Of extraordinary value has been the enthusiastic support of Nicholas Tapp, the most remarkable social anthropologist and Hmong specialist whose recent untimely departure from this world devastated me. Nick was most generous in giving time to my project from its very beginning and throughout every step of its development. In a conference in Thailand eleven years ago, Nick sat in a row behind me. Looking over my shoulder he saw the title of my research proposal and he asked whether he could have a look. Two days later, out of the blue I received five pages of comments from Nick. This was just the beginning of a series of long email exchanges between us in which Nick's comments on my writings, be they grant proposals, articles to be published or drafts of my book, were only getting longer. Besides their amazing detail and sheer quantity, Nick's comments were precious sources of information, of sharp and constructive criticism, or insightful suggestions and of brilliant ideas.

Another invaluable source of intellectual support has been Cô Huệ Tâm— Professor Hue Tam Ho-Tai—at Harvard University. Since 2012, she has helped me to revise the final manuscript of this book. Being a historian of modern Vietnam with a razor sharp analytical mind and an eager eye for details, Hue Tam has patiently showed me many ways to improve my argument and refine the presentation of the book. She and her husband, chú Patrick, helped to make my stay in Harvard Yenching Institute in 2012 productive and homey with their warm welcome and hospitality.

This book would definitely not have been written without the love, care, and support of a number of people who are dear to me. My deepest gratitude goes to my parents who created a love for books and for learning in me. It was my late father, Ngô Hữu Khoa who brought me to the Hmong and it is my deepest sorrow that I will never be able to tell him my own experience of being accepted by the people who had once accepted and loved him. My mother, Đỗ Thị Phấn, has made immeasurable sacrifices after my father passed away to provide my brothers and me with the education we have needed. My aunt, Cô Phương, has helped me to obtain all kinds of research permissions and necessary local connections to facilitate my fieldwork in Lào Cai. My grandmother, Bà Nội, whose recent passing has deeply saddened me, has given me a sense of protection and encouragement. Rob has given me much needed support and the confidence that I could pursue an academic career. My Hmong friend Ilean Her not only generously welcomed me to her home in Saint Paul and gave me the care of an older sister, she also helped me to understand the complex politics of being a Southeast Asian minority in America.

My most profound tribute goes to my beloved Peter. If it had not been for him, who encouraged me (and actually pushed me, especially when I seem too immersed in the joys of motherhood since late 2013), this book would not have been finished. His support came not only in words but also in written comments and brilliant advice after painstakingly reading every chapter and every draft of the book. I feel lucky to know that I can count on his intellect as an inexhaustible source of inspiration and on his witty humor to enlighten every day of our life together. In late 2013, our household became busier, and even jollier, with the arrival of Linh and Koos. I dedicate this book to my van der Veers.

Administrative divisions of Vietnam

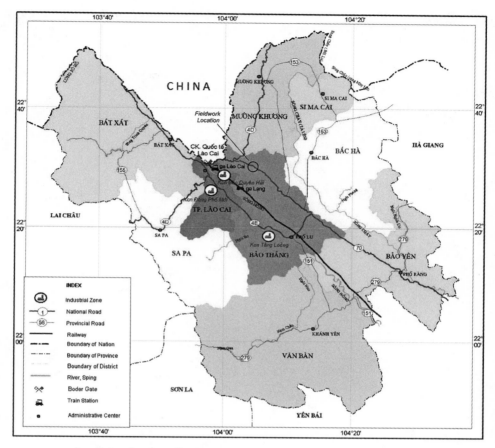

Lao Cai and surrounding areas

THE NEW WAY

The author, dressed up by Mrs. Gi for church on Sunday morning

INTRODUCTION

Old and New

Men make their own history, but they do not make it just as they please; they do not make it under circumstances chosen by themselves, but under circumstances directly encountered, given and transmitted from the past. The tradition of all the dead generations weighs like a nightmare on the brain of the living.

KARL MARX, *THE EIGHTEENTH BRUMAIRE OF LOUIS BONAPARTE*

O N the eve of the Lunar New Year, 2005, I helped Mr. Gi prepare the last ritual of the Hmong traditional New Year. He and I were alone in the house, and he was grateful for my assistance in setting up a new altar for the *dab txhiaj meej*, the spirit of wealth and prosperity, and the *dab roog*, the guardian spirit of the house. A bunch of freshly plucked chicken feathers and a ceremonial paper in his left hand, Mr. Gi slowly hoisted himself onto a wobbly wooden chair. Keeping the chair steady with one hand, I held out with the other a little bowl of glue made from cooked sticky rice flour. Dipping his thumb in the glue and smearing it on the paper, Mr. Gi carefully attached the ceremonial paper to the wooden wall outside and above the main door to the house, and then he attached the chicken feather to the paper. The door was significantly taller than those of most Hmong houses, so decorating its lintel was an arduous job, but finally, it was done. Still standing on the chair, Mr. Gi began to recite an incantation. The relatively short chant sounded melancholic. The night grew gloomier.

Ordinarily, the task of preparing for the New Year would be shared among all members of a Hmong family; but, after quarreling with him all afternoon

3

about his desire to carry out the ancient rituals, his wife and three adult children had gone to a neighbor's house to listen to an evangelical radio broadcast. Accustomed as I had become to the family's frequent conflicts since coming to stay with the Gis more than a month earlier, I was still taken aback by the intensely sad atmosphere in the house that night. Like the Chinese or Vietnamese, most Hmong avoid conflict at this time of year in the hope of ushering in a harmonious New Year. For them, the New Year is the most important time of the year, a vital moment in which ties with ancestors are renewed. The ancestral and domestic spirits of the family are honored through the ritual redecoration of altars in and around the house, and food is offered by the head of the family. The Hmong New Year becomes meaningful once these rituals have been performed in the household. For this reason, it is also the time of year when the unity of the family and the household is affirmed and ritually sanctioned. On New Year's Eve, it is essential that the family stay together. Yet, the performance of this all-important ritual had caused dissent and discord in the Gi family.

What had happened to this family? The brief answer is that after nearly a decade of "experimenting" with Christianity, Mr. Gi had chosen to return to his ancestral worship, while Mrs. Gi and their children preferred to remain members of the church. The divergent ways Mr. Gi and his family chose to mark the New Year—he by performing ancient rituals, his wife and children by listening to a religious program broadcast from the United States—encapsulate the tensions between old and new caused by the introduction of evangelical Protestantism to the Hmong of Vietnam in the 1980s. About a third of the more than one million Hmong living in Vietnam have converted to Protestantism. The rest includes some who have steadfastly resisted the appeal of Protestantism or, as in the case of Mr. Gi, have chosen to return to their ancestral faith. While Mr. Gi clings to the old religious beliefs and practices at the core of Hmong identity, his wife and children are connected via these radio broadcasts to the transnational Hmong diaspora, which came into being after the end of the Second Indochina War (1965–75) and now encompasses not only Vietnam but also Laos, Thailand, Myanmar, the United States, France, and Australia. Mr. Gi and his family are part of the story of the spread of evangelical Protestantism throughout the world, a phenomenon that is at once global and highly local.

This book addresses the interplay between the global reach of Christianity and the ways in which it is articulated in the Vietnamese Hmong society. It approaches the emergence of Hmong Protestantism from various perspectives, those of the Hmong converts and non-converts as well as those of the deconverted, of the Vietnamese state authorities, and of the missionaries. One of the classic narratives of Christian conversion is modeled on that of Saint Paul: a sudden flash of insight and a complete transformation. In fact, however, conversion is a complex social phenomenon that takes place in specific political circumstances. Conversion to Christianity in the Roman Empire is different from conversion from Catholicism to Protestantism in early modern Europe and from conversion under colonial or postcolonial conditions. In all these cases the relation to state power is crucial. In Vietnam, therefore, conversion not only means change of belief, but also a different relation to the state and, very crucially, to one's kin group. While the emphasis in the narrative of conversion is on the individual's change of heart it is actually the social realm that is first transformed. This is immediately clear in the fact that the Hmong have converted in massive numbers, although not in their entirety.

To explore the different social and individual aspects of what conversion means for the Hmong, this book pays close attention to the way in which Hmong people—converts and non-converts—make sense of their community, locality, and identity in space and time, especially in the face of the material and moral challenges that globalization presents to them. In describing the peculiar way in which the Hmong have received the evangelical message, I suggest a resonance with the Hmong's own messianic beliefs. I also address their longing to escape condition of marginality—geographic, socioeconomic, political—and their aspiration for modernity, however defined over the course of the twentieth century, by different actors: the Vietnamese state, with its sudden shifts in policy, the US–based Hmong diaspora which supplies both missionaries and audio-visual illustrations of global modernity. What is the impact of conversion on the converts' sense of self through their discovery of sin? The New Way, as converts often refer to evangelical Protestantism, reshapes crucial dimensions of Hmong lives; it even affects those who refuse to convert, or whom, having converted, decide to return to their old beliefs and practices. All must interact and be affected by the New Way, including the Vietnamese state authorities.

TIME AND HISTORY

The conversion of marginalized ethnic groups of people, like the Hmong, to Christianity is an important theme in the vast and fast-growing anthropological study on the process of modernization and globalization in postcolonial societies (Hefner 1993; van der Veer 1996; Aragon 2000; Steedly 1993, Tsing 1993, Keyes 1996; Robbins 2004; Keane 2007). Such conversion often involves the incorporation into a broader social order that brings not just technological and political transformations of traditional lifeways, but also far-reaching adjustments in the canon of divinity, identity and social ethics as well (Hefner 1993:3). The reformation of identity and morality that takes place through intellectual contact can be mediated by other sociocultural arrangements as well

(Hefner 1993:3). Ethnicity, nationalism, and political ideology, among others, can play such role. Religious, ethnic, and regionalist idioms are often interwoven in the same social movements (1993:35).

In this study of Hmong conversion, I do not attribute primacy to religious idioms in the reconstruction of Hmong macrocosmic identities. Rather I seek to place religion alongside other cultural media involved in the elaboration of the trans-local Hmong community. My analysis involves a discussion of the simultaneity of different perceptions of time and history that allows us to see the "coevalness" (Fabian 1983) of the Hmong (both in Vietnam and in the United States), the Kinh majority and the Communist authorities in Vietnam, and the Christian missionaries. The denial of the "coevalness" of the Hmong is clearest in the denunciation of the "backwardness" of the Hmong by the Communist authorities. It is the evolutionism in Marxist theory that puts the Hmong firmly in an earlier stage of historical evolution, so to speak. The Hmong practice swidden agriculture and are thus considered to be lagging behind the Kinh peasantry which itself is lagging behind the industrial nations of the world. The task of communism as a historical agent in the world is to bring the Vietnamese people to the same level as the capitalist nations, but without the great inequalities that characterize capitalism. The formulation of this task has become more problematic since Vietnam launched its program of economic reforms known as *Đổi Mới* in 1986 and now participates in a globalized market. Thus, a simple reference to Marxist conceptions of time and history is not sufficient to understand the complexity of the developmental strategies that are deployed to bring the Hmong up to speed. One of the challenges for the Hmong is that they are supposed to strive to achieve a level of development, that of the Kinh, which the latter are enjoined to leave (as soon as they can), creating a perpetual race to "catch up" that characterizes even the highest levels of Asian economies (see Miyazaki 2003).

Christian missionaries see themselves at the opposite end of the spectrum from Communist cadres, and the Communists agree. With the exception of the liberation theology movement in mid-twentieth century Latin America and other parts of the world, the anti-communist legacy of Christianity (especially American Christianity) and the anti-Christian legacy of Communism are enduring and deep-rooted. Ironically, they are each products of nineteenth-century Western notions of progress and modernity, and their understanding of history has much in common. Like the Communist state and its agents, Christian missionaries see the Hmong as 'backward' and consider their culture an "irrational" impediment to progress. Like the Communists, they want rid the Hmong of their traditions in order to bring them to the light. In the most practical terms, missionaries and the Communist authorities compete as agents of change. While the Communist authorities use the resources of the state, the missionaries use the resources of a global, largely US–based, transnational movement. The competition is couched in the language of communism versus individual freedom, of communism versus capitalism, of sovereignty against foreign interference, but at an ideological level Christianity and Communism share not only an understanding of progressivist history, but also of utopia and messianic time.

The Hmong are caught between these powerful historical actors and these different perceptions of time and history. Although they may not be seen "coeval" by missionaries or communists, the Hmong they are in fact acting and interpreting a history that is not of their own making. Their own perception of time and history is deeply embedded in the life of the community and in their kinship relations. On the one hand their sense of time and history is focused on the continuity between generations; on the other hand they have a strong belief in messianic time and anticipate a moment of revolutionary change. Their rituals are part of the maintenance of these continuities, but at the same time the belief in a revolutionary moment in which the Hmong king will return to unite the Hmong and create an independent kingdom. Both communist and Christian utopianism can be related to Hmong messianism, but the personal return of Christ fits Hmong messianism better than the ever-delayed paradise on earth promised by communism. Much of this book is devoted to the inner conflicts of messianism, Christian conversion, and the maintenance of community and kinship among the Hmong in contemporary Vietnam.

MILLENARIANISM THROUGH THE AIRWAVES

Like the Urapmin of Papua New Guinea who converted en masse to Protestantism (Robbins 2004), the Hmong of Vietnam were not initially missionized. But unlike the Urapmin, the Hmong did not seek out the Christian message by sending members to Baptist seminaries; it can almost be said to have sought them out in the form of the Far East Broadcasting Company's proselytizing program in the Hmong language in 1980. They were first exposed to the broadcast program by happenstance, as some fumbled with newly acquired radios and accidentally heard voices speaking in their own language. Later, Hmong missionaries came to Vietnam from overseas to spread the Protestant Gospel further, but the chief vehicle of Hmong conversion remains the religious broadcasts, which are unintelligible to the Kinh officials in charge of maintaining order.

The rapid adoption by local Hmong of evangelical Protestantism can be attributed to its heavy emphasis on the Second Coming of Christ which resonates with traditional Hmong millenarianism. During the early period of "accidental hearing" of the Christian proselytizing program broadcast by the Far East Broadcasting Company (FEBC), many Hmong interpreted FEBC's stories about God (or Vang Tsu, the Hmong name for both the traditional messiah and for God) as being about the mythical Hmong King. Another common name for Vang Tsu is Fua Tais. Enshrined in Hmong folklore as the "Lord of the Sky," Fua Tais has been the core of Hmong messianism, which, according to Tapp (1989), is an inherent part of Hmong traditional beliefs. The Hmong believe that in times immemorial, they had a country of their own somewhere in China, ruled by a kind-hearted and powerful Hmong king. The Hmong kingdom was once prosperous and unified, but then the evil Han Chinese came and treacherously trapped and then killed the beloved king. Ever since, the Hmong have lived a life of constant exodus and suffering. However, the king announced before his death that he would return one day to rescue the Hmong from their suffering and bring the righteous kingdom back to them.

Millenarian beliefs and practices are not unique to the Hmong. They have long been part of mainstream Chinese and Vietnamese popular religion and have always been interpreted by the imperial states of these two countries as potential inspiration for rebellion; they were banned as heretical and their followers were subjected to violent campaigns of suppression. The communist states inherited this tradition of suspicion and suppression to which was added the Marxist belief that religion is the opiate of the masses. But in Vietnam and China, there are significant similarities between the millenarian and communist messages (Tai 1983; Galbiatti 2005). In China, Peng Pai, one of the founders of the Chinese Communist Party, found that, in order to convert peasants to communism, he had to eschew Marxist terminology and adopt the more familiar language of traditional Chinese millenarianism. A very similar language was deployed a decade later by the Hòa Hảo in southern Vietnam, enabling it to compete for the allegiance of the peasantry against communist recruiters. A similarly uneasy dynamic can be found in Hmong receptivity to Protestant proselytization and the communist state's hostility to it.

COMPETING PATHWAYS TO MODERNITY

Both China, where the Hmong originated, and northern Vietnam, where the subjects of this book reside, spent much of the twentieth century striving to achieve modernity along Marxist-Leninist lines. When the State Commission for Electrification of Russia was established in 1920, Lenin (1920) famously proclaimed: "Communism is Soviet power with electrification of the whole country." Lenin's goal was "the organization of industry on the basis of modern, advanced technology, on electrification which will provide a link between town and country, will put an end to the division between town and country, will make it possible to raise the level of culture in the countryside and to overcome backwardness, ignorance, poverty, disease, and barbarism." Mao's China and postcolonial northern Vietnam under the Việt Minh did not succeed in electrifying the whole country or ending the division between town and country. But they assiduously pursued Lenin's agenda of eradicating "backwardness, ignorance, poverty, disease, and barbarism" through centralized planning and relentless mobilization campaigns.

A first step in the Việt Minh government's plan for political struggle and development campaigns was the creation of a classification scheme that distributed different ethnic groups along an evolutionary spectrum, in which some were more advanced than others (Harrell 1993; Keyes 2002). The creation of this classification scheme expressed the Kinh majority population's sense of ethno-cultural superiority and belief in the backwardness of ethnic communities, including the Hmong, who occupied "the most remote corners of the land." In the name of modernization and development, minority communities were subjected to a rapid series of campaigns aimed at radically transforming their traditional lifeways. Their religious beliefs and practices—the core of their identity as Hmong—were deemed superstitions that must be eradicated. Through campaign after campaign, tensions between Hmong and the state and its agents intensified.

Today, modernity, for both the Vietnamese state and the Hmong, has taken on new meaning. The previous developmental style of centralized planning and constant mobilization campaigns has given way to a market-driven economy combined with the retention of the communist one-party system. All over the country, billboards exhort the population to embrace "modernization with Vietnamese characteristics." This is the slogan of the Đổi Mới era, which began in the late 1980s. While the Đổi Mới reforms have raised the standards of living for the majority kinh population, some of their consequences have been deleterious to the Hmong, as for other minority communities, who continue to suffer from "backwardness, poverty, ignorance, disease."

When it made its way to the Hmong through the electronic medium of radio broadcasting, Evangelical Protestantism immediately presented a powerful vision of modernity, one that is highly competitive to the blurred vision promoted by Vietnamese state. With the same promises of modernity as communism, Protestantism offers the possibility of alternative paths to development that are not connected to the Party-State and do not seek the subjugation of personal interests to those of the state. Conversion to Protestantism, for many Hmong in Vietnam, is not just a means to remove themselves from their perceived marginalized situation. Conversion is also a type of passage, a passage via the channel of Christianity, which will lead them to the new landscape of modernity.

CONVERSION AND SUBJECTIVITY

In his introduction to *Conversion to Modernities*, Peter van der Veer (1996) notes that conversion "became a prime locus when technologies of the self and of colonial domination converged." Referring to the case of India in the nineteenth century, van der Veer points out that while there were substantial disagreements between missionary societies and colonial authorities, both parties fundamentally agreed that the colonized had to be converted to modernity. He also suggests that conversion to forms of Christianity in the modern period is not only a conversion to modern forms of these religions, but also to religious forms of modernity.

Whether under socialism or the new market-driven economy, the pursuit of modernity is not just about transforming objective living conditions, but also about creating new subjectivities. The moral understanding of progress and agency has always been embedded in the vision of modernity that the Vietnamese state has promoted. This moral dimension prevailed in the consciences of Kinh cadres who felt the need to convert the Hmong people to socialism and to mold them into the "New Socialist Person." In the post–Đổi Mới era, it has taken the form of judgment on the Hmong's failure to catch up with modernization and marketization. This book shows the extent to which the moral narrative of modernity can go as far as contributing to the formation of Hmong individuals' conscience in relation to modernity. What is often at work here is not only that Hmong people are subjects to be converted to modernity by political (state) and religious (missionaries) agents, but that Hmong converts themselves are agents who are actively seeking ways to embrace modernity. Marginality is what impels them to convert to modernity.

Webb Keane (2007) in his groundbreaking *Christian Moderns: Freedom and Fetish in the Mission Encounter* observes that across the ethnographical spectrum, the idea of the modern is crucial to historical self-understanding. In a concrete, though heterogeneous way, modernity is understood as a form of social imagination that features two distinctive characteristics: one of rupture from the traditional past and one of progress into a better future. Modernity is part of elite and popular discourses, imaginings, and desires. Christian imaginaries, as Keane (2007) shows, have had an effect across the postcolonial world that can be attributed to their coupling of religion with certain concepts of modernity and vice versa. This coupling is twofold: empirically, as a result of colonial and postcolonial circumstances during which many people first experienced what they understood to be modernity as having a Christian faith; and conceptually, in that both modernity and conversion are about the making of a new personhood, or individual subjectivity, both of which share the assumption of the superiority of the "new" over the inferiority of the "old." Keane (2007: 47) points out that there are aspects of the very idea of modernity that seem to have been shaped in a dialectical relationship to a moral understanding of progress and agency.

This moral narrative has affinities with aspects of Protestantism, especially as it developed in the era of evangelical and Enlightenment challenges. Religious perceptions of the self, of community, and of the state are transformed when Western discourses of modernity become dominant in the modern world (van der Veer 1996). A call for humans to act upon history, a call that in Foucault's (1984:42) terms would involve an "ironic heroization of the present" and demand that one produces oneself, is also often encompassed in the moral narrative of modernity that Keane (2007) discusses. When concepts and narratives of modernity are coupled with that of conversion, narratives of conversion are transformed and a central problem arises: the assertion of authenticity and sincerity (Keane 2002). The "authentication of the present is often in terms of continuity with the past, but in both modernity and conversion, there is a deep ambivalence about the past" (van der Veer 1996: 18). This ambivalence can also be seen as a novelty in the way religious conversion is perceived today.

Religious conversion appears to need explaining in a way that secular conversion to modern ways of being does not (Asad 1996: 263). Nonreligious persons today tend to think of the shift to modern life in a similar way. They want to know what is involved in living a modern life, not why people are motivated to become modern. Anthropologist Talad Asad points out that, like the truth, modernity seems to justify itself: "Religious conversion is usually thought of as 'irrational' because it happens to people rather than being something that they choose to become after careful thought. And yet most individuals enter modernity rather as converts enter a new religion—as a consequence of forces beyond their control. Modernity, like the convert's religion, defines new choices; it is rarely the result of an entirely 'free choice'. And like the convert's religion, it annihilates old possibilities and puts others in their place" (1996: 263).

In many respects, modernity is also as much a story people tell about their *own past* as about that of *others*—but it captures something important: something Keane (2007) names "the moral narrative of modernity," the narrative that often has a normative, even moralistic, thrust to it. It goes so far as to suggest that if one resists becoming modern, one can harm not only oneself but also one's community, or even one's nation, as in the case of Indonesia to which

Keane (2007: 48) refers. This story is certainly similar to other parts of the world that have been called "developing" and where developmental states have been the force of a nation's historical development. This book does not take a well-defined concept of modernity but instead pays attention to the way people like the Hmong and their lives and ways of thinking are shaped through the interaction with various "civilizing," "modernizing," and "globalizing" forces. The "moral narrative of modernity" is employed by state developmental agents, Hmong missionaries, and the Hmong themselves. For the state developmental agents, to make the Hmong modern is to make them submit their own interests, be it socioeconomic or political, to that of the nation-state. For Hmong missionaries from America, to convert their Asian Hmong fellows is to remit modernity to their homelands. For the Vietnamese Hmong converts, to convert to Christianity is to answer the call to modernize and to empower themselves against the backdrop of their group's deepening marginality.

For many Hmong people, the aspiration to become modern via the act of conversion conveys a deeper philosophical message, one that defines the role and meaning of religion in individual and community life. While acknowledging the theoretical merit of the recent literature on conversion that re-theologizes subjectivity invoking Derrida, Badiou, and Zizek who focus on the abrupt conversion of the Apostle Paul (Engelke and Robbins 2010), I want to make it clear that this perspective is not useful for a sociological understanding of what conversion means for the Hmong. Although, Christianity is known by the Hmong as the *new way* (*kev cai tshiab*), conversion in the Hmong case is as much about a rupture highlighted in the nascent anthropology of Christianity (Robbins 2006) as about the continuity and dialogues between the "Old" to the "New" selves. After two decades of Christianization, the persistence of the old way among at least two-thirds of the Hmong population poses complicated questions about change, continuity, religiosity, and morality.

For the converts, the aspiration to be modern and the moral narrative of modernity have impacted their sense of community commitment and their deepest sense of the self. This is clearly observable in discourses over sex that recently emerged and circulated among Hmong converts. Both modernity and conversion are about the making of a new personhood or the construction of individual subjectivity, and both assume the superiority of the "new" over the "old" (Keane 2007: 47). Under the sway of conversion, social mechanisms and concepts such as sex, soul, spirits, and just about everything else in Hmong society, are liable to change. Such transformation of Hmong subjectivity, of ways of being Hmong, is encompassing. In everyday life, conversion challenges traditional assumptions about proper sexual practice, alcohol consumption, gender roles and relationship between generations and between clan members.

A new sense of personhood of the individual is emerging against the background of traditional kinship relations and community bonds.

One area where the transformation of Hmong subjectivity is most profound is the attitude toward ancestors and nature (for example, the material embodiment of the spiritual world). Not all are willing to undergo such a radical transformation. The ongoing resistance to Christianity and the phenomenon of deconversion—the conscious act of undoing conversion after a significant period of experimentation with the Christian faith—are rooted in a belief in the indissoluble bond with ancestors among the non-converts and deconverted Hmong.

Conversion occurs either on an individual-basis or on a family-basis. It highlights the interaction—and, in many cases, the tension—between individuals' ideas and values and the structural requirements of the community. Conversion has ripped many families, clans, and communities apart as illustrated by the story of Mr. Gi's household. A problem for Christian converts is that they cannot simply abandon the past, since their sense of community and their status as a minority within that community continues to connect them to the Hmong tradition. This problem is exacerbated by the constant attacks on Hmong "barbarism" by their Kinh neighbors. One of the serious emotional and conceptual problems that Christian converts are facing is that Christian respectability looks very similar to Kinh respectability.

Images and descriptions of the life of the Hmong in the United States introduced by the media and through missionizing visits have also reshaped the desire for modernity of the Vietnamese Hmong. To them, the Hmong who return to Vietnam (or, if young, come for the first time) to spread the Christian Gospel represent "Hmong modern." For the first time in their modern history, the Hmong in Vietnam are informed of an alternative way of life in which one can be prosperous and still be Hmong. But for those Hmong who reject Protestantism, or, having experimented with it, choose to deconvert, it is not possible to embrace this new way of life and still retain their identity.

MINORITY/MAJORITY AND LOCAL/GLOBAL

One impact of the introduction of evangelical Protestantism involves a change in Hmong people's perception of their already precarious position within Vietnam. Despite their ranking as the eighth largest of Vietnam's fifty-four recognized ethnic groups[1] and having a number of members who rose to nationally prominent political positions, many Hmong people see themselves as members of one of the most marginal ethnic groups in Vietnam in economic, social, and cultural terms. The state recognition of ethnic minority status follows a

Communist model that was put into place by Stalin's nationalities doctrine and was followed by the Chinese in the 1950s. It recognizes "a nation" as a historically stable community, formed on the basis of common language, territory, economic life, and psychological make-up. This policy of recognizing ethnic minority status in a Kinh majority nation in fact underscored the marginality of the Hmong and their unfinished assimilation into the body of the nation. When Christianity as a foreign religion is added to this ethnic marginality, the distance with the nation is reinforced and in Vietnam leads to suspicion of potential separatism. The geographical location of many Hmong groups in the border areas heightens this suspicion.

From being one of the most dominant ethnic groups in the Northern Highland of Vietnam, since the late 1960s, Hmong people gradually became subjected to Vietnamese state rule and to thus to the Kinh group's economic and cultural domination. Their sense of marginality results from a comparison between their declining status and the increasing Kinh domination in their own land. This awareness of their own marginality is recently complicated for the Hmong by exchanges with their much better-off overseas ethnic brethren in the United States. Within the Vietnamese nation-state, the Hmong may occupy a marginal position in terms of their economic, political, and social status, especially in relation to the Kinh ethnic majority, but beyond the nation-state the situation is different. The remoteness of their location in the national space does not hinder them from becoming part of a transnational community comprising the Hmong of China, Laos, Thailand, and Vietnam. On the contrary, as the nostalgic sentiment of cultural authenticity premised on diasporic identity-politics has developed, the Hmong in Vietnam have started to find themselves occupying a central place in this newly imagined community. In addition, as contact with Hmong missionaries from overseas intensifies, Hmong converts now also imagine themselves to be at the center of a global Protestant community.

The United States is often seen as the most advanced nation, and one of the contradictions explored in this book is that members of the Hmong population have migrated to the United States and are thus simultaneously part of a backward ethnic group (in both Vietnam and the United States) and of an advanced nation. One of the ironies involved in Protestant proselytization is that the American Hmong tend to romanticize the traditional lifestyle of their brethren in Vietnam, while at the same time desiring to bring Christianity and thus change to that lifestyle for them.

The Hmong in Vietnam not only compare their situations to that of their Kinh neighbors, but also to their Hmong brethren in the United States who are considered to be more advanced than the Vietnamese Kinh. Thus, the vagaries of transnationalism create different time scales and understandings of national and global history that allow the Hmong to cross borders and jump over stages of historical development. In this context, conversion to Christianity may be seen as an attempt to move beyond the nation-state frame of reference as well as the act of moving beyond the nation-state itself.

In a number of Asian countries where the majority population is non-Christian, the conversion of people from the ethnic and geographical margins of society often leads to tension and conflict.[2] Not only does the Christianization of these minority groups further widen the ethnic gaps, but it also leaves the nation vulnerable to the penetration of foreign cultural and political forces. In Vietnam, the combination of the transnational nature of Hmong identity, the converts' membership in a global church, and the Hmong's millenarian tendencies have intensified the state's deep anxieties about sovereignty and national security. The state fears the potential development of a separatist movement aimed at a Hmong kingdom ruled by the mythical Hmong king whom converts have identified with Jesus Christ. Adding to these fears are the long distant nationalist movement of the diasporic Central Highlanders in the United States who reject Vietnamese nationality and advocate a separate Dega kingdom (Salemink 2006). The conflation of traditional Hmong millenarianism and evangelical Protestantism has led Vietnamese state analysts to blame missionaries and foreign activists for enticing and even coercing the Hmong into conversion. The spread of Protestantism is viewed as a scheme to provoke ethnic conflicts, spark anticommunist sentiment, and create social and political instability. Imputing economic poverty as the motive for Hmong to convert, the Vietnamese state employs "a politics of poverty" (Escobar 1995; Procacci 1991) to invalidate conversions and, at the same time, validate its own intrusive intervention in the revival of Hmong traditions and justify the imposition of propaganda campaigns and efforts to "rescue" the Hmong from Christianity.

CONDUCTING RESEARCH IN A VIETNAMESE HMONG VILLAGE

I came to the Gi home in the late afternoon of a sunny day in early November 2004. The house is at the elevated end of a 700-meter potholed trail that connects the hillside with the big road, the National Highway 70, which runs through the commune. After I had failed in the previous weeks to settle in with two other Hmong families, the Gis represented almost my last hope of finding a home in this commune. Accompanying me was Mr. Chung, my Hmong teacher and de facto research assistant, who happened to be Mr. Gi's former boss. A young woman with a toddler sleeping in a sling attached to her back was gathering the maize kernels spread out to be dried on the cement yard in front of the house. She halted on catching sight of our motorbike struggling to climb the trail. We greeted her when we finally stopped at the yard, and Mr. Chung asked in Hmong whether Mr. Gi was home. She coldly nodded her head, then quickly walked away, disappearing into the kitchen attached to the main house. It would have been awkward for us to be left standing in the yard had Mr. Gi not emerged from the house and warmly welcomed us in.

Hmong people are known for their hospitable and polite manner toward visitors, so the reception of the young woman, who we learned was Chau Thi Cu, Mr. Gi's daughter-in-law, startled me. The reason for her manner soon became clear: For a number of years, Mr. Chung had been responsible for many anti-Christian campaigns in the province, some of which directly affected Mr. Gi's family. Using clan connections, Mr. Chung had visited frequently and persuaded Mr. Gi to deconvert. Mr. Chung himself admitted that it was his idea to promote Mr. Gi to the vice-chairmanship of the commune's Fatherland Front, a post that is directly responsible for anticonversion campaigns at the commune level, and thus to effectively put Mr. Gi in direct confrontation with his Christian wife and children. After retirement, Mr. Chung continued to come to aid Mr. Gi in his struggle to bring ancestral worship back to the house. Except for Mr. Gi, the rest of the family was unhappy to have Mr. Chung visit. It did not take long for me to understand that having been brought to the family by Mr. Chung, I had scant prospect of being accepted by the family.

Gaining entry into the field proved to be a highly challenging part of my fieldwork, both in terms of securing research permission and establishing rapport with my informants. Hmong conversion in Vietnam is considered by the state to be an extremely sensitive political issue. After obtaining research permission to stay in a certain village, the next most difficult task I faced was gaining entry into a "field" that was so fragmented, not only at the village level, but even within a single family like the Gis. Since conversion has resulted in social and cultural conflict and division among converted and unconverted Hmong, I needed to gain access at least twice: entrance to the community of the converted and, then, to groups of unconverted Hmong. Two weeks before I met the Gis, local authorities arranged for me to stay with a non-Christian family. The head of this family was working for the commune police station. After two days in their home, I had to find a pretext to leave. Despite the hospitality of the family and their willingness to show me around the village, the head of the family not only voiced his anti-Christian opinions, but also intended to give his neighbors, who were Christians, the impression that I was a "cadre researcher" (*cán bộ nghiên cứu*) sent by the government to study how Christianity was destroying Hmong culture. I realized that if I did not remove myself, my ability to conduct research would have utterly undermined. Via the introduction of a

Christian acquaintance, a week later I was invited to stay with a Christian family in another hamlet, only to find out that neither my host nor I benefited from the arrangement. Local policemen began to interrogate us about my host's reason for accommodating me, a "person with foreign connections." Word quickly spread among non-Christian residents who soon become hesitant in their dealing with me.

Before going into the field, I was anxious to learn all possible strategies that my teacher and colleagues had used to gain access and establish rapport with their informants. During my fieldwork, I came to realize that the Gis and most of my informants accepted me and eventually trusted me with their stories and thoughts not because of any strategy that I employed, but because of my honesty about my intention to learn about their lives and predicaments. The political nature of religious conversion made the task of establishing rapport with potential informants difficult. As there was critical antagonism between the government and the converts, I found myself caught in a dilemma. In order to stay long enough with the converts, I needed permission from the government. Yet, if I showed my affiliation with the government, I risked being rejected by the converts. This situation was further complicated at the beginning of my stay with the Gis. In order to be accepted and allowed to stay, I needed permission from Mr. Gi, the head of the household. Given that I had arrived at the house in the company of Mr. Chung, the rest of Mr. Gi's family, especially his children, were convinced that I had been sent by the government to spy on them and propagate "anti-Protestantism" ideas to their father. Just like Mr. Gi's daughter-in-law, Chau Thi Cu, all the other young people in the house ignored me, though they kept a close eye on the people with whom I talked, what I did, and where I went in the village.

After persistent efforts to show that I was not from the government—or more precisely, after witnessing me being followed and questioned by the local policemen—the Gi family slowly began to trust me and talk to me more openly. In winter 2007, they adopted me to their family. The adoption was yet another occasion on which I became the source of family conflict. Mr. Gi had insisted on formalizing this event with a ritual ceremony in which a name would be chosen for me and I would be introduced to the ancestors of the Sung clan. Although she agreed with the decision to adopt me, Mrs. Gi objected this ceremony. After nearly a week of quarreling with one another, they told me at one dinner that they could not find mutually agreeable ritual procedure for adopting me. But that did not change the way they felt about me. With or without an adoption ritual, I am, in their words, already like a daughter to them.

The way I was accepted into the Christian Hmong community in Phong Hải is similar to the experience of Clifford Geertz (1973) in Bali. Only after witnessing Geertz and his wife fleeing from the scene of a cockfight and hiding from the police in a courtyard did local Balinese accept them into their community. Similarly, only after seeing me being tailed and harassed by the local police, the Christian Hmong of Phong Hai, beginning with those from Mr. Gi's family, started to speak to me and slowly accept me into their community. I had yet to face another problem, which was that, at one point during my stay, Mr. Gi became uneasy when he saw me growing close to his wife and children and joining them in sneaking out for evening bible gatherings. It took him some time to come to accept, or more precisely turn a blind eye to, my involvement with his wife and children's religious life. In return I tried my best to be discreet about my participation in church activities.

METHODOLOGY, LANGUAGES, AND ORTHOGRAPHIES

This book is based on eighteen months of ethnographic research in Vietnam and over six months of fieldwork in the United States, which stretched out over seven years. In Vietnam, this included a period of preliminary summer research in 2004, follow-up fieldwork in 2005, an extended period of fieldwork from September 2007 to July 2008, and shorter return visits in the spring of 2009, 2010, and 2011.

I began my research in the United States by attending the first International Hmong Studies conference organized by Concordia University in Saint Paul, Minnesota, in March 2006. In the summer of the same year, I returned to the United States for Hmong language training at the University of Wisconsin, Madison, and also took the opportunity to visit Hmong communities in Wisconsin and Minnesota and to attend Hmong church gatherings, fundraising events organized by Christian and non-Christian Hmong communities, and the conference of the Hmong District of the Christian and Missionary Alliance (CMA) church in Saint Paul. In 2008, I returned to the United States for another three-month fieldwork trip in which I conducted more interviews with Hmong missionaries, the FEBC's former president, Jim Bowman, and many Hmong pastors. I also attended another annual conference of the Hmong District of the CMA church in Denver, Colorado, and several Hmong community events in Sacramento, California. In addition to the fieldwork in Vietnam and in the United States, I took one short fieldwork trip to visit various Hmong communities in Laos, two trips to Thailand and several trips to China to interview Hmong missionaries and radio preachers.

The major methodology employed throughout the fieldwork in Vietnam was participant observation and personal in-depth interviews. I attended countless Thursday and Sunday church gatherings during these research periods. I observed and took notes on the content of homilies and sermons by deacons and church leaders and the interactions between church members. The information that I collected was mainly qualitative, and includes personal narratives, life stories, and descriptions of relationships, behaviors, and interactions that I observed in the field. I also analyzed a considerable number of scholarly works to develop a better understanding of different perspectives on Hmong conversion. In Vietnam, three attempts to use questionnaires to gather quantitative data failed mainly because the interviewees were afraid that information they provided down in such an official way could be used against them later. The quantitative information used in this book is mainly second-hand data and data from the government census.

To conduct this fieldwork, I used Vietnamese and Hmong inside Vietnam and English and Hmong outside of the country. In Vietnam I have often had to rely on my far-from-perfect Hmong to engage in daily conversations. But in discussions about Christianity, conversion and its effect on Hmong "traditional" culture, my informants often insisted on speaking in Vietnamese with me. After a while I realized that the ability to speak fluent Vietnamese about these important issues is key to the leadership and charismatic authority of these informants, who are mostly male leaders or active female members of church groups.

At the beginning of my research, I had a series of Hmong language lesson with Mr. Chung, a retired Hmong politician who spoke Green Hmong. There are a considerable variety of dialects spoken by different Hmong groups. White Hmong (Hmoob Dawb) and Green Hmong (Hmoob Ntsuab) are the two main dialects spoken by the Hmong population outside of China. Although Hmong people believe that they once possessed an ancient form of writing, only at the end of the nineteenth century did orthographies appear, mostly through the invention of outsiders, using Chinese, Vietnamese, Russian, Lao, and Thai characters and alphabets to transcribe their languages. An exception is the eighty-one-symbol alphabet called *Pahawh*, which was invented in 1959 by Yang Shong Lue, an illiterate Hmong farmer who lived near the Vietnamese-Lao border. Followers of Chao Fa, a messianic anti-Laotian movement, used this writing system and honored Yang as the "mother of writing" and their spiritual leader.

Around the same time that Yang Shong Lue invented Pahawh, Vietnamese ethnologists and linguists were also sent to Sapa, Lào Cai, to study and devise a Hmong script.[3] Their script is closest to the Green Hmong dialect spoken by the majority of the Hmong population in Sapa. A song titled "Meo People [Now] Have Writing" was composed by Huyền Tâm, a Kinh cultural cadre, to celebrate this invention. The script was presented as a "gift" to Hmong people to symbolize "the care of the Party and the state" for them. Official reports claimed that at least 9,000 people in Lào Cai alone became literate as the result of various campaigns to disseminate this script between 1959 and 1979. However, there is very little evidence that the script actually took root in Hmong society because soon after the last campaign to disseminate it ended, officials complained about how difficult it was to find a Hmong person who could use the script (Trần 1996). Today, despite a number of attempts to revise it, the script is declared dead as it can only be used in very limited way by a handful of Hmong people (Trần 1996:196).

Mr. Chung is one of the few in Lào Cai who can still use this script, which he used to teach me Hmong. My acquisition of the language was very limited although Mr. Chung always encouraged me by saying that as an educated Kinh, I should be able to learn this script without much trouble.[4] I soon realised that only few people in my fieldwork area were able to use the Vietnamese Hmong script while most, especially the Christian Hmong, could only use the Hmong Romanized Phonetic Alphabet (RPA). In 2006, I attended the Hmong language course at the Southeast Asian Studies Summer Institute at the University of Madison, Wisconsin, to learn this writing system, which was devised in the 1960s by the Catholic missionary Yves Bertrais and two American Protestant missionaries, Linwood Barney and William Smalley who worked with White Hmong people in Laos (Heimbach 1979). The system was mainly used to transcribe the Bible and religious materials into dialect spoken by the White Hmong, although systematic variations are noted for the Green Hmong dialect. Since 1975, the RPA has been widely used by Hmong diaspora in the west to facilitate their transnational communication. The RPA is the Hmong script that has the richest literary base today.

Throughout the research for this book, I used the RPA system to transcribe selected Hmong vocabulary items. To ensure the anonymity of my Hmong informants, I have encoded their names in aliases, using equivalent English spelling.

A Hmong village high on a mountain slope in Lung Vai commune,
from which most of the Hmong people in Phong Hải came

Tourists visiting Hmong homes in a Hạ Sơn village in Phong Hải

Costume of Hmong Leng women

A Christmas celebration held in a mountain cave in order to avoid government surveillance

Two Protestant Hmong women visiting the ruins of a Catholic seminary near Sa Pa dating to the French Colonial period

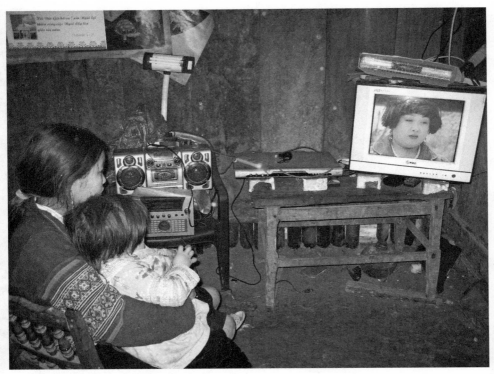

Watching a Hmong American soap opera

Singing Christmas carols

A Sunday service

A protestant New Year sports Tournament

A government-sponsored New Year celebration for non-Christian Hmong

A Christmas Feast

THE HMONG OF VIETNAM

ORIGINALLY from the mountainous regions of southwest China, the Hmong arrived in Vietnam about four centuries ago. The largest wave of Hmong migration from China into the Indochinese peninsula and Burma took place in the wake of the Miao rebellion of the 1870s. After 1975, at the end of the Second Indochina War, a large number of Hmong people, mainly from Laos, fled as refugees to various Western countries.[1]

In China, the Hmong are a subset of the larger Miao group (Miaozu), numbering three million. Whereas the term *Miao* has no negative connotation in China, and the Hmong members of the Miao group have no objection to this term (Schein 2000), the situation is quite different outside China. Hmong populations in Southeast Asia and in Western countries commonly resent being called Miao, or its variants Miêu and Mèo, because of the term's negative connotation and prefer to be called Hmong. Among themselves, they have their own nomenclatures for their cultural subdivisions.

The Hmong of Vietnam are officially classified by the government's Committee for Ethnic Minorities and Mountainous Affairs into six subgroups: White Hmong, Flowery Hmong (or Hmong Leng), Red Hmong, Green Hmong, Black Hmong, and Na Miểu (CEMA 2011). In addition, various smaller groups identify themselves as Hmong Shi, Hmong Pua, and Hmong Xau. However, as elsewhere in Asia, this classification is problematic (Keyes 2002). Ethnographers agree that there are at least four main groups: the White, Green, Leng, and Red Hmong. Members of the Na Miểu group do not consider themselves to be Hmong, although the government classifies them as such (Nguyễn 2007).

A close-knit clan-based pattern of relations is the most important aspect of Hmong social organization (Đặng 1998; Trần 1996; Ovesen 1995; Tapp 2001). Hmong society is divided into about twenty named exogamous patrilineal clans. The members of each clan observe certain food taboos and, irrespective of residence, regard one another as relatives. These ties, which bind persons sharing the same ancestral spirit, cut through all sub-ethnic and linguistic divisions and go beyond political and state boundaries. A Hmong family from the Yang clan in Vietnam can expect support and help from a Hmong family of the Yang clan in Laos or China, and vice versa. Despite attempts by various states to contain Hmong population within national borders, Hmong people continue to crisscross the borders between Vietnam, China, Laos, Thailand, and Burma.

Since the early 1980s, many Asian Hmong communities have also included in their transnational network the American Hmong who went to the United States in the aftermath of the Second Indochina War. Exchanges with Hmong people from the United States have had a profound impact on the Hmong community in Vietnam. One direct impact is the massive number of Protestant conversions that began in the last few decades of the twentieth century.

Although Hmong people today reside in sixty-two of the sixty-three provinces in Vietnam, they are to be found in greatest number in the Northern Highland region, in areas considered "highly sensitive" by state authorities, such as along the Laos-Vietnamese and Sino-Vietnamese borders. They are the largest group in the provinces of Hà Giang, Điện Biên, and Lai Châu, and the second largest group (after the Kinh majority) in Lào Cai and Sơn La. Smaller populations of Hmong also live in border areas with Laos in Thanh Hóa and Nghệ An, in northwest-central Vietnam. Since the late 1970s, increasing numbers of Hmong people have migrated to Central Highland provinces such as Đắc Lắc, Gia Lai, and Lâm Đồng.

PHONG HẢI

Hmong people have until very recently made up the majority inhabitants of Phong Hải, although this is not reflected in the administrative name of the place. Despite being surrounded by mountains, the commune has been called Phong Hải—literally, Ocean Screen—since its establishment in 1963. The name expresses the nostalgia of a small pocket of Kinh immigrants for their native villages in coastal provinces of Hải Phòng and Thái Bình. Beginning in 1977, all Kinh families in Phong Hải were organized into the Phong Hải Tea and Pineapple Production Corporation and lived in the stretch of flatland alongside twelve kilometers of National Highway 70. The administrative center of the commune, a combined-levels school, a simple health clinic, and a military station were also located there. In 1979, when China invaded Vietnam in a brief but bloody border war, all Kinh residents of Phong Hải fled. Only a few of them returned after the war, so the tea and pineapple hills of the commune remained deserted for almost two decades.

Members of eight ethnic groups—Hmong, Dao, Nùng, Dáy, Phù Lá, Mường, Tày, and Hán—dwell in the mountainous parts of Phong Hải. The Hmong, with a little more than two thousand members, were the largest group until the massive arrival of new Kinh immigrants in the last two decades to the area. Most of the Hmong homes can be found in villages on the lower altitude hillsides of the high, rocky limestone mountains on the east side of the road. Hmong villagers turned these high mountain slopes above their villages and small valleys nearby into cornfields and dry rice terraces. Running along the west side of the road is a medium-size stream that provides water for wet rice fields in a sizable valley below. The rice grown in these wet fields makes up 90 percent of the entire commune's rice production, yet most of these fields belong to the Kinh and the Nùng groups. In the early 1990s, within the framework of a program called Hạ Sơn (literally, "Moving Down from the Mountain"), authorities forced many Hmong residents in the hilltop villages to relocate to villages at lower altitudes. But since very little was done to allocate arable land in the lower valley to these villages, the program yielded more damage than benefit to those who moved.

Throughout my research, I mainly stayed in Tiền Phong village with the Gi family while attending the meetings of a church group in the village of Tòng Già. The Hmong term *lub zos*, is meant to refer to a single-clan village and one that also is religiously homogeneous. However, both Tiền Phong and Tòng Già are far from being *lub zos*, since they are not 100 percent Hmong. In Tiền Phong, besides fourteen Hmong families from four clans, the village also has three Nùng and fifteen Kinh families. Tiền Phong, which literally means "pioneering," was originally set up by three Kinh families in the 1960s who were joined by other Kinh families in the early 2000s. All Hmong families of Tiền Phong and Tòng Già were relocated here by the authorities during the 1990s through the Hạ Sơn program.

Protestant conversion has further diversified this small Hmong community. Altogether, the Tiền Phong–Tòng Già–Sảng Pả house church had 150 members in 2006. They attended two house churches weekly, one in Tòng Già village and one in Sảng Pả village. Both in Tòng Già and Sảng Pả, about 30 percent of the inhabitants are still "traditional" (người Hmong truyền thống), and they continue their "ancestors' way." This demographic division between Christian and non-Christian of the Tòng Già–Sảng Pả area reflects that of the whole Phong Hải commune, in which some 60 percent of Phong Hải's Hmong are Christian converts and 40 percent remain unconverted.

Today Phong Hải finds itself between two booming major urban centers near the Sino-Vietnamese border: Lào Cai city and Bảo Thắng township. While the traffic of goods and people between these two towns takes place on the Provincial Highway No. 151/4E on the west side of the Red River, Phong Hải is 13.5

kilometers along the National Highway 70, which is on the east side of the river. The 1991 opening of the border for trade between China and Vietnam made the National Highway 70 the main road for transporting people and goods between Lào Cai and Hà Nội. This peculiar situation produces a common feeling among Phong Hải people of being excluded from reaping the benefits of the flow of goods in the province while being rather well informed about Vietnam's recently growing economy.

The booming tourism industry in Lào Cai has recently included Phong Hải, to a very limited extent, in its development agenda. Beginning in around 2005, tour guides added a stop at Phong Hải Hmong villages near the highway to their daily tour itineraries. These visits provide tourists with smoking breaks, time to relax their cramped muscles, and the opportunity to compare the lives of the lowland Hmong, which the Hmong in Phong Hải have suddenly come to represent, with those of the highland Hmong, who are identified with the two tourist sites of Sa Pa and Bắc Hà. Although Phong Hải residents have become accustomed to seeing Vietnamese tourists in fancy clothes and strange-looking foreigners traveling by minibuses and expensive cars, Hmong villagers complain about the indecorous lenses of tourist cameras poking into their homes and tour guides pointing to their quotidian affairs as representative of "lowland Hmong" customs.

A military station is located at the entrance to the commune. Like many of its kind in rural areas elsewhere in post-war Vietnam, the military station provides the main and most viable source of romance for young girls, mostly from the Kinh group in the commune. Beside its romantic function, the station also engages in more serious affairs with the ethnic locals. When conversions began, for example, the military station worked closely with local government in campaigns to stop them. The villages around the station, such as Tiến Phong, Tòng Già, Cửa Cải, and Sảng Pả, became the first and most immediate targets of those campaigns, which were carried out intensely for almost two decades. Today, even when control on conversion has abated, both Christian and non-Christian residents in the areas are fully aware of the government's continuing surveillance on and interest in their religious life, and this is due to the work of the military station.

The origins of the Vietnamese state's suspicious attitude toward the religious life of Hmong people in Phong Hải and elsewhere in Vietnam lie not only in the state's ideological antagonism toward traditional Hmong beliefs and practices, considered by the state to be mere superstition, or toward organized religion such as Protestantism, but also in the Hmongs' role in both the colonial and the socialist history of Vietnam during the last century. Although I came to know the members of the Hmong community in Phong Hải by happenstance, the particular history of their community, their experience with socialism, their marginalization due to the process of economic reform (Đổi Mới) since 1986, and their recent encounter with Christianity made them ideal informants for my research purposes. Their experiences and memories of major social and political changes that have occurred since the end of the colonial period bear much resemblance to those of Hmong people in other parts of the country. By the end of the 1980s, when one-third of the Hmong community in Phong Hải decided to follow Protestantism, they, like those elsewhere in Vietnam, had been under the rule of the Nguyễn imperial state, then of the French colonial regime in the Protectorate of Tonkin and then under the Việt Minh–led Democratic Republic of Vietnam which became the Socialist Republic of Vietnam. Each change of regime at the center led to changes in the administration of the border areas and in the fortunes of the people living in those areas.

COLONIAL LEGACIES

Soon after large numbers of Hmong fled into Vietnam from Yunnan in the wake of the Miao Rebellion of 1873, the Sino-French war (1883–85) engulfed the borderland between Vietnam and China where they had resettled. The Sino-French war marked the end of Vietnamese independence (as well as Vietnam's traditional tributary relationship with China) and the formation of the Protectorate of Tonkin in northern Vietnam and Annam in the central region of the country (the south had been the French colony of Cochinchina since 1867). When the French entered the northern upland in the 1880s, they maintained the imperial system of using tribal chieftains known as Thổ Ty (*tusi* in Chinese)[2] to exercise control over local populations. Under this system, most of the Thổ Ty were of Tai ethnicity (related to the Zhuang ethnic group in China). Members of the Đèo clan of the Sip Song Châu Tài (the Twelve Regions of the Tai) were given control of the Black River basin and the upper west side of the Red River (Lentz 2011; Le Failler 2011), in which were living not only the Tai but also members of the Khmu, Dao (Yao), and Hmong ethnic communities (under the French, the Hmong were known as Meo). This system gave additional power to the Tai, who then came to exert harder control on the Hmong population and exploit them and other minority groups. In turn, the Hmong from the west side of the Red River resented the French for privileging the Tai; Hmong living in the upper east side of the Red River, however, were not under Tai control and maintained good relations with the French who supported their opium production.

As a result, during the First Indochina War (1946–54), different groups of Hmong allied themselves with the Vietnamese or the French. Because of their different experiences with Tai control, Hmong leaders on the west side of the Red River gave their support to the Việt Minh relatively more readily than those on the east side. In 1948, in a bid to prevent minority communities from joining the Communist-led Việt Minh, the French created the Thai Autonomous Zone, still with the Đèo clan in control. The Interzone covered most of the Red River Delta and areas bordering China and Laos. In 1952, the provinces of Yên Bái, Lào Cai, Sơn La and Lai Châu were detached from the Interzone to form the Northwestern Zone.[3]

As the French and Việt Minh battled for control of the area, many Hmong tried to avoid involvement altogether by abandoning their homes and villages, which became battlegrounds, and relocating across national or regional borders. This strategy was mostly unsuccessful, as virtually all the areas in which the Hmong live were in strategic locations along the border, and because the Hmong were primary producers (if not traders) of the opium that funded military efforts on both sides of the wars (Lee and Tapp 2010: 14). Even today, state authorities consider this strategy of avoiding conflict to be unpatriotic and anti-revolutionary, equating the Hmong with those who were allied with the French in the battle against the Việt Minh.

Another important legacy of French colonialism that affects Hmong people is the impact of Catholicism. Catholic proselytizing started in Vietnam as early as the beginning of the sixteenth century, although the mountainous region of Upper Tonkin (North Vietnam) was left untouched by European missionaries until the late 1800s (Michaud 2004, 2007). This situation changed after the French colonial implantation in the second half of the century. With the support of colonial authorities, the Société des Missions étrangères de Paris began to send missionaries to work among different ethnic groups in Upper Tonkin. The Hmong were among the first indigenous groups to be targeted by Catholic missionaries, the most prominent of whom was Father Francis Maria Savina (Tuck 1987). Savina spent two decades in Lào Cai working among the Hmong population; he become fluent in their vernacular and made systematic study of their society and religion. While his scholarly work resulted in perhaps the most important colonial ethnography of Hmong society in Vietnam, the yield of Savina's missionary work was rather disappointing. Savina himself never mentioned how many Hmong people he converted, but it seemed that the harvest of his decades of evangelical labor were only a few dozen Hmong Catholics (Tran 1996).

Although the number of Savina's converts was indeed small, those conversions have engendered a lasting suspicion on the part of the Vietnamese government toward the Hmong. Today, Vietnamese scholars and government officials do not hesitate to point out the religious-cum-political ambitions of

CHAPTER ONE

Catholic missionaries and the Hmong conversion to Catholicism as proof of the Hmong's eagerness to form alliances with French colonizers (instead of resisting). After the 1954 evacuation of French Catholic missionaries and clerks in the North, a handful of Hmong Catholics in Sapa and Trạm Tấu, Nghĩa Lộ (now, belonging to Yên Bái province) were left without a priest. Between that time and the late 1980s, not only did their religious community cease to grow, but the number of Hmong who claimed to be Catholics dwindled to just over a few dozen (Tran 1996).

Two decades later, the number of Hmong Catholics in Lào Cai soared to thousands. According to the statistic provided by Lào Cai state authorities, as of 2012, there were 2,451 Hmong Catholics in Lao Cai, coming from 389 families and making up 33 percent of the Catholic population in the province. This number is, however, just a tiny fraction of the estimate of 20,000 Hmong Catholics in the Hưng Hóa Diocese, which was reported by Father Daniel Taillez, is based in Thailand, who visited Vietnam in 2011 shortly after a millenarian unrest in Điện Biên province. While the Vietnamese government has the tendency to underestimate the number of adherents to any religion in Vietnam and Christian missionaries tend toward overestimating their flocks, the difference between the two accounts is too stark. Regardless of the actual number of members, the Hmong Catholic community in Vietnam has witnessed a remarkable growth over the last few decades, and, like their Protestant counterparts, they have established a close relationship with their oversea Hmong Catholic fellows.

ELIMINATING THE BANDITS:
THE BLOODY PATH TO CITIZENSHIP

While the French had attempted to divide and conquer by creating an autonomous zone peopled by minorities, as soon as independence was declared in 1945, the Việt Minh sought to establish control over the same populations. The new state's agenda of political control and sociocultural transformation was carried out through some of the bloodiest episodes in a history of tense relations between the Hmong and the postcolonial state. These episodes were part of a program called "Eliminating the Bandit/Rebels" (Tiễu Phỉ). *Phi* or *thổ phi* derives from the Chinese word for bandit (*tufei*). In the past, *thổ phi* was the name given to the terrifying bandit armies who perpetrated ambushes and robbery and over which the central Vietnamese authority had little control. *Phi* were clearly active in the northwest before 1945 but communist writers such as Vũ Ngọc Kỳ (1999) considered their attacks on French military posts and seizures of food and weapons to have been perpetrated for "economic reasons" and thus were beyond reproach. Thus, most of the armed movements that occurred prior to 1945 such as the ones led by Giàng Chỉn Hùng (in Bắc Hà), Giàng San (in 1918 in Sa Pa), Thào Nù Đa (in Mù Căng Chải, Yên Bái), are exalted as heroic revolts against the wicked colonial rulers. This line of argument allowed Vietnamese scholars to draw conclusions about the Hmong's consciousness of being Vietnamese and to depict these Hmong leaders as anti-colonial heroes (Trần 1996; Nguyễn 2008). In fact, the leaders of these movements were often self-proclaimed messiahs in the Hmong messianic tradition, and their political outlook was anything but anticolonial.

When, after 1945, the Việt Minh sought to establish its control over the region, the same activities undertaken against them by Hmong or any other ethnic groups became indefensible and the meaning of *phi* changed. The word was no longer limited to banditry but was now used to denominate a counter-revolutionary movement. Any Hmong who endorsed *phi* movements was regarded as a reactionary rebel. The Tiễu Phỉ (Eliminating the Bandits) program was thus launched in 1950, and it was only in 1978 that the last campaign of this program came to an end. In four years, from 1951 to 1955 alone, it was reported that during the five grand Tiễu Phỉ campaigns nearly one thousand ambushes and surprise attacks were organized. The result was the "disintegration of 8,788 *phi*, thousands of guns, and a hundred tons of ammunitions."[4]

Tiễu Phỉ is, to this day, the program that has left the deepest scars in the relations between the Kinh and the Hmong. A blurry handwritten document, dating from 1971, which recorded "The Opinions of Mr. Đồng from the Supreme Court on Tiễu Phỉ in Lào Cai," reveals that following the year 1955 many *phi* arrests were made, mostly of Hmong people.[5] Those arrests increased the distrust and tension between the Hmong and the new government, and consequently, more *phi* movements emerged. From 1959 to 1962, the number of Hmong arrests became so great that the central government took strict measures to stop them, fearing that they would alarm the Hmong in the entire northwest region and could lead to their mass flight into Laos. In addition, the central government noticed that the province had arrested a large number of people without any documentation (*hồ sơ*) and that the accusations were not supported by sufficient evidence. Only several years later was evidence sometimes provided; the crimes prosecuted were mostly 'old crimes' (crimes that were not crimes before the establishment of communist rules). According to central government instructions, regardless of how serious the punishment for these crimes, they should not carry the death penalty. Yet, in Lào Cai in 1962, from among more than seventy arrests, mostly Hmong, four Hmong men were given the death penalty and another forty-two men received heavy punishments. Mr. Đồng, the author of the document also recalled that the central government had to constantly warn Lào Cai province officials of the political sensitivity of such mass arrests and persecution and of the bad influence that such actions had on Hmong communities in other regions. For the central government to take such a cautious stance was not unwise; anxiety indeed intensified in Hmong communities. Some Hmong who had connections to Kinh cadres tried to inquire about the reasons for such arrests and why most people arrested were Hmong. Given no answer, many of the Hmong who were also cadres started to wonder whether they were "out of use" for the state and withdrew from their posts.

From the late 1970s onward, the Vietnamese government redefined *phi* as a problem of ethnic relations instead of counter-revolutionary activity. On the positive side, this redefinition advocated a more active program to combat the antagonism between Kinh cadres and Hmong local leaders. In Lào Cai province, instructions were given to pay special attention to "the issue of recruiting cadres of minority origins [*vấn đề cán bộ người dân tộc*]." This was by no means an easy task owing partly to the inflexibility of policy implementation by local authorities and partly to the limited trust that Kinh cadres continued to have in their ethnic minority comrades. On the negative side, viewing ethnic tensions as the reason for *phi* activity, Kinh cadres often condemned the disagreement of Hmong people with state policy as phi conduct. Phi began to be named as a form of ethnic revolt. As before, the shift in the meaning and status of *phi* reflected the progress of state formation in the Northern Highland. As the modern state of Vietnam gradually became established in the region and pushed its boundaries further to include ethnic minorities like the Hmong into the space of the nation-state, those who stood up against this expansion were labeled rebels.

While seeking to eradicate banditry, the Việt Minh government put in motion a plan to bring the Northern Highland under firmer control. Even before the victory at Điện Biên Phủ in 1954, the region experienced a string of intense communist campaigns such as Land Reform (1953–56), Rectification of Errors, Plan for Economic and Cultural Development of the Highland, Storm the Hill, Clear the Hill by Torchlight, the New Life Movement, the Rural Hygiene Movement to name but a few. Sometimes carried out intensively and sometimes discreetly, these campaigns were, in Patricia Pelley's (1998: 386) words, designed to transform, "both the economy and culture of everyday life" of the Highland. To hasten development of the northwestern Autonomous Zone and its counterpart in the east, from 1961 onward, Kinh (Viet) volunteers were mobilized to serve as leaders of the minorities in a newly launched program called Strengthening the Highland (*Củng Cố Vùng Cao*). It was within the framework of this program that three Kinh families from Hải Phòng came to establish the pioneering Tiền Phong village in early 1960s. By 1966 there were one million of these volunteers. A slogan that is still used today, "The Three Togethers: Eat Together, Sleep Together, Work Together" (Ba Cùng: Cùng Ăn, Cùng Ngủ, Cùng Làm), was created to boost the morale of those participating in this campaign. However, lack of mutual understanding and poor communication between the Kinh cadres and the local people led to poor results. In some cases, the two camps even had to be separated because of mutual distrust and hostility. For Kinh cadres, the perception of Hmong people as *phỉ* (i.e., always ready to "hit and run" like a bandit) proved to be particularly harmful and hindered their mission to work with them. A cadre who had spent several years carrying out a "mobilizing the masses" *(vận động quần chúng)* campaign in a Hmong area commented in a September 2007 interview:

> The Mèo [Hmong] always lived in anxiety. They always felt they were threatened, not necessarily by any particular party [we or other]. This anxiety formed throughout their thousand year history of fleeing en masse from the persecution of the Chinese. This anxiety made them always ready to fight back. If they were afraid of us, they ran to the jungle. If they disagreed with us, they ran to the jungle. If they fought back against us and failed, they also ran to the jungle. Hmong men always had guns with them. They always thought that if they fought against us, regardless of how few or how many men they have, they shall fight till their last breath, thinking that if they didn't fight, they would die anyway. . . . The way they lived also reflected this anxious attitude and the readiness to flee. Their houses were very simple, very closed up, with only a front door and a back door. Their furniture was virtually non-existent. Their clothes and cooking utensils were always packed or ready to be packed. The knife that they used was not a normal kind of knife but one that can be turned into a dangerous weapon immediately when needed. When they slept, husband and wife lay with head and feet opposite each other. When they worked on their field, they always had their gun next to them, and constantly kept alert eyes on everything around.

If taken out of the context in which they were given, these comments seem to confirm exactly what James Scott (1985) sees as "weapons of the weak" commonly utilized by hill people in what he calls Zomia (Scott 2009; Michaud 2011). They were however articulated by a Kinh cadre to illustrate the tense relations between the Hmong and the Kinh cadres during these violent campaigns. They tell us more about the Kinh cadre's cultural prejudices and ethnic stereotypes in which the Hmong are portrayed as mountain nomads. It is this portrayal that formed the cadre's and his colleagues' paranoia about the Hmong. He went on to tell an example of such paranoia and misunderstanding. Together with a colleague he once came to visit a Hmong family, an important target of his mobilization. The family prepared a bed for them in the main hall of their house, very close to the ancestral altar. Then the father and son took their knives and gun and left. Not understanding what was going on, the two cadres were terrified, thinking that the family had gone out to get help and would return to butcher them. So they quickly packed up and ran only to find out later that the family had gone out to hunt for food to host them as honored guests.

Still, on the whole these campaigns were hailed as successful by the government. By the end of 1961, more than 70 percent of families had reportedly joined cooperatives of a semi-socialist type. But in the memory of my Hmong informants, the Democratic Reform (Cải Cách Dân Chủ) program, which was part of the larger Land Reform campaign, and the Renovating the Highland project were among the most unforgettable. In the name of building a "socialist cultural life," these campaigns had a destructive impact on the social structure of Hmong society. The Democratic Reform program, for example, set a record in the number of Hmong people arrested and persecuted in the history of modern day Vietnam.

FIXED CULTIVATION AND RESETTLEMENT

The Hmong, with their shifting cultivation and their regular migration, came first in the government's list of priorities for sociocultural reform. In 1968, a grand program called "Fixed Cultivation and Settlement" (Định Canh Định Cư) was promulgated. It began with the perception that the Hmong's indigenous mode of cultivation, 'slash and burn,' resulted in deforestation and unstable societal conditions and kept them in backwardness and superstition. The swidden mode of production also exacerbated the Hmong's social and cultural isolation.

Vietnamese scholars and policy makers see the implementation of the Fixed Cultivation and Resettlement programs, which involved forcing the Hmong to abandon shifting cultivation and settle in sedentary villages as a necessary step to help them create a stable life. This would be the first step to incorporate them into the modernization and socialist programs of the nation and, for the last two decades, to prevent deforestation (Đặng Nghiêm Vạn 1975: 11–12; see also Trần 1996; Vương Duy Quang 1996). Foreign scholars see this program as an example of the state's assimilation efforts (Keyes 1987: 19; McElwee 1999; Salemink 2000). Perhaps the ideology and motivation for Fixed Resettlement and Cultivation was a mix of both. Whatever the motivation, after decades of implementation, its achievements are rather modest. By 1988, of the total 118,799 Hmong people living in Hoàng Liên Sơn (now separated into three provinces—Yên Bái, Nghĩa Lộ, and Lào Cai), only 42,343 people had settled into sedentary farming (Nguyễn Anh Ngọc 1989). In Lai Châu Province, by 2002, 4,436 households comprising 28,699 people (mostly Hmong) continued to maintain their "nomadic" life and to practice shifting cultivation.

Reasons for the limited success of the Fixed Cultivation and Resettlement program vary. Lack of arable land near the sedentary villages was often cited by my Hmong informants as the most important reason why the program did not work for them. This was because another state program called Clearing the Wilderness (Khai Hoang) was simultaneously implemented. In this program the central government encouraged Kinh people from populated coastal and delta provinces to resettle upland.[6]

In the mid-1980s, a program designed specifically for the Hmong population was introduced. It was unabashedly called *Move [the Hmong] Down from the Mountains (Hạ Sơn)*. A continuation of the Fixed Cultivation and Resettlement project, it aimed to more forcefully relocate Hmong families from 'undesirable locations'—for instance, too close to the borderlines and too scattered and far up on the mountains—to concentrated villages in lower areas where the Four Modernizations—"Electricity, Roads, Schools, and Health Clinics" (Điện Đường Trường Trạm)—could be built.

A number of Hmong villages, including Phong Hải, were relocated to lowland areas within this program. Despite some immediate achievements, the program also negatively affected the life of the Hmong. One was the inconvenience and hardship they experienced during the transition from one mode of production to another. The Hmong needed a great deal of time to clear new fields and to adapt to sedentary cultivation, not to mention the fact that the land assigned to them was often much smaller than what they were used to having. More critically, living in the lowland area meant an absolute repudiation of opium production, which, for many Hmong, was still the main source of cash income until recently. After 1986, the state introduced the "Self-Provision, Self-Reliance" (Tự cấp Tự túc) policy. This policy change affected the Hmong in the lowland areas the most. In general, financial and commodity subsidies for the Hmong and other minority groups were reduced dramatically; worse, the resettled Hmong were no longer considered residents of a high and remote area and therefore were no longer entitled to subsidies and welfare designed specifically for such regions.

Lack of available land in lowland areas forced most Hmong families to keep their fields in the old areas up in the hills long after they were forced to resettle.

Most of the villagers in Phong Hải, for example, preferred to maintain their fields up in the mountain. Even the first Hmong family who resettled in the area in the late 1970s, when "there was enough land that you could make it your own" still keeps its field in the old village or went back to the mountain area to open new fields without seizing fertile land near the road or with easier transportation access. At that time, when most of the harvest and animals were kept in huts in the field, there was no real need to transport the crop back to the house. Presently however, this distance has turned into a disadvantage as most Hmong families who grow maize as a cash crop need to sell their harvest and this can be done more easily if their field is near a road.

LAND LAW AND OPIUM

The "Self-Provision, Self-Reliance" policy was part of the Đổi Mới program launched in 1986 when Vietnam's national economy was on the brink of collapse. Đổi Mới was a set of comprehensive and ongoing market reforms that eventually would turn Vietnam into another capitalist economy while still under the one-party system. Đổi Mới encompasses a large range of policies and laws facilitating the industrialization, modernization, and commercialization of all economic sectors.

To achieve those goals in agriculture, a land law was implemented in 1993. Under this law, agricultural and forestland were allocated to households, individuals, and organizations for management. This process effectively privatized land ownership and hence commoditized land. The allocation of land to households was carried out on the basis of land quotas and the status quo, that is, each household in the northern mountainous areas was allotted no more than three hectares of productive land and thirty hectares of forest land. In fact, in the northern mountainous areas, very few households were allotted the entire allowed amount of land as the areas were populous and there was not much arable land. All the land now had its own specific owners and therefore was no longer available for rotational cultivation as in the past.

For ethnic minorities and particularly the Hmong, this land law had far-reaching consequences. First and foremost, it made their system of rotational shifting cultivation increasingly difficult and eventually impossible. The privatization and commoditization of land allowed by the 1993 land law subjected land prices to market forces, and this again placed the Hmong and many other ethnic minorities at a disadvantage. As Kinh immigrants from lowland provinces who resettled in the mountainous areas often had cash to buy land for farming, they drove land prices up. They made it harder for members of the Hmong community to save enough to purchase new fields for their grown children to separate their households. As a result, many Hmong families have been on the move again since the late 1990s in search of new land in remote areas, far away from authorities and in 'protected' natural forests. These forests are still under the loose management of forest enterprises and state farms. Indeed, this is partly the reason why the Hmong migrated to the Central Highlands.

After 1954, the Vietnamese state sought control over opium production by the Hmong and other ethnic minority and profited from this lucrative crop through taxation (Lentz 2013). In 1992, however, the state began to prohibit the cultivation of poppy and this was a real blow to the Hmong economy. Opium has been grown in the uplands and mountainous regions of some north-western provinces of Vietnam, notably Sơn La, Lào Cai, Lai Châu, and Nghệ An since the nineteenth century. The majority of opium producers are Hmong. This lucrative crop has been both a blessing and a curse for them in the past. Various agricultural products such as maize, cassava, yam, taro, fruits, and herbal medicine were selected by the state officials as substitutes for opium production. Yet, very few Hmong families benefited from such programs. Then as market demand escalated, cardamom became a popular substitute crop even though it was not promoted by the government. Currently, however, profit from cardamom production fluctuates strongly depending on market demand as well as on the influence of lowland traders. Moreover, owing to recent weather unpredictability, the production of cardamom has been significantly reduced.

Although government reports claim that 98 percent of Vietnam's opium crop has been eliminated, there are numerous cases of people shifting back to poppy cultivation owing to a lack of processing facilities and markets for the substitute crops. Ten years have elapsed since the implementation of this provision in the Constitution, and poppy re-cultivation is still seen in some localities especially in distant valleys along the border with Laos and in mountainous areas. In Sơn La, according to local authorities, by February 21, 2002, 204 villages in 74 communes from 9 districts had re-grown poppy crops on an estimated 650,000 square meters area. In Lai Châu province, the acreage under poppy plants in 2001 was 60,000 square meters. These figures most likely do not represent the real situation. As of late December 2009, opium fields were still being discovered in remote valleys of the province's mountain region (Vietnam News Agency).

BLAMING THE VICTIM

The return to opium production led to renewed morally-laden charges in the political discourse and popular media that hold the Hmong responsible for their own poverty. Some scholars-cum-government officials equate opium production with "the interest and traditional culture" of the Hmong. Lamenting that such "interest and traditional culture" contradict national ideas and that opium cultivation prolongs the poverty and addiction of this group, they see the Hmong's stubbornness as the main cause of their own plight (Vương Xuân Tình 2002). Similarly, they argue that Hmong culture is to be blamed for the limited success of the Fixed Cultivation Fixed Settlement campaign (Đặng Nghiêm Vạn 1998; Trần Hữu Sơn 1996). These scholars argue that Hmong stubbornness (jokingly and negatively expressed in Vietnamese by the phrase: "*Cái lý anh Mèo*" [Mr. Meo's reasoning]) and their traditional culture prevent them from reaping the benefits of development projects on which the government has spent a huge amount of resources. Government officials have also lamented that in spite of the enormous financial assistance and care from the Party and the state (*sự quan tâm của Đảng và nhà nước*) in addition to so much support of their Kinh brothers—the model members of the nation—the results of economic development, education, and scientific knowledge and technology acquisition among the Hmong are still rather limited.

Explanations for why ethnic minorities in Vietnam, including the Hmong, continue to do so poorly in spite of various development efforts often fall into two camps (Taylor 2008: 10). The first camp mainly comprises foreign scholars who remain focused on the state and its defective vision as the most influential actor in the drama of development failures. Indeed, both at the level of conception and implementation, development is carried out by Kinh cadres who know little about Hmong society and culture and fail to gain the trust of local people. In contrast to this explanation, Vietnamese state agents and scholars have consistently identified the recalcitrance of the ethnic minorities, who continue to practice their "backward" ("*lạc hậu*") and "ignorant" ways, as the cause of their own failure to bring development to them. One of their arguments is that the Hmong are old-fashioned self-sufficient farmers and thus unfit for the free market economy. Vương Xuân Tình (1996), for example, claims that self-sufficiency is one of the unchangeable customs (*tập quán cố hữu*) that "indicate[s] the state of under-development and unsuitability to the market economy" of the Hmong. In the market economy, he asserts, the key is to generate income and it is the income that contributes to ensuring food security. For this reason, the "autarchic food system" of the Hmong, as Vương sees it, will reduce their dynamism and will not tap the local potential and strength to create more income. Vương does not take into account that, little more than fifty years ago, the Hmong were the major Indochinese opium producers and were an integral part of global trade networks and economies.

The reason Hmong farmers were unwilling to sell their products often had little to do with an "autarchic food system," but rather with their distrust of

Kinh traders. In recent years, urban Vietnamese have become aware of the unregulated industrialization of the agricultural sector in the country, which leads to lower quality and unsafe food products. Nowadays, since chickens at the market come mainly from either chicken farms where the producers use industrial food (*cám con cò*) of suspect safety to feed their stock, consumers, believing that minority people are still not yet commercially-orientated and not clever enough to use industrial feed, prize chickens which are said to come from minority households. Poultry and other foods produced by ethnic minorities in mountainous areas have become very popular because of the belief that they are both tastier and healthier.[7] In all big cities in Vietnam one can find restaurant billboards advertising "chicken raised by ethnic minorities" (*gà mòi*) or "hillside raised chicken" (*gà đồi*), "clutch-under-the-armpit-size piglets" (*lợn cắp nách*), "wild stream fish" (*cá suối*), and "river fish" (*cá sông*). The authenticity of products is highlighted or even fabricated. Vietnamese tourists who travel to the Northern Highlands are often after "exotic local products" (*đặc sản địa phương*), not just for the sake of health but also for an "authentic" experience. Tourism marketers are more than willing to cater to them so that, with the recent skyrocketing growth of domestic tourism, demand for local authentic food is much higher than the available supply.

Yet the Hmong are unenthusiastic about selling their home-produced products. When I spoke to some Kinh traders, I frequently heard the Hmong's refusal to raise chicken for sale described as "stupid" (*ngu*) and showing the local population as "lacking economic mentality" (*không có đầu óc kinh tế*). One trader explained: "One kilogram of chicken nowadays [in 2007] costs at least 50 thousand dong [US $3.50] on average. Chickens raised by minority people [*gà bản*] can command a much higher price, at least 20 to 30 percent more. I do not understand why those Mr. Mèo, who work the entire month on the field for an income that is as much as what three chickens cost, still prefer to keep these chicken to eat rather than to sell. You know, poor people sometimes are very ignorant and wasteful."

My host family provided a different perspective. Every year they raised a large number of chickens; like many other Hmong families in the area, it was mainly for their own use. The only time I saw Mr. Gi sell something was when he brought two piglets to the market because the family had too many and needed cash to pay two Kinh carpenters to build a new house so that the oldest son of the family could have a separate household. The rest of the cattle raised by the family were used as food. Every now and then, there were Kinh traders who came into the village and asked every household to sell their poultry. My host mother said she, like other Hmong people, did not want to sell anything to these Kinh traders. According to her, they always tried to pay very low prices and used inaccurate weighing machines. The Hmong commonly regard the Kinh as smart (*khôn*) but tricky (*lươn lẹo*) and entrepreneurial (*con buôn*) people who only wanted to rip off their Hmong providers. Some Hmong complained that Kinh merchants were rude and treated their customers with total contempt. Currently, in various isolated Hmong communities, especially those that cultivate cardamom, one can still encounter Kinh merchants who behave in exactly this way. Of course one can argue that when Hmong farmers refuse to sell their products they have a "non-commercial mentality" and can be blamed for their own poverty, but one would underestimate the extent to which the Hmong distrust Kinh traders and consumers.

KINH CONDESCENSION AND CONCERNS

Despites the state's official advocacy of equality and brotherly relations between all ethnic groups in Vietnam, Kinh condescension and even outright racism toward the Hmong is pervasive and often unconscious. I remember, as a five-year-old, joining in the games other Kinh children played on the street in Lào Cai where I was born and, taunting Hmong children as they passed by us: "Who wants to buy a cat?" (*Có ai muốn mua con mèo không?*). In Vietnam, the Hmong people are pejoratively called "Mèo," a homophone for "cat." As kids, we had no clue how much the Hmong people hated to be addressed as "Mèo," but we certainly knew that it is objectionable to call a person *con*, a generic particle denoting an animal or an animal-like thing. Adults around us did not object to our game or to our conduct. That we, the Kinh, were civilized (*văn minh*) and they, the Hmong, as well as other ethnic minorities, were backward (*lạc hậu*) was a common and unquestioned idea. Only after I was brought to stay with my father's Hmong friends in the early 1990s did I begin to feel ashamed of my racist attitude.

Kinh racism toward ethnic minorities has much more serious consequence than the hurtful feelings that our children's game had generated among our Hmong fellows. Mr. Thanh, a former official from the Fixed Resettlement and Cultivation program recalled in 2007:

> We spent enormous effort on the Fixed Cultivation and Resettlement program, yet the result was rather limited. In Nghĩa Lộ, in a Mèo village, we already built a health clinic [which facilitated both the use of traditional herbal medicine and Western medicine], a school, which was subsidized 100 percent for students from the first grade up and four water storage pools. If the villagers did not have enough rice, we sold

them rice at very low price. . . . For their farming, we helped them with technology but they were not used to that. In fact, they are still not used to it nowadays so the result was very meager. From the outside, the village looked very clean and neat, but inside, villagers were still ready to move at any moment. This is because the Mèo are a very proud people and they are proud of their self-reliance and independence. They did not want to receive things from other people, which they saw as "charity." In some places, we brought people from elsewhere to build the road and they did not like it; they wanted to make their own roads. In some places, officials from trade departments brought goods to the village to give away or to sell without immediate payment [*bán nợ*]; the people who came to receive these goods were very few. A cement pool to store water, if it was said to be built from money borrowed from the government, the village agreed to make use of it; but if it was described as a gift from the government, they would not like it and would not make use of it. For the Mèo, money couldn't buy their trust.

In this rare and honest assessment, this former official acknowledged that top-down development programs designed by Kinh officials failed to address local needs because of their patronizing attitude. The 2009 World Bank report *Country Social Analysis: Ethnicity and Development in Vietnam* suggests that it is perhaps one of the explanations for the failure of development programs for ethnic minorities. Filed by scholars and experts who have significant experience with ethnicity and development in Vietnam, the report maintains that the racist views of the many Kinh cadres, the main representatives of the Vietnamese state and of society at large, are to be blamed for the failure of anti-poverty programs among minorities in Vietnam. Though the report leaves out the cultural effects of World Bank–sponsored market reform and neo-liberalization, I agree with its assessment that racial and cultural prejudices are a major cause of the shortcomings of state-run development programs in Vietnam. During my fieldwork, I often encountered Kinh officials who saw their work as "doing development for the Hmong," as charitable acts, something Hmong people should be grateful. Such patronizing attitude has been regularly broadcast in the government official propaganda. For example, in almost all public occasions in which the Hmong are the subject, the song "Mèo People Are Grateful to the Party" (*Người Mèo ơn Đảng*) would be performed. Written in 1956 by a Kinh revolutionary songwriter, pen-named Thanh Phuc, the song is supposed to be a narrative in the voice of the Hmong people about how grateful they are to the Party. Its lyrics go like this:

Here perching on the mountain pass, we Mèo people are singing.
Stars lighten the sky, we Mèo are grateful to [the] Party.
After generations and in poverty and suffering,
Mèo people's life is brightened from now on.
Grateful to the Party, we Mèo are now prosperous,
We no longer abandon fields, burn houses, and live a nomadic life in poverty.
From now on, we Mèo live prosperously together,
in villages [where] the sound of flutes chant,
Mèo people are forever grateful for the Party.[8]

Ever since it was written, "Mèo People Are Grateful to the Party" has been used as a propaganda tool for various state-run social campaigns to "civilize" and "modernize" Hmong society. While very little evidence points to its propagandistic efficacy, the song set the tone for the way Hmong people would be represented in Vietnam. In many ways, this presentation fits the prevailing image of ethnic minorities in Vietnam as subjugated, disciplined, and circumscribed (Taylor 2008: 5). The song is but one of many examples showing how from the point of view of the state, the Hmong should be grateful to the government for implementing policies that have freed them from their traditional shackles of dependency, ignorance, and outmoded livelihoods and customs.

†

More than half a century has passed since the state of Vietnam determined to bring socialism to ethnic minorities in the Northern Highland, yet, not much has changed for the better for the Hmong. More than any other ethnic minority in Vietnam the Hmong have been marginalized by programs that purport to develop them. Vietnamese communism is controlled by the ethnic majority, the Kinh, and mutual distrust characterizes relations between Kinh and Hmong. The Kinh distrust the loyalty of Hmong and point to a long history of strategic manoeuvering of Hmong between foreign powers (French, American) and Vietnamese communists. The Hmong are located in mountain areas that are the most sensitive for national sovereignty and have kin across borders in Laos and China; that is enough reason for the Vietnamese state, to distrust them. For their part, the Hmong have only heard pretentious rhetoric from Vietnamese communists, but experienced very few positive results. They have been arbitrarily persecuted in the fifties; their lucrative opium crops have been taken away from them; they have been deported and then brought back. Their customs and kinship structures have been under attack. The development programs that have been initiated by the Party-State have all unfolded under the assumption that the Kinh have a superior civilization and need to 'help' their 'younger brothers', the backward Hmong, to reach a higher level of development. That all these programs have failed to bring progress to the Hmong is considered by state officials who both designed and carried them out to be caused by the stubborn resistance and stupidity of the Hmong

It is the pervasive association of Hmong with a previous barbaric state of warfare and independence that impels the Vietnamese communists to follow an ambitious course of control and repression under the rubric of "development." These policies are not geared to local circumstances or Hmong participation, but top-down plans that are meant to transform the Hmong into new citizens of Vietnam. In their daily life, however, Hmong feel that they will always be secondary citizens. The time-lag that is assumed in the development programs can never be overcome. In relation to Kinh Vietnamese, Hmong are forever behind. To conclude his assessment of the Hmong situation, Mr. Thanh said; "Many Hmong I met during the resettlement process were much poorer and often did not have enough food to eat. They did not see a better future or, more precisely, they didn't believe in the future that socialism could bring to them." While the state and its agents expect them to be grateful for "the care of the Party and the State," Hmong express their frustration with the state's civilizational agenda either through overt or covert resistance, through migration and flight, or, in some cases, through conversion to Protestantism. Through conversion, they reach an understanding of time and history, of the place of Hmong in the world, and a different model of what it means to be modern than that offered by the Vietnamese Party-State and its local Kinh officials.

THE SHORT-WAVED FAITH

I N the late 1980s, when his home village of Sa Pả became overpopulated, Grandpa Ceem and his family packed their few possessions and moved up to the sparsely populated mountains of Than Uyên, where there was still some unclaimed arable land. Joining them were the family of Grandpa Meeg and two other families. As a low ranking government cadre, Grandpa Ceem received from his work unit (*tổ công tác*) a small radio with AM, FM, and SW frequencies, which became his family's only source of entertainment after they settled down on their remote mountain. That radio, a precious and rare object among the poverty-stricken Hmong, was intended to keep Grandpa Ceem in touch with his Kinh colleagues and superiors, and, through them, with the state. Instead it connected him and his fellow Hmong to a world beyond Vietnam, to the Hmong diaspora and to global Christianity.

One day, not long after arriving at their new home in Hua Tra, while turning randomly through the channels, Grandpa Ceem was startled to hear a Hmong voice. Since nearly a decade before, when the last government Hmong radio program had stopped broadcasting, he had heard no Hmong voices on the air. Moreover, there was something special about this voice. It was warm and loving. Calm and relaxed, the voice spoke like a Hmong father telling a story to his children. Unfortunately, before Grandpa Ceem could understand what the story was about, the voice announced that the morning program would end here, but would continue at 6:00 that evening on the same frequency; the speaker introduced himself as Pastor John Lee (Xwb Fwb Vam Txoob Lis).

Worried about not being able to find the channel again, Grandpa Ceem left the dial at the same place, turned the radio off, and spent the rest of the day anxiously waiting. The hour finally arrived and he turned the radio on; his whole family was speechless to hear beautiful music as a prelude to Pastor John Lee's story. This time Grandpa Ceem understood that the story was about Vang Tsu, a Hmong king he had heard about in his childhood but under the name Fuab Tais. Pastor John Lee said that Vang Tsu loved the Hmong and he would return to help them one day. Other details—concerning sin, the teaching of Vang Tsu's son, Lord Jesus Christ, who was sent by God to die to save mankind, and the discussion of the evil Satan—required many more days of listening for Grandpa Ceem to grasp. Yet the message about Vang Tsu struck Grandpa Ceem at once.

When I met Grandpa Ceem, twenty years after that fateful day, he was an affirmed Protestant. Although the route to this affirmation was bumpy, Grandpa Ceem assured me that he never regretted a single part of it. He was especially grateful for the opening of that trajectory; the accidental encounter with the radio broadcast that led him to a life in Christ. Grandpa Ceem's story runs counter to traditional conversion narratives. Classic missionary narratives suggest that the conversion of indigenous people is achieved only after a lengthy and complicated process which requires missionaries to stay close, both physically and spiritually, to their targeted groups and to have a great deal of charisma, bravery, love, compassion, patience, and devotion towards their flock. To understand how Protestant conversion, like Grandpa Ceem's and that of thousands of Hmong people in Vietnam was made possible by a radio broadcasting program, we need to step back in time, to the last three decades of the twentieth century, when in the context of the post-Vietnam war, a Hmong evangelical radio program was created to broadcast to the Hmong in northern Vietnam.

INTENTIONAL PROJECTS: THE WORKS OF
THE FAR EAST BROADCASTING COMPANY

Missionary outreach is a Christian calling, but for American Christians it is even more of a life goal (Keyes 1996). Religious broadcasting, since its very beginning, has been an integral part of American culture. Though at first Christian broadcasting organizations focused on domestic markets, it was only a matter of time before many of them sought to extend their activity to other parts of the world where Christians were in the minority or altogether absent. This is the context in which the Far East Broadcasting Company (FEBC), a non-denominational, international Christian radio broadcasting group, was founded. The organization was created in 1945 by a US evangelical organization, and it became the third largest international broadcaster in the world.[1] According to the FEBC, US soldiers were returning home from the Pacific theater with the new sense of the great spiritual need of Asia so the FEBC's response was to try to meet this perceived want. From the beginning, the FEBC's goal was to reach both the converted and the unconverted, with an emphasis on the latter. It choose a foreign location—Manila—and its program schedule was rich in evangelizing messages, religious music, and specific stories of listener conversions to Christianity. Today, the FEBC broadcasts the Gospel in 158 languages from 36 transmitters located throughout the world. Their programs reach across areas in which two-thirds of the world's population lives, and the FEBC receives in excess of 750,000 listener responses annually. The focus on international proselytizing is what distinguishes the FEBC from other existing Christian broadcastings.[2]

Among FEBC's programs, the Unreached People Groups (UPGs) is a special one to which FEBC devotes particular attention and strategies. An "Unreached People Group" (also referred to as "Hidden People" or "Forgotten People") is a missiological term commonly used by evangelist Christians to identify groups of people distinguished by a distinct culture, language, or social class who lack a community of Christians able to evangelize them without outside help. The only opportunity for these groups to hear about salvation is through an "external witness." Historically, an external witness was a Western missionary committed to sharing the Christian message with a group of people, but these days "indigenous missionaries" and "gateway" groups are able to reach their non-Christian neighbors. An indigenous missionary is a person who shares his faith with his own people. He has a great advantage over foreign-born missionaries because he understands the language and culture and is thus more effective in leading people to Christ. [3] Likewise, "gateway" groups live in close proximity to other minority groups. When gateway groups are exposed to the Gospel and become believers, they become conduits to surrounding groups. Two examples of gateway groups are the Khmu of Laos, who are successfully evangelizing neighboring Laotian minorities, and the Chin, a minority group living in Burma, who are reaching out to the Shan also of Burma.[4]

According to the FEBC, radio can also serve as an "external witness." "Many regions that are inaccessible—either geographically or politically—can easily be reached by radio waves. Radio is resource efficient: a few dollars pay for one minute of airtime, touching the lives of those in remote areas where most have never seen a pastor, teacher or missionary; the skills of just a few workers can reach thousands who have not even heard the name of Jesus."[5] Seeing the efficiency of radio, the FEBC has called for support from donors for a program to give radios to its listeners. "Portable Missionaries" (PM) was a term coined in the early 1950s when staff members from the FEBC in the Philippines designed and constructed transistor radios for the purpose of giving them to people in remote areas. The "box that can talk" brought them the Good News in their own language. PM radios continue to be effective means of sharing the Gospel with people who live in countries with restricted access and those unable to attend local churches.

Aware that there are still so many more UPGs in the world who have not heard of the Gospels, the FEBC presses on, one language and one people group at a time, following Jesus's commandment to "go, therefore, and make disciples of all nations."[6] Today the FEBC claims to minister to over one hundred different UPGs in Asia. Explaining why the UPGs seem to respond so favorably to the Gospels, the FEBC suggests that one of the reasons for the massive growth in Christianity among minority groups is the sense of dignity and worth that indigenous broadcasts offer them. People from these backgrounds "grapple with persecution and discrimination most of their lives, but when they hear a radio message spoken in their own language, it validates them. Many minority groups see the broadcasts as their only means of access to Christian instruction and fellowship."[7]

THE HMONG MISSION: INDIGENIZATION OF CHRISTIANITY IN THE TRANSNATIONAL SPHERE

Since the 1950s, as Keyes (1996: 286) observed, there has been a concerted effort on the part of almost all Protestant denominations in Southeast Asia to "indigenize" their local congregations. "Indigenization has meant, first and foremost, replacing Western missionaries by local clergy and lay leaders. At a deeper level it also involves re-working the religious message of Protestantism in indigenous languages using local meaningful idioms and expressed in rituals linked to local social processes." On the basis of this definition, can we see the FEBC's program for the Hmong as also a kind of indigenization of Christianity? And if we can, what are the implications of this as it concerns the indigenization of world religions to local practice in the transnational sphere?

The history of the development of the Hmong program of the FEBC clearly shows a tendency toward the indigenization of Evangelical Protestantism in Hmong culture (Clifford 2001). Moreover, the particularity of Hmong twentieth century history in Asia makes it possible to understand this "indigenization" as performed in the transnational sphere. First, in terms of personnel, there has been a gradual replacement of Westerners by Hmong pastors/speakers. The FEBC began broadcasting from Manila to the Hmong hill tribes in Laos as early as 1953. In those early days, the "God loves the Hmong" stories were not heard by many Hmong because they were told by a Westerner in the Laotian language. At first only a few educated Hmong, who also spoke Laotian, were able to listen to the broadcasts; some of these formed the first generation of Hmong Evangelicals in Southeast Asia. Even though the broadcast's success in those early days was modest, its importance should not be underestimated. From this group, a crucial human resource was developed, and it was this first generation that provided important Hmong agents and missionaries to help advance the FEBC's mission to the Hmong, not only in Asia but also among overseas Hmong communities.[8]

After the evacuation of Laos in 1975, programs for the FEBC Hmong broadcasts were made in a makeshift studio in a trailer caravan in Loei in northeast Thailand, just across the Mekong River from Laos. But this was only a temporary measure. Perceiving a great need to encourage and support the Hmong Christians back in Laos, the FEBC saw the necessity to establish long-term production facilities not only to meet this need but also that of thousands of Hmong refugees in camps in Thailand strung along the Laos border. Indeed, this community continued to grow in size years after the end of the war in Laos. The Laotian Hmong certainly had great needs and a lot of uncertainties, especially about the future. In 1979, the FEBC set up the Hmong programming department in California with the aim of better serving the spiritual needs of Hmong refugees. Also in 1979, members of a newly formed Hmong refugee community in the United States became involved and helped to expand this project, thus becoming a decisive factor in its success. Pastor John Lee, whom Hmong people in Vietnam respectfully called xwb fwb Vam Txoov Lis (Teacher Lee), and his wife, Pail, were the first and most important Hmong broadcasters of the FEBC. From their home in California they recorded more than a hundred hours of preaching which were sent to the Manila FEBC station to be broadcasted to Hmong regions in Asia.

The Lees made changes to the content of the Hmong programs, taking the indigenization of the FEBC's Christian message to the next level. Various elements of Hmong traditional culture were incorporated into the programs, and details of Hmong legends and folkloric stories were used as references to explain the Bible. John Lee brought hope to his listeners by telling them of Fuab Tais [another name for Vang Tsu]—the God of Heaven—whom they could know for themselves. He told them that there was a way back to him through faith in Jesus. Hmong people knew through their oral history that they had become separated from Fuab Tais—but now Lee was assuring them of a way back. The Lees also featured on their radio program a female Hmong missionary famous for singing biblical stories using Hmong traditional ballad style *kwv txhiaj*. Once Christian messages were indigenized into Hmong culture, they were received by a much wider audience than had been initially expected. The Hmong public was "self-organized" and was comprised of Hmong listeners not only in Laos and Thailand, but also in China, Burma, and Vietnam. The FEBC only recognized its own range of impact when

> [l]etters began to pour in from these countries. They spoke a common
> language of fear of evil spirits, and release from the spirits, from sick-

ness, and from appeasing the spirits by costly sacrifice. Letters poured in faster than John and Pail could answer them—but they became excellent program fodder for John as he spoke about their questions and gave answers based on Scripture. Little did anyone know at that time that the programs were having a profound impact upon Hmong living in the mountain provinces of northern Vietnam. The first news of any stirring among the Hmong of Vietnam came through a surprising source—an article in a Hanoi newspaper in 1991 written by a Communist cadre lamenting the fact that many Hmong were becoming Christians. They were selling their livestock, going out and buying radios, and tuning in to Christian broadcasts from Manila. More than that, they were turning to the God of Heaven and becoming Christians. Large numbers were suggested: 250,000 was the Communist estimate.[9]

UNEXPECTED RESPONSES: PROTESTANTISM AND THE HMONG IN NORTHERN VIETNAM

Once they came back to their senses after listening to the FEBC broadcast for the first time, even though it was already after dark, Grandpa Ceem sent his second son to the house of Grandpa Meeg who lived two hills away to ask him to come over, for "important business." When Grandpa Meeg arrived, the two men, surrounded by Grandma Ceem and the children, talked until late that night trying to make sense of the message. Next morning, they got up together very early, turned the radio on and waited for the voice of Pastor John Lee. From that day on, Grandpa Meeg came over to Grandpa Ceem's house often to listen to the radio because he didn't have one himself. Their wives and children also loved to listen, especially to stories that were told by a female pastor. They cried and agreed with the pastors when they described how difficult and filled with suffering Hmong lives were and how tired the Hmong were from having to satisfy the endless demands of spirits (*dab*). They were touched when the pastors said that they would pray to Vang Tsu to help them. They loved the music that was played between stories, and they thought the advices of the pastors on the ways of eating and doing (*kev noj kev uas*) were convincing.

Since all members of the two villages in Hua Tra are in one way or another related to one another, the news about the Hmong radio program not only immediately spread throughout the first Hua Tra village, but very soon Grandpa Ceem's house was also filled with people from the second Hua Tra village. Several months after that, at the Sunday markets in Than Uyên, Grandpa Ceem began to hear of a widespread rumor that Fua Tais, or Vang Tsu, was about to return. Only Hmong people who believed in him and prepare well for his arrival would be saved by Vang Tsu and be brought to his promised land. All others shall be destroyed in total chaos and destruction. People were discussing how to prepare to go with Fua Tais when he returned. Some said that they should go to Bắc Quang, Hà Giang, to look for Vang Tsu while others said that it would be best to stay home, stop going to the fields to work, and eat all the cattle and stored food because when Vang Tsu came he would take the people to the Hmong land where it was foretold that houses filled with food and tools awaited all of them. Some suggested hanging Hmong handmade hemp clothes in front of their houses so that Vang Tsu could find them. At the beginning of the following year, groups of people gathered to learn how to fly so that when Vang Tsu return, they could fly with him to his glorious kingdom. Feeling anxious, Grandpa Meeg asked around and learned that these rumors were supposedly coming from listeners to the Hmong radio broadcasts. Yet, the rumors didn't make sense to Grandpa Meeg. He could not recall the radio pastors ever mentioning anything like that. All he had heard from the radio program was that Vang Tsu loved the Hmong and would be sending his son with a book to teach the Hmong a new way. Learning that there were Hmong villagers in Lai Châu who had stopped working in the fields and who had ended up having to dig banana roots to eat, Grandpa Ceem, Grandpa Meeg, and other villagers became quite concerned. A village meeting was held at Grandpa Ceem's house to decide what to do. One option was to kill all the cattle for food, stop working, and to learn to fly. The other option was to contact the Evangelical Church in Hanoi as pastor John Lee at the FEBC advised. After the FEBC learned of the impact on Hmong people in Vietnam, the Hmong daily broadcast program included instructions for Hmong listeners to contact the Evangelical Church in Hanoi. The majority of villagers voted for the second option, and Grandpa Ceem was elected as the representative of Hua Tra to go to Hanoi. Today, Hua Tra people still talk animatedly about that period, the anxiety that they experienced, and their great relief when the year 2000 came and went and no one from the village was hurt, as the prophecy of those millenarian movements had predicted. In retrospect, many Christian Hmong became convinced that the millenarian rumors were spread by non-Christian Hmong out of resentment toward conversion.

Among the things that the Hua Tra people heard from the radio was a story about why evil existed in the world. Once upon a time, the story went, the Hmong were tricked by the Han (Chinese). They lived in fear after this and asked the *dabs* (spirits) for help. Grandpa Ceem's family had worshipped the *dabs* and sacrificed animals for them in order to prevent them from causing miscarriages among the women in the family. But there was a way to avoid the malignant power of the *dabs*, said Pastor John Lee. The Hmong neither needed to worship the *dabs* nor worry about not doing so because the powerful Vang Tsu would protect them. After years of traditional healing, Grandpa Ceem and his family members still suffered from illness and misfortune, so when the village elected him to go to Hanoi, he was eager to do so.

When Grandpa Ceem arrived in Hanoi, he was received warmly by a Kinh pastor. The pastor spoke to Grandpa Ceem about Christianity and told him that the greatest sacrifice that God had made for mankind was to let his only son die to redeem mankind from its sins. The pastor instructed Grandpa Ceem on how to become a Christian. Also during his visit to Hanoi, one of Grandpa Ceem's life dreams came true: he saw Uncle Hồ (Hồ Chí Minh) albeit not alive but in his mausoleum.

Upon returning to Hua Tra, Grandpa Ceem gathered the people from the two villages and announced his decision to burn his family's ancestral altar to become a Vang Tsu follower. With very little protest, the heads of every household in the two villages agreed to do the same. Whereas there were numerous conflicts in other clans and villages regarding the decision of whether to convert or not, Hua Tra's homogeneous decision was partly a result of contingency and partly because Grandpa Ceem was respected as the only shaman in the Hua Tra area. Years later, some villagers told me that whatever "way" he took, they would follow. Those who at that moment were not completely convinced said that they felt that they had no other option. After this historic meeting, all 150 people belonging to the 27 households in the Hua Tra villages identified themselves as Vang Tsu followers. Their way from then on, as far as they saw it, was "the New Way" or Kev Cai Tshiab—the Hmong phrase for Christianity— and they took themselves to be "new Hmongs" (*peb Hmoob tshiab*) as opposed to traditional spirit worshiping "old Hmongs" (*lawv Hmoob kub*).

The relatives of the Hua Tra villagers mostly lived in Sa Pả, too far away to influence their relatives in Hua Tra. Grandpa Ceem was thus saved from social conflict with the non-Christian members of his clan. Despite initial resistance, some of these Sa Pả relatives ultimately converted, although many of them did not. The first five or six years after their conversion, Hua Tra villagers were also left in relative peace by the police of the Mường Khoa commune to which Hua Tra belongs. The two villages were simply too far out of reach to local policemen. As Grandpa Ceem laughingly recalled, policemen were sent to Hua Tra several times to raid church gatherings. When they arrived at Grandpa Ceem's house after half a day climbing the mountain, they were too tired to do anything, so Grandpa cooked dinner for them and then they went back down the mountain again without having carried out their mission.

The story of Grandpa Ceem illustrates the way in which many Hmong in Vietnam received and responded to the evangelical programming of the FEBC. Although the FEBC began broadcasted the Gospel in the Hmong language in the early 1980s, it was only in the late-1980s and early 1990s that the Hmong in Vietnam began responding to its message. One explanation, as one Hmong informant told me, was that only a few Hmong at that time had radios. In the 1980s, radios and most electronic items were considered luxury commodities that only rich Vietnamese in the cities could afford. By the mid-1980s, as a result of significant economic achievements in China, some industrial commodities including battery-operated radios became available through black markets along the border between the two countries, although it had officially been closed after the border war in 1979. As a result, some Hmong, whose wealth came from opium production, could purchase radios and other goods at border markets. As the number of radios increased in these communities, the only station broadcasting in the Hmong language remained the FEBC. In scanning through the radio dial, as Grandpa Ceem had done, more Hmong discovered the FEBC and many were soon attracted to the Lees' stories. From this point on, and partly thanks to word-of-mouth, many more Hmong joined the regular audience of the Lees' morning and evening programs.

The appeal of the FEBC programs to the Hmong was due not only to the Lees' charismatic and elegant style of storytelling, but also to the content of these stories. As previously noted, the messages about Fuab Tais or Vang Tsu meshed with folk tales about the legendary Hmong king from whom the Hmong had been separated since they lost their kingdom in China. The Hmong's hopes and imagination had been nurtured by the folkloric repertoire and the idea that Vang Tsu would come back one day to save the Hmong from their life of suffering and bring them happiness, wealth, prosperity, and eventually a righteous kingdom. When the personage of Vang Tsu was presented as the father of Jesus Christ and the Hmong were told that believing in Vang Tsu required believing in Jesus Christ as well, thousands of Hmong converted to Christianity. When word came that Pastor John Lee had died, a Vietnamese Hmong wrote to the FEBC:

> Dear Mrs. Lee,
>
> Everyone that accepts the faith does it through your radio program exclusively. After Pastor John died, it seemed as if we were without a father. Because we feel that all of this is a family. However, we want to thank God that we have come to accept the faith. Many of us in fact.

But despite us being sad, we are happy that one day we will meet Pastor John in Heaven.

There is so much to like about your programs, be it the music you put on or the gospel that you preach. It encourages all of us greatly. The program does very much to feed our hunger for Christ.

Please pray that more of us will come to know the Lord. Thanks.

[Mr. X, Hmong from Vietnam, August 2004][10]

Religious conversion is a complex cultural process entailing the multifaceted and ongoing transformation of a person's patterns of behavior, way of thinking, and daily life. The conversions initiated by the FEBC were just the beginning of a complicated trajectory through which a converted Hmong asserted him or herself as a Christian. While prompted by FEBC's broadcasting programs in vernacular language, conversions, or at least in the first wave of conversions, were only the beginning of the Christianization of the Hmong in Vietnam. From roughly the mid-1980s to the first half of the 1990s, most Hmong people heard Christian messages via the FEBC. During this period, some listeners interpreted the FEBC's message as millenarian news brought to them by their overseas Hmong fellows, and this interpretation spawned various social unrests. In general, when the prophecy failed most of millenarian movements eventually died as well (Festinger 1956). In the Hmong case, while one set of followers became disillusioned and returned to previous belief practices, others continued on their search for truth even after the prophecy failed. Many of them crossed the border into Laos and were given information, instruction, and religious materials by Christian Hmong in the country.

Upon realizing the existence of a mass audience in Vietnam in 1991, the FEBC began tailoring its Hmong program to further develop a close audience relationship. The letters that were sent to the FEBC by the Hmong in Vietnam as spoken messages recorded on cassette-tapes helped the Lees to redesign their program to better match their audience's needs. Hmong missionaries were sent on field trips to visit Hmong communities in Vietnam. A cooperative relationship was established with the Northern Evangelical Church in Hanoi. This church soon became the major channel facilitating the flows of Bibles, tapes of recorded sermons, and other religious materials between the FEBC and the Hmong. The church received Bibles and religious materials in Hmong language, which were smuggled into the country by overseas Vietnamese networks, Korean missionaries and businessmen, and American Hmong evangelists pretending to be tourists. These materials were then widely distributed to Hmong villages by the FEBC's listener-turned-village-evangelist leaders. Along with the radio broadcasts, these materials instructed listeners conversion and on how to conduct rituals to burn ancestral altars. The Evangelical Church also provided leaders of newly converted communities hundreds of registration forms. When a Hmong convert filled in his or her name and address on the form, this became the certificate legitimizing their new faith. With this, they could expect support from the church. Many of my informants recall how helpful the radio was in instructing them on what to do during this period and in the following years when the government began to show increasing disapproval of their conversion.

In the period from 1991 to 1998, larger numbers of Hmong started to identify themselves as Christian and met with strong disapproval from the Vietnamese state. Theological training and instruction were banned, and the government carried out harsh persecution and frequent house-church raids with the goal of preventing the formation of a Hmong Christian community. The FEBC played an important role in shaping the new converts' faith and helping them to get in contact with Hmong missionaries, either by secret encounters in China, Laos, and even Thailand, or through mail correspondences. Because a large number of Hmong people were illiterate, the "letters" they sent to the FEBC were mostly their own recordings on cassette tapes that were readily available. These recorded tapes were taken to China or Laos in order to elude the Vietnamese police. From there they would be sent to the FEBC's international office in Hong Kong, which classified them before sending them on to Hmong broadcasters like the Lees in the United States. Starting in the early 2000s, increasing numbers of audiovisual media products produced by overseas Hmong or dubbed into the Hmong language in Laos were made available to those living in the Northern Highlands of Vietnam. Many of the audiovisual media products were religious, and their novelty triggered huge interest among Hmong audiences especially among the youth. The new delivery format brought another wave of evangelical enthusiasm. To some extent, the interest in the new audiovisual religious media rivaled interest in the FEBC. Although still very popular among Hmong listeners—especially among older Hmong Christians who preferred its personal form—the FEBC lost quite a few listeners to the new audiovisual media, and not surprisingly most of these were younger people. Hmong youth, like any others, could hardly resist the alluring visual content offered by new media. Not only did many previously uncertain converts become self-assured Christians, but also, thanks to the new media, Christianity was redefined with visual glamour and aesthetic canons of modernity that differed from the offerings of Kinh officials who preached the State's rhetoric of "modernity with Vietnamese characteristics."

Pastor John Lee's death in 2002 was a loss for the FEBC. John Lee had founded and defined the Hmong programming. Even today many Hmong converts in Vietnam still say that when they die, they will go to heaven to meet God, Lord Jesus Christ, and Pastor John Lee. After Lee's death, several Hmong pastors were selected to replace him and continue leading the program. In around 2006, the FEBC decided to stop having a Hmong pastor replicate John Lee's program and began to search for suitable pastors to launch an entirely new Hmong broadcasting project. The time slots that had been John Lee's were used to rebroadcast his old recordings, which, thanks to his diligence, were plentiful. In addition, a new program was launched that consisted of new recordings by various Hmong pastors from the United States, Laos, Thailand, and China. The program has been daily broadcasted from Chiangmai's station in several time slots—both from 8:00 to 8:30 a.m. and from 8:00 to 8:30 p.m. The ultimate impact of this program remains to be seen, but its creation and development has already led to a shift in the evangelical direction for the Hmong in Vietnam. Beginning in 2005, as the changing laws in Vietnam began to allow the Christian community to practice its faith relatively freely, the new FEBC program started to shift its focus. Instead of instructing church leaders on how to engage in underground evangelical missionary work in their villages and regions to capture new converts, the new FEBC program began to focus on teaching Christian theology, the ways of conducting rituals and prayers, and the ways of living a proper Christian life.

RELIGION AND MEDIA: A DIALECTICAL RELATIONSHIP

Contrary to the modernist idea that linear modernization, secularization, and differentiation all contribute to the disenchantment of the modern world, "the return of religion" today is often characterized by the use of media rather than by its rejection (Weber 2001: 55). In fact, various forms of mass mediation of religion all over the globe challenge the hitherto widely held assumption that with the global spread of "modernity," societies will become less differentiated and religion will retreat into its own domain of "the sacred" and "the private" (Clark and Hoover 1997). In the twenty-first century, it is difficult to conceive of religion as being detached from the dizzying array of media that amplify and circulate its ideas and practices. Among the pioneering works concerning religion and media so far, visual media are still the main focus, and many questions still need to be answered about the role and nature of radio and voice in religious movements.[11]

In the existing scholarship on the conversion of tribal and non-state peoples to more expansively organized "world" religions, it is surprising to find how little is written about the mass media's contribution to this development. Perhaps this is because the idea that missionary work through media could generate conversions is hard to imagine in that conversion is often seen as one of the most profound transformations an individual or a community can experience.

But is the evident connection between religion and media today something entirely new? Religious ideas, as history records, have circulated through a variety of media for millennia. This can be explained by the fact that mediation is inherent in religion itself. Mediation of magic and miracles has never been possible without introducing a certain technique and, quite literally, manipulation (De Vries 2001: 24). Crucial in shaping religious experience, spectacles such as the crucifixion or the revelation of divine knowledge have been brought to religious adherents through various forms, from textual to contextual and from aural to visual. Thus, rather than assuming the connection between religion and media to be uniquely modern, we should try to understand their original relationship. As is increasingly noted by scholars of religious studies, revealing the key nature of this relationship may help us to explain a broad range of phenomena: from the historical circulation of portable print texts such as Buddhist sutras and the Jewish Torah to the spread of Koranic tafsir throughout the Muslim world on audiocassettes and the worldwide circulation of Christian evangelical broadcasting, of which the FEBC is but one example. To this list we may add the more recent proliferation of a wide variety of religious practices on the Internet.

Numerous scholars have studied media as an aspect of religious practices (Hirschkind 2006; Meyer and Moors 2003; De Witte 2003; De Vries and Weber 2001; Eickelman and Anderson 1999; Hackett 1998; Hoover and Lundby 1997; Stout and Buddenbaum 1996). Representing different intellectual traditions, these new studies move beyond a prevailing intellectual prejudice against popular media as a degrading influence on, if not an antagonistic competitor with, religious life. Yet, even when a relationship between religion and media is acknowledged, there is still a tendency to perceive the assumed link between religion and media as the instrumentalization of one by the other. In other words, this relationship is often seen as non-dialectical, as if media formed the mere vehicle of religion or perhaps, as if the medium were endeavoring to create religion in its own image. As De Vries (2001: 19) critically points out, "Medium is not secondary, nor is the religious mere epiphenomenon. This is what even the most promising theorizations of the contemporary social and cultural work seem to overlook." The dialectical relation between religion and media should also raise the question of "semiotic ideologies" (Keane 2007), such as basic assumptions about the nature of images or the voice in religious life.

Scholarship that regards the relation between religion and media also often asks why the global mediatization of religion that we are witnessing today is more fundamentally Christian than Jewish, Islamic, or Buddhist. Apparently, no other group has been so quick to realize and embrace the potential of electronic communications as the Evangelical Christians (Harding 2000). To what extent does this fact raise the question of whether there are historical structures of possibility that are more available in one religion than in others, especially in the technological development of media? If there are such potentials, what do they mean in terms of knowledge and methodology for the topic we are addressing?

Evangelical Christians take the Biblical demand of the Great Mission quite seriously: "Go into all the world, and preach the good news to all creation" [Mark 16:15]. Yet, this does not really explain why Evangelical Christians were the first to view the ability to communicate over the airwaves as a gift from God intended to fulfill the Great Mission. There are similar messages in Islamic, Judaic, and Buddhist traditions but the first transmission of the human voice over the air in December 24, 1906, was a religious communication not about Abraham the Patriarch or Buddha but about God and his son Jesus Christ. This early religious broadcast proved to be the beginning of a tradition. A century later, Christian broadcastings, especially Evangelical Protestant programs, are still dominant in the worldwide religious mediascape. In the United States, religious broadcasting has been an integral part of American culture since the very beginning of radio.

Even if the biblical potential is not enough to warrant the Christian advantage, we may want to ask what other factors could explain such a huge achievement by these religious groups in using mass media to undertake their mission in the contemporary world? First, if one regards it as a "medium"—be it technological and/or religious/spiritual—aimed at creating a connection between the present and the absent or between the visibly present and the invisibly present or between the physical and spiritual (De Witte 2003: 174), then, at its very core, every religion is a kind of mediation between, first, the physical and the spiritual world and, second, the individual person and the religious community. In this sense, a religion's success in using technological media to fulfill these functions depends on the structural potential of the religion itself. Evangelical Protestantism is structured around the idea that individuals can directly connect to God through the Bible—God's words—and around the emphasis of personal interpretation of the Bible. This feature meshes very well with the character of the radio medium that it is also—in many ways—very personal. More generally, many Protestants follow what media historian Jonathan Sterne (2003) has called a long-standing "audiovisual litany" with deep roots in Christian civilization, according to which the voice and the word are felt to be less material and instead, the site of intimacy and truth. By contrast, vision and image are cast as exterior materiality, as distancing and sometimes even alienating from truth and the presence of the divine.[12]

CHAPTER TWO

To some extent, this "audiovisual litany" can also be found among the Hmong. For example, in the experience of many of my informants, receiving the Gospel through the voices in the radio provides a space that they can fill with exercises of their own imagination to define the connection they have with God. This space is larger than that created by television or by other forms of visual mediation since images have, as their downside, the possibility of narrowing the gap of imagination or of creating an "inactivity of imagination," and de-personalizing the message they carry. For the last decade or so, various audiovisual and printed outlets were made available for the Hmong converts in Vietnam through underground missionary networks. Some of this material has also become quite popular. Such is the case of the movie *The Story of the Life and Times of Jesus Christ* (1979), which was dubbed into the Hmong language. Although the movie is widely watched, many Hmong people told me that they were somewhat disappointed when they saw Jesus Christ in the image of a white man. An older Hmong woman told me that she used to close her eyes while watching the movie. In addition, the concept of medium also implies the existence of an audience, which underscores the importance of receiving God's words in one's own language. If the word of God is in a language that one does not understand or in the language of one's ethnic rivals or competitors—such as, for example, when Hmong listeners receive the message in Vietnamese—mediation can only be partial and the message has negative connotations. This is not only a question of correct understanding, but of linguistic intimacy with God who uses one's own language. Evangelical Protestantism is the religion with the longest history of translating the Bible into various vernacular languages; along with this tradition of translation, the Evangelists have also acquired a considerable amount of knowledge about the cultures in which the vernacular languages are embedded. Missionaries like Francis Maria Savina and Samuel Pollard, for example, were the first to collect ethnographic information about the Hmong. Missionaries generally preceded colonial officers and anthropologists in collecting ethnographic knowledge about indigenous people (Comaroff and Comaroff 1991). This explains why most of the Evangelical Protestant radio ministries, of which the FEBC is among the largest, have the necessary skills and assets to design programs that fit the cultural and psychological tastes of various indigenous peoples, that is, to effectively indigenize Christianity.

THE SEMIOTICS OF LISTENING

Anthropological literature about conversion to Protestantism in the non-Western world emphasizes the clash and struggle between different semiotic ideologies in the process of missionary proselytism (see, for example, Meyer 2010;

Keane 2007). Often Protestant missionaries and the people they seek to convert have different ideas of the value and function of images, of the voice or of the word in religious mediations. This is one of the most visible cultural dimensions of Western colonialism and imperialism and a source of constant struggle. For example, a focus on dramatic visibility in traditional religious practices in West Africa was met with great skepticism by the established Protestant mission churches, who stressed the value of the word and the hermeneutics of the biblical text as the site of the divine (Meyer 2006). As a response, new Pentecostal-Charismatic churches have emerged that integrate preference for dramatic visibility in Protestantism through religious uses of audiovisual media.

In his unique study, Charles Hirschkind (2009) shows how cassette sermons—a popular Islamic media form—serve as an instrument of ethnical self-improvement and as vehicles for honing the sensibility and effects of pious living. Although the FEBC does not represent seamless domestication of Protestantism, in the case of the Hmong program, it is fairly successful in shaping an "ethical soundscape" that nourishes the sensory knowledge and susceptibilities to Evangelical messages. This success is partly traceable to differing assumptions about the power of the voice and the radio as a medium for it. It is also partly because there is a very strong elective connection between such assumptions among the Hmong listeners, the media, and the semiotic ideologies of American Hmong missionaries engaged in radio broadcasting. It is also the result of unanticipated and unintended convergences. For example, although the FEBC staff often praise radio as God's gift and credit their success to God's grace and the miracle of the Holy Spirit, they have still had to make quite an effort to convince their conservative fellow evangelists about the usefulness of radio in missionary work. Frank Gray, FEBC's radio engineer, has published a number of papers and essays to justify the use of this technology, something seen as belonging to the world of science and of the secular and not for the spreading of sacred messages. After asserting the standard position—"it is God's plan"—he told me a fascinating technological detail about the (accidental) success of the FEBC.

In shortwave broadcasting, the signal is first "shot up" by a transmitter until it reaches the ozone layer, then it "falls down" to be "caught" by radio receivers. The quality of the broadcast thus depends on the distance between the transmitters and the receivers. The best signal can be achieved when this distance is between roughly 2,000 to 3,000 kilometers. If the distance is too short or too long, the signal will be "shot over" or will drop before it reaches the receivers' locations. In 1949, because of the communist victory in China, the FEBC was forced to relocate to Manila. Only later did the FEBC realize that this forced relocation was fortunate. Manila turned out to be an excellent location from which the FEBC's beamed signals could best reach most of China's mountain borderland region, where most of FEBC's UPG listeners live, and in mainland Southeast Asia. Vietnam's Northern Highland region lay within optimal distance for FEBC's reach. This explains why the Vietnamese government's attempts to jam the program (using both FM and SM military jamming techniques) failed.

There were still plenty of rough edges and conflicts in this process. One of the difficulties that the FEBC and its Hmong audiences faced was their different assumptions about the nature of the voice. For the FEBC it was God's words that were important, but for the Hmong it was John Lee's charismatic voice and his "Hmong way" of explaining the message. In the beginning, there was significant opposition to Lee's adoption of various Hmong myths and terms to explain certain biblical stories. Another issue was temporality and the generic conventions for public speaking that most radio broadcasts carry with them. Radio broadcasts, even if they involve the use of minority languages and the telling of "traditional" myths and the like, often involve generic conventions that are at odds with the recounting of myths and storytelling as well as with other public linguistic performances in many of these societies. For example, broadcasts start and end precisely in one-hour or half-hour intervals. Voices are clearly audible to all and there is no prolonged silence and only brief pauses between speakers and turn taking (Scannell 1992). This generic convention was systematically applied to the Hmong program. First, the choice of broadcasting time (6:00 to 6:30 a.m. and 6:00 to 6:30 p.m.) was the result of careful consideration from the very beginning, following the advice of many Hmong pastors and the Lees. Having firsthand experience of living in a Hmong village in rural areas, they know that these are the time that Hmong families in rural areas are likely to be at home to listen to the radio. A broadcast also starts and ends precisely at the half hour. Music is used to pave the way to the broadcasting pastor's preaching and to end the program after the pastor prays. Some Hmong informants told me that the broadcasting schedule has become the daily schedule of not only their religious but also secular life. In the morning, they made sure to complete all the housekeeping chores and then everybody sat down, relaxed, prayed before the meal, and started eating as the program began. Roughly around the time the pastor prayed, their meal was also finished. They would then pray along with the pastor. In the prayers, the pastors often mentioned the names of Christian Hmong people in different places in Vietnam, Laos, China, and Thailand, to be prayed for. This made them feel that listening to the broadcast was similar to being in a church gathering except that the "virtual" radio church was much bigger. The same routine was followed for the evening program.

Linguistic differentiation was another area in which the Hmong broadcasters and listeners constantly had to negotiate a middle ground. While the majority of Hmong broadcasters speak White Hmong, the majority of listeners in Vietnam are Hmong Leng and speak the Green Hmong dialect. This created some difficulties in the beginning stages of broadcasting. Once the FEBC established contact with its Hmong audiences in Vietnam, effort was made to insert more Green Hmong materials into the program. Female pastor Dua Her's *kwv txhiaj* telling of biblical stories in Green Hmong is but one example. Since 2006, broadcasts in Green Hmong have been scheduled regularly on the new FEBC program. In turn, more and more Hmong Leng listeners are making the effort to learn White Hmong. This, however, has led to some conflicts with Hmong politicians, who are mostly Hmong Leng and anti-conversion. Not only have they explicitly criticized the use of White Hmong on various occasions, in the last decade these politicians have fervently supported the improvement and dissemination of the Vietnamese Hmong orthography, which is based on the Green Hmong dialect.[13]

RELIGION AS A MEDIUM

Traditional Hmong religion embedded in itself a mediatic function that was for Hmong the most important part of their culture. This is *kevcai*, a term which can be translated as "customs" or "tradition," but which literally refers to "ways" in the sense of "roads or paths," classified predominantly as those of marriage and death, but also including those of the New Year celebrations and, more broadly, of birth, subsistence, litigation and dispute (Tapp 2003). In this sense, it is the medium—the ways—that is important for them. For the Hmong in Vietnam and in contact with Christianity, it is the *kevcai* which formed and is still forming the site of conscious modern struggles over which traditions should now be preserved and which ones rejected. Christianity is most commonly translated as *kevcai tshiab* or "new way," and the felicitous coincidence of this translation is that it corresponds—albeit inversely—to the words *kevcai qub* or "old way," which are used to call the Hmong traditional religious beliefs and practices. For a third of the Hmong community, Evangelical Protestantism is perceived as the "new way," a new road or a new "medium," which is "modern" and capable of providing them with new perspectives or a new philosophy of life. Conversion to Protestantism, in the case of the Hmong, is clearly a project of modernizing oneself and one's world. And the FEBC's message or the "good news" may actually be itself the medium—the middle ground, and the means whereby and within which a new Christian Hmong society and culture can be constituted. Even though they resist the call for faith in Jesus Christ, many members of this part of the Hmong community, which still is much greater in size, are attracted to the FEBC's broadcasts. A number of my non-Christian informants admitted that they listen regularly to the broadcasts because "they are very interesting, from the music to the stories. They are also very informative. You can learn a lot about what is going on with the Hmong abroad." Despite their failure to convert these members of the Hmong community, the FEBC broadcasts have had a definite impact on their sense of themselves. They increasingly share the view that their traditional *kevcai* is "old," "backward," and disjunctive in regard to the world around them. As a result, unconverted Hmong increasingly face a "crisis" in defining for themselves the right medium, the middle ground and the means whereby and within which their society and culture can be reconstituted.

†

The relation between religion and media is dialectical as well as instrumental. Evangelical Protestantism's success in using the FEBC to spread the Gospel to indigenous people would not be possible without the religion's biblical, historical, and structural potentials. Yet, FEBC's success in gathering large audiences—some unexpected—would not be possible without the radio being the messenger who brings the "Good News."

Another factor that led to the success of the FEBC is the way it indigenized Christianity and its message, as well as its entire evangelizing process. Christian messages were translated into the Hmong language and the Hmong medium and then broadcasted by indigenous broadcasters shaped by typical Hmong manners and forms. Even today John Lee is sometimes admiringly referred to as the "Billy Graham" of the Hmong by his colleagues. Cultural repertoires such as myths and legends of the Hmong were exploited as being the best way to attract audience's attention. Modern media techniques like public relations and audience response were employed to enhance the attractiveness of the program. Last but not least, despite being a media ministry, the FEBC works in close cooperation with local churches and agencies that act to "ground" the "aired faith" both for and into the Hmong community.

The conversion initiated by the FEBC is just the beginning of a complicated trajectory through which a converted Hmong has asserted himself or herself as a Christian and it requires the on-air missionaries to be continuously active. Even though the Hmong conversion context is far from any post-theological or post-theistic context, it provides us with some of the most helpful conceptual and analytical tools for understanding the complex structure and dynamics of the field. What escapes us in an exclusive focus on media and the message, however, are the socio-political and cultural motivations of the messengers. A number of questions surrounding structure and agency are relevant to Hmong missionary encounters and conversions, particularly those involving the Hmong missionaries who came to Vietnam to evangelize their Vietnamese Hmong fellows.

REMITTANCE OF
FAITH AND MODERNITY

O N a spring day in early 2007, two men were roaming around an area I shall call Cardamom Hill pretending to be tourists. They were looking for Hmong who "worship God" (*ntseeg Vang Tsu*), and they were directed to the home of a man I will call Sua. Sua was a recent and active convert to Christianity who since 2006 had been the leader of a large congregation in Cardamom Hill. By the time the two men sat down in Sua's kitchen, which also served as his living room, the guests, whom Sua called called *xib fwb* (pastor) Pao and Fu, and he had mapped their "kinship" connections (rather distant) and ways of addressing one another. It happens that Fu's wife was from Sua's clan and that Pao's aunt-in-law was from the Viet-Laos border village where Sua's grandmother was born. Sua was pleasantly impressed by the pastors' rhetorical skills and quickly took a liking to them. They talked and prayed for a while, and then the pastors hopped on the back of two motorbikes driven by Sua and another member of his congregation and went on to visit nearby Hmong Christian communities.

Two decades after first hearing the "good news" of evangelical Protestantism via the airways, the Hmong in Vietnam began receiving visits from a network of underground evangelists. The origin and background of these evangelists has varied; the majority of them have been overseas Hmong: some from Thailand, Laos, or China, but most from America. To carry out the risky task of evangelizing the Hmong in Vietnam in the face of government hostility, these missionaries must be able to mobilize resources both locally and transnationally. The informality of their evangelical networks as well as the conversions they accomplish depends on the strength of ethnicity and kinship among the

Hmong—something that the Kinh agents of the state do not possess—and the transnational aspects of their mission

Everywhere that Pastors Pao and Fu went they established their various kinship ties with the people they met and were received warmly. To their local Hmong brethren, they represented many different yet interconnected things. Hailing from the United States where Pastor John Lee had lived and produced his broadcast programs, the pastors brought further doctrinal enlightenment; they represented the wide world beyond the remote location of the village, beyond even Vietnam; they represented as well modernity and prosperity beyond what the Hmong saw the Kinh enjoy. For the missionaries, the villagers were brethren whom they came to evangelize. Having spent their lives struggling to adapt to American life while preserving their ethnic and cultural identity, for them the poverty of the villagers—their very backwardness—represented a more authentic way of being Hmong, one that evoked in them feelings of nostalgia.

ETHNIC ORIGIN AND DOUBLE TRANSNATIONALITY

Like their on-air radio colleagues, such as the Lees and other FEBC Hmong broadcasters, many of the on-foot Hmong missionaries had been former Laotian war refugees who came to the United States in the second half of the 1970s. Their decision to serve as missionaries in Vietnam, an act that is highly political and often dangerous, can be understood in the context of their double conversion both to Christianity and to American citizenship.

Although Hmong converts in Vietnam and overseas Hmong pastors lived in two different countries, they were bound together by their shared ethnic identity: being Hmong. Regardless of region or country of origin, all Hmong who bear the same clan name are supposed to consider each other as brothers and sisters. Ethnic ties are further reinforced by the shared experience of living as part of a marginalized ethnic minority in all of the countries in which the Hmong live (Schein 2004, 2007). In all of these locations, the Hmong are known for their persistence in resisting cultural assimilation and preserving their ethnic identity. This shared experience of ethnicity configuration has helped to strengthen ties between Hmong groups from different countries. Such transnational connections in turn help to transcend locally constructed ethnicity (Barth 1969; Eriksen 1993) for the possibility of a global Hmong identity (Julian 2003; Lee 1996).

Besides ethnic ties, which create transnational linkages between local and diasporic groups and individuals, the Hmong also embody what I shall call "double transnationality." Since they are also part of an older Southeast Asian diaspora, the Hmong in Vietnam share with their Laotian, Thai, and Burmese Hmong counterparts a history of southward migration from China and the cultural memory of a historic "homeland" situated in China. This memory continues to influence messianic tendencies (Tapp 1989a; Trần Hữu Sơn 1996). This southward migration constituted the "first transnational wave" of the Hmong in Vietnam and elsewhere in Southeast Asia. The "second transnational wave" began after the end of the Secret War in Laos in 1975 as hundreds of thousands of Hmong and other upland Laotians were forced to leave the country and become political refugees in the West.[1] The result of this "double transnationality" is the ambiguity of homeland. There is a strong tendency among American Hmong to imagine and conceive of a double homeland in both Laos and China (Schein 2004). Similarly, although these Hmong came mainly from Laos, the notion of national boundaries does not converge with their notion of ethnic boundaries.

As various forms of global connections have emerged in the past decades thanks to the availability of communications tools and the increasing affordability of travel, the vision of a geographical homeland has been enlarged to include other locations in Southeast Asia where there are Hmong residents, such as Thailand and Vietnam. Today members of the Hmong diaspora in the West tend to reconstruct their group identity by erasing cultural and linguistic differences between themselves and all the Miao in China.[2] By reclaiming a common identity for all Hmong and Miao in the world, diasporic Hmong assume membership of a much larger community, as there are about ten million Miao compared to three million Hmong. Many Hmong in the United States told me that they or their relatives were born in Vietnam and then moved to Laos, and that many of them still have relatives living in Vietnam. This is why one of the American Hmong missionaries who came to Cardamom Hill could claim the same place of origin with one of the Vietnamese Hmong villagers despite having fled to the United States from Laos.

Hmong whom I encountered in Madison, Milwaukee, St. Paul, and Minneapolis often told me about recent visits to Vietnam to look for long separated relatives. One successful banker in St. Paul told me about a trip she made in early 2007 with her husband to a village all the way up in Hà Giang province in Vietnam to visit her father-in-law's younger brother. The brothers were separated for more than sixty years because of war and migration. Only in early 2000 did her father-in-law learn that his brother was still alive, but he was too old to make the trip himself to see him. After much difficulty, the banker and her husband managed to establish contact, first by sending cassette tapes via the missionary networks and later by phone. In 2006, her father-in-law passed away without realizing his dream of seeing his brother again. On the father-in-law's deathbed, he asked his son to go to Vietnam to find his uncle. The banker told me this story in tears, but, remembering her later visit to Vietnam, she soon became quite joyful and talked excitedly about how beautiful, how traditional, and how "authentic [her] Hmong people" back in Vietnam were.

I witnessed another example of this kind of enthusiasm for the ancestral homeland at the First International Hmong Studies Conference held at Concordia University in St. Paul in 2006. A Hmong high school teacher who had led a group of Hmong students on a school tour to Vietnam gave a presentation about the Hmong population in Vietnam. Although it was not an academic presentation, her talk was among the best attended of the entire conference. The teacher proudly presented general background information on the socioeconomic and cultural life of her "Hmong brothers and sisters" in Vietnam despite the fact that she did not manage to visit any Hmong areas during her stay but just remained in Hanoi. She used pictures and printed materials that she had gathered from Hanoi bookstores and from the Vietnam Museum of Ethnology to illustrate her talk. Her talk praised the "authenticity" and the "traditional" way of life of the Hmong in Vietnam. During the discussion, several young Hmong audience members commented on how admirable it was that the Vietnamese Hmong could be so poor and yet still preserve their—"our"—beautiful Hmong culture.

THE MISSIONARY ZEAL

During my fieldwork among church communities in Wisconsin (2006), Minnesota (2006 and 2008), and Colorado (2008), I often encountered churchgoers who expressed the desire to go to Asia to do mission work.

Most of our knowledge today of Protestant missions in Southeast Asia is limited to research on those that took place in the colonial and neocolonial era (Tapp 1989b; Keane 2007; Kammerer 1990; Aragon 1996, Salemink 2003). Much less studied are the missions carried out in the context of postcolonial and contemporary societies like the underground missions established by American Hmong missionaries for Hmong people in Asia. Whereas Protestant missionaries working during the colonial period mostly benefited from the protection and encouragement of colonial authorities—with few exceptions in French Indochina, Thailand, and India—Hmong missionaries today do their work in secretive circumstances to avoid arrest. Their work has been strictly forbidden by state authorities in Vietnam, China, and Laos. The charismatic aura that surrounds the act of becoming a missionary in the colonial era works differently from of Hmong evangelists from the United States today. For colonial missionaries, this job entailed leaving home, perhaps for good, working among people of wholly alien cultures, and undergoing the hardships of physical discomfort and disease (Keyes 1996: 282). For the Hmong missionaries, the secretive and dangerous nature of the underground missions gives the undertaking a heroic aura. Unlike their colonial predecessors, contemporary missionaries do not see going to Asia as a lifetime commitment, but rather more of an extended trip abroad; this can make them appear to be more cosmopolitan in the eyes of their community in the United States as well as in the eyes of their marginalized peers in Vietnam, Laos, and China. While hardships of physical discomfort and disease were life-threatening factors for colonial European and American missionaries, today these factors are rarely as extreme and often help to add the aura of adventure to missionary narratives.

The most important difference between the Hmong missionaries and their colonial forerunners is their relationship to the people and the culture they aim to influence. For European and American missionaries, being missionaries meant working among people of wholly different languages and cultures. In the alien worlds of Southeast Asia, "they were outsiders whose spoken language, much less written language, was totally incomprehensible to almost everyone they sought to convert" (Keyes 1996: 282; Rafael 1988). By contrast, the fast growth of the Hmong Christian population in Asia today is attributed to the fact that it has been Hmong missionaries who have evangelized other Hmong. This is the concept of "homogeneous unit principle" that Pastor Timothy Vang (1998) coined to explain this missiological mechanism. The principle is drawn from the idea that "people become Christian most rapidly when the least change of race or clan is involved" (McGavran 1955; cited in Vang 1998: 129). That is, people are more likely to convert to Christianity, presumably, if they do not have to deal with ethnic, racial, linguistic, or other social differences during and after their conversion. Quoting McGavran, Vang writes that "people like to become Christians without crossing racial, linguistic, or class barriers" and "they want to join churches whose members look, talk, eat, and dress like them" (1998: 166). Vang argues that the Hmong Christian and Missionary Alliance's (CMA) application of this principle has contributed "significantly" to the growth of the Hmong CMA in Laos from the 1950s to the 1990s.

Despites the differences between colonial and contemporary Hmong missionaries, there are some obvious similarities. First, to some extent, both share the conviction that they have a moral obligation to bring the truth of the Gospel to those who have not yet heard it. Second, their missionary zeal has its roots in their own conversion. This is something similar to Brumberg's (1980) finding when he pointed out that the roots of the first American foreign missions could be traced back to the Second Great Awakening of the early nineteenth century. The American social context of members of the Hmong diaspora is crucial to explaining their motivation.

Incomplete Conversion

Some of the Hmong in the United States are descendants of those converted in Laos in the mid-twentieth century. Although Catholic and Protestant missionaries were already active among upland Laotians at the end of the nineteenth century, only in the late 1950s did conversion begin to spread. George Linwood Barney (1957), a linguistic anthropologist and missionary, characterizes this mass conversion as a "people's movement" in which several families or entire villages converted to Christianity within months, and immediately organized themselves into churches and sent their children to Bible schools. Half a century later, while asserting that it was the "outcome of the mysterious movement of the Spirit of God," pastor Vang also admitted that the devastating destruction of the Secret War on the Laotian highlands that turned thousands of Hmong people to Christ (1998: 59).[3]

In the refugee camps, another massive segment of the Hmong population converted to Christianity.[4] Pioneering studies on the Hmong community in the United States also reveal links between marginalization in the context of the refugee camps in Thailand and the growth in the number of Christian converts among Hmong refugees (Culhane-Pera et al. 2003; Hones 2001). Nancy Smith-Hefner (1994) in her study of Khmer refugees observed that the core of Boston's Khmer Christian community, including virtually all of the ethnic Khmer pastors, was comprised of individuals who converted to Christianity in refugee camps before coming to the United States. Many linked their conversion to the suffering and pain they experienced during Pol Pot's time in power and to what they regarded as their miraculous escape from Cambodia to Thailand. It was common for them to be tormented by the question of why they survived their ordeal when so many of their friends and family members did not. After reaching the border camps and meeting Christian missionaries, these Khmer were exposed to a new religious narrative, one that offered them the possibility of interpreting their difficult experience in redemptive terms and reframed their ordeal in terms of the divine designs of the Christian God who had deliberately chosen to save them from death (1994: 27). This redemptive interpretation of past difficult experiences was also very common among the Hmong refugees.

After coming to America, although many Hmong resisted Christianity or gradually distanced themselves from the faith, others actively converted. Besides obtaining a new interpretation of their past suffering, some saw their life in Christ as a fast track to American cultural citizenship. Either way, most of Hmong refugees I interviewed in the United States pointed out the important role of religion in their diasporic life. This accords with Raymond Williams' claim that "Immigrants are religious—by all counts more religious than they were before they left home" (cf. Casanova 2005: 13). Many studies on migrant societies in the United States indeed demonstrate that religious spaces and rituals serve as core cultural institutions in which ethnic, religious, and thus cultural identities are negotiated, reinforced, or reconstructed in accordance with and in reaction to local conditions (Guest 2003; Jeung 2005; Levitt 2002). The religion and religious practices of these diasporic societies play a critical role in enhancing refugees' diasporic identities and cultural citizenship (Clifford 1994; Cohen 1997; Ong 2003; Rosaldo 2003; Westwood and Phizacklea 2000; Vasquez 1999; van der Veer 1996, 2001, 2002). In many cases, migrants carry their religions from their homelands to their host society, where their religiosity tends to be enhanced and becomes more sincere (Levitt 2007). In her study of Cambodian refugees in a Mormon church, however, Aihwa Ong (2003) sheds light on how conversion to Mormonism, an American religion, has aided the assimilation process of Cambodian refugees into American society. Conversion in this case amounts to a rite of passage from traumatized Cambodian war refugees to modern Mormon-Cambodian-Americans and as such, it is the process of re-articulating these refugees' personhoods. Ong's findings show that for many diasporic Cambodians, Evangelical Protestantism is an important modernizing culture in the United States (2003: 220). Becoming American is thus also a process of becoming modern.

Most Hmong immigrants, in both processes of resistance and conversion, have been active agents of the transition of their identity to their modern American selves. Upon arrival, the Hmong were scattered across the United States as the federal government attempted to evenly distribute their economic burden on any given state's welfare system. Many Hmong were supported by government assistance or worked multiple minimum wage jobs. They also experienced a certain amount of resentment from the surrounding communities; they were seen as "sponges" on the American system (Fadiman 1997: 191). For older Hmong immigrants, many of whom have never learned English, living in the United States was completely disorienting and remained confusing even many years after immigrating (Faruque 2002: 92). Most adult Hmong immigrants had never previously seen a house with electricity or indoor plumbing. Immediate assimilation was therefore simply not an option as it might be for immigrants from more modern countries or regions. Adrift between different living environments—all drastically different and, on account of this, often incomprehensible—many Hmong people found in their traditional religion and cultural practices a supporting force, a communal bond, and a sense of home. Consequently many did all they could to maintain their culture and religion in the face of Western influence.

In contrast to those who fiercely maintained their ethnic, cultural, and religious identities, many others actively converted and formed Hmong Christian communities. There are numerous explanations for this phenomenon. Some Hmong openly stated that they became Christian because, back in the 1980s, the only way for them to get from the refugee camps to the United States was through sponsorship by a Protestant church. Once they arrived, they joined the church to please their sponsors and to enable their children to qualify for scholarships to private Christian schools. Others joined Christian relatives and managed to find a sense of community in the church with non-related Hmong community members. Some converted because of the difficulty in finding traditional healers and ritual specialists, because of the difficulty of performing rituals prohibited by local laws, or because of the need to protect themselves from illnesses caused by spirits.

More abstractly, a number of Hmong people in Minnesota and Wisconsin explained that for them, a life in Christ seemed closer to what they perceived of as a life in America. To become Christian was understood to be a faster way to become culturally American. Faruques's (2002) analysis of the Hmong community in the Midwest also shows that Christianity is generally seen by members of this community as an instrument that they can use to assimilate themselves into American society. To some extent, the gaining of religious citizenship is thus a means of gaining access to cultural citizenship in the view of many Hmong Americans.[5]

The reality of conversion is, however, more ambivalent for many American Hmong who described to me how they attempted to "make a complete break with the past" (Meyer 1998) and to become modern (van der Veer 1996) while feeling constantly pulled by a desire to reinforce the importance of being Hmong and to formulate a new kind of Hmong identity. As a result, many seem to feel that their conversion is not complete. A middle-aged women whom I accompanied to Church in Madison, Wisconsin, in the summer of 2006 tried to explain this feeling of incompleteness, using the example of a public testimony we had both just witnessed. As in other CMA and Lutheran churches, testimonies, carried out in the style of public confession, were the moment in which church members were encouraged to speak up in public about the ways in which God had changed their lives. These presentations were often very emotional and ended up in public breakdowns as the confessors and those listening to them became carried away by painful memories of the past and wept openly over memories of their suffering during the war, while in Laos as refugees or as new immigrants in the United States. Although the confessors would usually end their story with a statement about how their lives had become much happier since the discovery of God and Christ in their hearts, past wounds were reopened during these public confessions, which seemed to be painful for the speakers and other church members.

While Christianity offers a discursive method to express the sorrow and pain that many of these Hmong refugees had undergone during their exodus, it is not always able to alleviate their suffering. In an article reviewing literature about the animistic and Christian practices of Hmong people in the United States, Hilary Watt (2008: 22) concludes: "Perhaps the desire to 'forget' old customs is rooted in the desire to forget the trauma of warfare, refugee camps, and relocations. Many immigrants have experienced one or all these traumas, and conversion may be the simplest way to forget what, for many, was a very difficult set of experiences." But it is possible that the desire to be Christian may have little to do with the desire to forget traumas of warfare. To the contrary, the confessors and their churches, audiences and fellows knew beforehand that they would be encouraged to recall painful memories from their past, yet they allowed these emotional wounds to be opened up. The consequence of this confessional practice is a reproduction of vivid imagination and memory about the past, including that of cultural and religious practices that belong to that past.

As neither conversion nor assimilation to American life are perhaps never entirely completed, becoming a missionary in Asia maybe one way some American Hmong converts try to assert the authenticity of their conversion—both to Christianity and to their new American Hmong selves—and reconnect with the place where they believe that authenticity of Hmong culture is still intact. All they need is to receive a sign of the calling.

The Calling

The "melting pot" is a metaphor commonly used to illustrate the American cultural tradition wherein immigrants from all backgrounds are encouraged to give up their traditional culture and identity in order to assimilate fully into American culture. In an influential study of ethnic identity in the United States, Glazer and Moynihan (1963), however, stated that the most important point to be made about the "American melting pot" is that it was never actually achieved. They argue that rather than eradicating ethnic differences, modern American society has actually created a new form of self-awareness in people, which is expressed in a concern about their roots and origins. Moreover, many immigrants in the United States continue to use their ethnic networks actively when looking for jobs and spouses. In the case of Hmong in the United States, even among those who made the effort to acculturate through Christian conversion, it is quite clear that the "melting pot" mechanism does not work effectively.

After some time, many Christian Hmong have in fact rejected Christianity and returned to their traditional religion. This is partly because for some the conversion to Christianity, albeit their conscious choice in the effort to adapt and integrate into mainstream American society, has also brought about new problems causing conflicts within their families or clans (Lukens 2008: 35). For others, after the first few years of settling in America, life became less difficult and they could now afford to give offerings to spirits and return to practicing shamanism. Some returned to traditional practices after realizing that Christian prayer had not been effective in curing chronic or life-threatening illnesses. Many half-hearted Christian Hmong decide to return to traditional Hmong religion during life-cycle rites and rites of passage such as marriage, birth, and death. Some former shamans who had converted to Christianity returned to practicing shamanism because they felt that even after becoming Christian, they couldn't escape the calling of spirits and the demand for their services in traditional healing rituals by their non-Christian ethnic fellows. More and more Hmong people in the United States perceive shamanism not only to be the religious affiliation of the Hmong people but an inherent part of Hmong culture and thus of Hmong identity.

Because of the sensitivity of these conversions and deconversions in the Hmong community in the United States, people will generally only discuss them in private. Mr. Long Yang (pseudonym), a respected community leader, shared with me his life story. Born a Christian in Laos, he was given an English name at the end of the Secret War. His father was a high-ranking soldier in General Vang Pao's army and a very devoted Christian. Before leaving home for battle, he would always kneel down and pray before the cross and there were times he asked the whole family to observe a fast for him. Even today, whenever father and son get the chance to talk, the father's main goal is to get his son to join his church:

> Sadly, religion has torn our family apart. Today, I choose to follow in my relatives' footsteps, which are shamanism, because I believe that it is they [my shaman relatives] who will be there for me when I am in need of [cultural] assistance. However, I will never forget all the positive things that I've been taught as a Christian person. What did I learn as a Christian? I think that the most valuable lesson being taught in the church is that we learn how to fear the consequences of our actions. What did I learn from shamanism? Unity! I have learned how being part of a clan can have its benefits when the majority is present. The closeness of a family-oriented structure is ever so important. Being raised as a Christian, I never knew what it was like to have relatives from within our own family tree. For a long time, I thought we were on our own and that our family was the only one remaining. Our father had separated and divided us from contact with anyone and everyone

that was ever related to us because they were non-Christians. I still hear the Christian teachings and preaching today about leaving your kindred behind if they choose not to follow you, which I think is a misconception.

Religion and culture for many Hmong are intimately intertwined. In fact, this entanglement is still common in many non-western societies (Kammerer 1990, 1996). In traditional Hmong society, religion is a comprehensive system of socialization and support, which extends beyond the boundaries of faith and rituals. Religion enables Hmong people to strengthen not only relationships between the living and their deceased ancestors but also among the living. Nowadays, in the American Hmong community, not only do many elderly Hmong immigrants fear the disappearance of Hmong culture and identity, young Hmong people also express concerns over the division in their community based on religious differences. As artist Mayli Yang aptly puts it "Growing up exposed to both Animism [Shamanism] and Christianity—the two most dominant religions in the Hmong culture—I've realized how divided we are due to religion. Religion is a paradox, particularly in the Hmong culture, because it separates us from our families yet connects us to perfect strangers" (Vang 2003).

Racism is another pervasive phenomenon with which Hmong immigrants and their religious practices are confronted. One immigrant, Pastor Chang Tao Vang, complained that "one thing that made us worry in the US was that Americans didn't know how much we helped them during the war. When we first got here, the Americans hated us because we looked different from them. When they saw us, they spat at us. When they saw us driving newer-model cars, they cursed at us. When we were driving old rusty cars around, they also cursed at us." As I observed among many of my sources, confronting racism has made many Hmong immigrants more defensive with respect to their religion. For the non-Christian Hmong, this entails the struggle for the recognition of their animistic/shamanic belief as a religion with equal rights and freedoms to those of others. In *Slaughtered in Hugo,* a fascinating documentary about the conflict over a Hmong funeral home in Hugo County in Minnesota, filmmaker Vam Meeg Thoj brought to the public the sentiments of many Hmong immigrants who feel their religious practices are discriminated against by their white American neighbors and by a Christian-based government.[6]

For Christian Hmong, racism has also resulted in the idea that religious freedom is a domain, which, as upright Christians, they should fight to protect. Yet, for Hmong Christian converts in a Christian dominated land, the fight for religious freedom is given an interesting twist. According to Pastor Chang Tao

Vang, it is a concern over the faithless future for those Hmong Americans who are not Christians. "The generation that was born here will become Americanized and will lack the close family bonds that we used to have. They will isolate themselves and live as they choose. In the future, when the Hmong who were born here become able leaders, they will no longer keep to the traditional religious culture but become Christianized. Those who do not want to be Christian will have no faith of their own any longer."[7] Pa Mang Her, a Hmong man in Lansing, Michigan, saw things in a less pessimistic light. With good Christian optimism, he said, "there is still hope":

> I see myself as a second generation Hmong, but also a Christian Hmong
> person, and I think there is a great calling I feel that the Lord has called
> me to. And as Christians we have our responsibility to fulfill, to bring
> our family to know God and to understand, to be a light and a salt to
> the world. And because I would say that I am maybe 1 percent of my
> family, and 99 percent are the others who are still non-Christian or are
> curious about becoming Christians. I don't separate myself from them,
> as Christ said: you know his commandment was to love your God with
> all your heart, your soul, and your mind but [also] to love your neigh-
> bor as you love yourself. I would go and help them out as much as I can
> and I do have the free time to do so.

The outcome of the kind of calling Pa Mang Her spoke about is perhaps shown in the willingness of many Hmong Christians to be missionaries; first, to go in missions to other non-Christian Hmong in the United States and later also beyond. According to Deacon Fungchatou Lo, it is "unfortunate" that only 25 percent of Hmong people are Christian, thus his and his congregation's mission is to reach out to non-Christian and the un-churched Hmong. In a call for donations and financial support for his mission, Dr. Lo from the Hmong ministry in Brooklyn Park, Minnesota, notes that "since over 85,000 Hmong live in the Twin Cities, the mission work is sizeable." Dr. Lo and his congregation provide Hmong immigrants and their families with biblical tracts and make home visits. They share audiotapes of the Lutheran Church Missouri Synod (LCMS) doctrine as well as of the book of Romans, and they are working on recording the entire Bible in Hmong on audiotapes. They also reach out to Hmong people in Thailand through the Bible Institute, which trains spiritual leaders to become pastors.

The interpretation of past difficulties and personal trials in redemptive terms, as the sign that a Christian God has deliberately chosen them to be saved from death—is something very common among the Hmong refugees. Like many other Hmong missionaries, Dr. Danai, who returned from the United States to run the Hmong Overseas Mission in Chiang Mai, Thailand, gives a creative twist to this concept, turning it into a call for missionary zeal in various fundraising speeches in Wisconsin and Minnesota:

> Like I said to the Hmong in America in my last speech in St. Paul, thirty-three years ago, when the Hmong first came to the United States, they came because of starvation, the war. That is the reason why they came. But many years later, yes there are more opportunities in the U.S. . . . like a hundred more opportunities. Opportunity, you can be better financially, education, job, and opportunity of being able to give, to help our people. If you don't live in America you don't have the opportunity to give financially to support other people. Being in America is being in the land of opportunity for education. The law makes that possible. Now you have a chance to share your knowledge with other people, with your own people in Asia here, the Hmong in Asia who do not have opportunity. That is the message I gave to people in St. Paul.

Dr. Danai's rhetoric seems to work very well and that perhaps can be explained by the ambiguity of being immigrants in the Hmong diaspora. Immigrant communities are not the same as diasporas.[8] Ashley Carruthers, looking at the Vietnamese in Sydney, argues that diaspora and transnationalism are two different moments in a single process. The first generation are truly "diasporic"; they have lost their homeland, there is (for them) an irretrievable break and sense of rupture and loss, and at the same time it is their relationship with the homeland that defines their identity in their new homes and their general failure to assimilate. But members of the second generation move back and forth more easily, opening businesses in Vietnam, etc., and being "transnational." What Carruthers (2002) argues for the Sydney Vietnamese applies to the Hmong as well. Like the Sydney Vietnamese, though to a lesser extent, second generation Hmong in the United States do take advantage of their ability to travel back and forth between Laos and America, opening businesses and leading "transnational" lives.

But while in the case of the Sydney Vietnamese, diasporas and transnationalism are two different moments in a single process, Hmong Americans are simultaneously a diaspora and an immigrant group. For them, being diasporic and immigrant are two identities that continue to exist in parallel and are related to one another. Unlike the Sydney Vietnamese who have a clear sense of where their homeland is, the one they were exiled from—which defines their diasporic identity—and the one that they can always return to, which makes them immigrants as in the case of the second generation Vietnamese, the Hmong in America have a much less clear sense of where their "homeland" is. Before they became refugees in the United States, they had already been part of the Hmong diaspora that left China long ago. Through their death rituals and folklore, their identity has always been defined by their imagined relationship to a homeland in China. Obsessions with authentic Hmong culture, origins, and nostalgic sentiments for homeland(s) have defined Hmong identity throughout history (Julian 2003). This explains why from the beginning of their resettlement in the United States, many Christian Hmong long to go back—both to visit and to evangelize—to the place where they came from in Asia and beyond. If Laos—their immediate previous homeland—is closed to them, Hmong American refugees still manage to reconnect with their cultural homeland in China (Schein 2004a, b; 2002a; 1999a, b; 1998).

This longing is well recognized by missionary organizations. The Hmong Ministry states, "most of the first generation Hmong American students have many close contacts with relatives back in Southeast Asia, and many have a willingness to return to Asia if they are called." During my fieldwork among church communities in Wisconsin (2006), Minnesota (2006, 2008), and Colorado (2008), I often encountered churchgoers who expressed their wish to go to Asia to do mission work.

When I met Mi, a jolly, baby-faced, nineteen-year-old girl, at a 2006 fundraising event at a Wisconsin CMA church, she told me that she felt that God was calling her to do missionary work. God's calling coincided with Mi having recently quit an accounting program at the local community college after developing a passion for flower arrangement. With great enthusiasm, Mi said:

> My big plan is first to set up my own business and then get some money. I will give some to my parents who I know love me, and some to my family, and then become a missionary. I also want to travel around the world. That's what I want the most. Just to see God's other creations out there in the world. But if I have to choose, I will go to wherever there are Hmong people. I know our Hmong people need me and people like me. While traveling I will spread God's words. I want to do that for the rest of my life. [First I will] get my own shop, get rich [giggling], then become a missionary for my people for the rest of my life...When I saw Maiv's [her friend who just returned from a holiday in Laos with her family] video, I really feel that God is calling me. My parents may have problem with the missionary things. By the way, they are not real Christians. They just converted to please their sponsors. Maybe, if it is all God willing, they will one day hear His calling too.

The enlarged, transnational Hmong diaspora is closely associated with Christian evangelical broadcasts such as those of the FEBC, which in turn are closely linked to the conversion of the Hmong in Southeast Asia (Ngo 2009). Every year the CMA Hmong district organizes an annual church conference that attracts large crowds; at the 2008 conference in Denver, Colorado, there were over a thousand attendees. In recent years, missions among Vietnamese Hmong increasingly have become the major theme of the conference.

Fundraising events like this one that support missions to Asia are often well attended. Despite all the anti-missionary obstacles, the Christian Hmong in diasporic communities can still manage to send the "good news" to their ethnic fellows in Vietnam by embracing their common ethnic identity and also drawing upon the organizational and communicational strength of the global Protestant church. Consequently, the practice that they develop is based on transnational connections that they sustain between America, the location of their exile, and their Asian lands of origin.

At the 2008 CMA conference, a session called "Prayer for Mission" was organized in a large hall on the ground floor of Denver's Renaissance Hotel with no fewer than five hundred participants. Four large maps of the world were put on the walls of the hall. The session started with long prayers, speeches by missionaries who were working mainly in China, Thailand, Laos, and Vietnam, and a video made for fundraising purposes about a mission among the Dahua Miao in Guizhou, China. At the end of the session, all participants were called to group themselves and stand under the part of the map that had the country or region where they were either doing missionary work or wished to do missionary work. After several chaotic minutes with people running from one side of the room to the other, the groups were formed. Because the maps were not sufficiently large and the groups were unevenly formed, someone suggested that one person from each group should write the name of the country where his/her group was intending to go on a piece of paper and hold it up. All participants started praying for each group. The two most popular regions were Vietnam and China.

REMITTANCE OF FAITH AND MODERNITY: THE DOUBLE IMPACT OF EVANGELISM

Examining various transnational ties between the Hmong diaspora and the Hmong in Laos and China, Schein (2007: 10) observes that Hmong Christianity generates a transnationality that departs from the sensibility of much of the other transnational practices. Whereas importing costumes, seeking homeland women, touring and returning to Asia are premised on desire and nostalgia for the intact culture and authenticity of the homeland, the proselytizing impulse is fundamentally about changing it:

> It is about designating the country of resettlement as unequivocally superior in its religion and therefore as a legitimate base for impacting the rest of the world. This perspective on the resettlement country intersects interestingly with the economic perception of transnational relations. Both remittances and conversions are premised on improving the homeland rather than consuming it as is. Likewise, the seeking of homeland women, much as it is about the romance of their traditionality, is often driven by the desire to remove them or their families from poverty. All of these relations are not only recognized but are also premised on political economic asymmetries. It is precisely because of their material resources that Hmong Americans can initiate activities that impact their homelands, and not vice versa. (2007: 10)

Schein points to something quite important, namely the desire to reshape the homeland. But there is some ambiguity and ambivalence in this desire. While there is a desire to remake the homeland, there is also, like elsewhere, nostalgia for its authentic purity. It is this ambivalence that is at the heart of the impact of the Hmong homeland on Hmong immigrants in the United States. Moreover, while Hmong Americans can initiate activities that affect their homelands thanks to their material resources, they are themselves also deeply affected by the missionary encounter. The power to influence others is not, as Schein said, an exclusive privilege of the American Hmong. At least in missionary encounters, the identity of the diasporic Christian Hmong is under transformation as well. This is similar to what Peter van der Veer (1996, 2001), Jean and John Comaroff (1991) and Birgit Meyer (1999) have argued regarding conversion and missionary encounters elsewhere in the world. Van der Veer (1996: 7) suggests that in order to understand the interactions between the developments in the colonizing and the colonized worlds, which he later named *Imperial Encounters* (2001), one should avoid the simplicities of theories of modernization and secularization in which modern Europe unilaterally modernizes its "Others," whose role is limited to reaction both in the sense of weak responses and retrograde action:

> The immense creativity in colonial encounters, both on the part of the colonizers and the colonized, is often done little justice in accounts that rather stress failure than innovative practice. The colonial era makes new imaginations of community possible, and it is especially in the

religious domain that these new imaginations take shape. In that sense, conversion to another faith is part of a set of much larger transformations affecting converts, non-converts, and the missionaries themselves. Conversion is an innovative practice that partakes in the transformations of the social without being a mechanical result of it. And again, this is true for the colonizer and the colonized, the missionaries and the converts. (1996: 7)

Referring to the history of Christianity in Europe, van der Veer also points out that while conversion of others is gradually marginalized in modern Europe and transported to the non-Christian colonized world, the rise of missionary societies accompanied by intensive fundraising and missionary propaganda, deeply affects Christianity "at home." For many Hmong Christian communities in the United States the situation is similar, namely that the *missionarization* of other Hmong in the United States proves increasingly difficult, and they are therefore shifting their energies toward their Hmong fellows in Asia. During these missions, the encounters between American Hmong missionaries and Vietnamese Hmong converts are two-sided processes in which not only the converts but also the non-converts, and the missionaries themselves, are equal actors who bear the consequences of their actions equally.

The first and most consequential impact of missionary encounters is the unsettling confrontation with Hmong culture in Vietnam for the American Hmong. During the coffee break after a presentation about Vietnamese Hmong at a Minnesota conference at Concordia University, I had a conversation with several college students. One woman was particularly interested in the fact that I was from Vietnam and was doing research about Hmong people there. She said that hearing the presentation made her feel ashamed of herself for failing to do her part to preserve Hmong culture despite the opportunities she had been given as an American Hmong. Living in a rich society like America, she said, one has all the material means to preserve Hmong culture and the possibility to learn and do research about Hmong folkloric songs (*kwv txhiaj*) and to take lessons to learn to play *qeej* (a Hmong musical instrument).

While we were talking, a Hmong man cut in. As I learned later, he was a Protestant missionary who made occasional trips to a number of Hmong villages in Vietnam. According to him, Hmong people in China and Laos have been, to a considerable extent, assimilated into larger societies and their culture has become less traditional owing to the influence of modernity brought about by economic development. The Hmong in Vietnam, on the other hand, could still preserve their culture and traditional lifestyle because of their economic poverty and isolation. They are by far "the most traditional Hmong in Asia." He

then went into detail about how the Hmong in Vietnam still wear Hmong traditional clothes (with elaborate embroidery on handmade indigo cloth) daily,
and not just during festive occasions like the American Hmong. He described
Hmong markets and the way Hmong youngsters still sing passionately to each
other during courting and how warm and kind people are to one another. "They
are truly amazing, so different from us here in America," he added regretfully.

The missionary's admiration of the Hmong people in Asia for their ability
to keep Hmong culture alive perhaps also has something to do with a certain
regret concerning the loss of Hmong culture in the US Hmong community. In
fact, the experience of being an immigrant and a marginal ethnic minority in a
pluralistic society such as the United States is discussed by Hmong missionaries in their preaching programs. In missionary encounters, these individuals
are seen as powerful, confident and successful "brothers." But, in fact, for some,
the experience of social marginalization in the United States may have been a
factor in their decisions to become missionaries.

Although the Christian Hmong compose a relatively successful and thus
powerful and vocal part of the Hmong population in the United States, they are
still, by far, the minority in this ethnic group. And even when successful and
powerful as an individual, a Christian Hmong will first and foremost remain a
Hmong and thus a member of one of the most marginalized Southeast Asian
immigrant groups in the United States. This very element puts them in an
ambivalent situation in Asia where their hosts see them as part of the successful overseas Hmong community while they themselves are aware of their own
marginality in the United States.

The patriarchal structure of Hmong culture and society is reflected in the
proportion of male missionaries to female missionaries. From my encounters
with male missionaries I got the impression that they, more strongly than their
female colleagues, felt that they were received in a more respectful way and
that their position was more honored among their Hmong fellows in Asia than
among those back home in America. This might explain Schein's (2004) observation that the Hmong's choice to travel "back home" seemed to be one of their
best hopes for empowerment. She argues that Hmong people resist their socioeconomic marginalization within the societies in which they live by forging
transnational ties that yield economic advantages, political alliances, and even
mobility at home (2004: 286).

The second impact of the missionary encounter on the American Hmong is
the formation of their self-perceived role as guardians of religious freedom and
human rights for the Hmong in Asia. In responding to a Hmong woman whose
family members were victims of religious persecution in Vietnam, a missionary made a promise that he and many others in the United States would do

CHAPTER THREE

their best to influence the Vietnamese government to stop the persecution of the Hmong. In fact, perceiving themselves as guardians of the rights and religious freedom of the Hmong in Vietnam is another way the American Hmong connect with their Vietnamese Hmong counterparts. The reasons for this are twofold. One is connected to the antagonism between the American Hmong and the Communist Vietnamese state and the other is connected to the general rhetoric of American Christianity and worldwide religious freedom.

Most of the American Hmong missionaries are Laotian Hmong who hold a negative view of the Vietnamese communist state. Given the history of the war and the Hmong exodus to the west, many Hmong immigrants in the United States are still haunted by painful and bitter memories of the Vietnamese communists. During the war in Laos, Vietnamese troops were said to be taking part in the fighting. As the Pathet Lao and Vietnamese troops advanced at the end of the war, Hmong villages in northern Laotian territories were under occupation by the Vietnamese army. The suffering of Hmong villagers during this period and after the war was blamed on the Vietnamese. It was said that the Vietnamese army wanted to punish the Hmong as retribution for their cooperation with the CIA. Sometimes in the midst of interviews, my informants often got carried away with strong emotions that emerged in the course of recalling memories of past dealings with Vietnamese and made angry remarks about Vietnam and its people. Realizing that I was Vietnamese, some of my interlocutors would recoil and apologize. To lighten the mood, when I arrived to an interview or gathering wearing a red shirt, my sources would sometimes announce my arrival with a joke: "Nyaj Laj liab tuaj os!" (Here comes a red Vietnamese).

In the White Hmong language spoken by Hmong people in Laos and in America, Vietnam is called Nyaj Laj, a near synonym to the word "enemy." Nick Tapp has noticed, in the past ten years, an interesting phenomenon.[9] The American—and Australian—Hmong are "forgetting" that they fought against other Hmong and the Lao in Laos. This, according to him, must be because so many of them now identify with the Lao as coming from the same place. They usually say they only fought the Vietnamese in Laos. There were indeed many Vietnamese troops in Laos supporting the Pathet Lao, but the main enemies were surely the Pathet Lao—and the Hmong who helped them. Today, to most Hmongs in the diaspora, especially those I encountered in the United States, the Nyaj Laj—the Vietnamese—are remembered as the enemy. This perhaps could be explained by the regional politics of Indochinese refugee identity in which anticommunism is a major element (Zake 2009; Vang 2009). By making promises to stop the persecution of the Hmong in Vietnam, the missionaries attribute a great sense of power and political clout to the Hmong diaspora, implying they are capable of making a difference in the life of their powerless

Vietnamese Hmong brothers and sisters. At the same time, this idea has driven the participation of the Hmong in the American public sphere. Hmong media devotes significant attention to issues of religious freedom and has thus driven many Hmong individuals in the United States to think of themselves as freedom fighters and protestors. If it is true that immigrants can only truly look forward to building a future in the country of residence once they are able to let go of their wishes to return to their home countries, being bound to the idea that they need to fight for either political or religious freedoms for their Hmong fellows in Asia may not seem the best strategy for American Hmong. These struggles for an overseas community of origin can be seen as a distraction from focusing their effort towards building a new life in America. However, one could just as well argue that it is precisely their fight for the religious freedom—and right to conversion—of their fellow countrymen in Asia that makes them into real Americans.

Peggy Levitt (1996) has pointed out that the impact of remittances on the sending communities is more than just economic in nature. She argues that "social remittances, which encompass flows of ideas, behaviors, identities, and social capitals between transnational communities" play a key role in bringing about multi-level changes for communities that stay behind (2005: 6). For non-Christian Hmong immigrants who have arrived in the United States in the last few decades, Christianity often appears as a modernizing force (Ong 2003; Faruque 2002). Chan (1994) notes that unlike their co-ethnic Catholics, Hmong who become Protestants are compelled to renounce all of their old religious practices. Instead of incorporating such practices as additional elements as Catholicism seems to do, Protestantism completely replaces—or does its best to replace—animism. She points out several significant effects that Christianity has not only had on the Hmong's religious practices such as polygamy, the practice of paying a bride price, arranged marriage, bride kidnapping and the tradition of girls marrying within a year or two of reaching puberty, but also on gender relations within some families. Such practices are frowned upon—indeed, are deemed uncivilized—by the Protestant church, and those Hmong who have converted to Christianity have either modified such traditions or abandoned them altogether. In encounters with the Hmong in Vietnam, the portrayal and presence of Hmong missionaries—for instance, Hmong Americans coming from a modern country with a certain lifestyle and perceptual framework—actually presents a vision of modernity in itself. This vision is sometimes quite explicitly articulated. Dr. Danai's vision is one such example as he insists that

> I will try to put this in a simple way. Animism is a life that is living with the past because Hmong traditional belief, religion, everything is typed

with the past. How our grandfather, great grandfather, our clan did the ceremony, we have to do the same. When you die you go back to the same root. You live for the past, with the past. Christianity, on the other hand lives for the future. If you want to live a life with the future, for the future, you need to walk with the future, go into the future, not just with the past. That is why the Hmong developed so slowly. I have one professor who knew that I was Hmong – by the way *I am* the first Thai Hmong who was educated abroad, not Dr. Prasit. Through him I understood that tribes, clans, are among lots of things that prevent us from living in unity. Christianity helps to unify people of different backgrounds, races and countries. I shared that message with Hmong leaders. What we are doing now is the good course that we do for the community.[10]

Missionary encounters in Vietnam not only bring motivation and inspiration, but also peer pressure to the Hmong who are repositioning themselves in the historical progress to modernity. By insisting on the wrongness of practicing a "traditional life" and by demonizing traditional religion, missionaries like Dr. Danai—quite indirectly—blame their Asian Hmong fellows for their failure to catch up with modernity and for their own poverty.

Some of the Hmong missionaries with whom I spoke emphasized the humanitarian side of their work and saw themselves as development agents. They spoke of their religious teaching as the teaching and delivery to their Hmong brothers and sisters in Asia of the "New Way." The narrative of "new" versus "old" in missionary discourse is often featured as a zeal for a break with the traditional past and to progress to a better future. Like immigrants who send remittances and wish to make a change in their homeland, the Hmong missionaries hope that by sending Christianity to their Hmong fellows, they can bring about change and development in the life of their Vietnamese brethren.

In a sense, this remittance of Christian faith to the Hmong in Vietnam and elsewhere in Asia by their Christian fellows from the United States can also be seen as a "remittance of modernity." Since an obsession with authenticity is also found in Hmong modernity and conversion narratives, the desire to help in the development of their fellow Hmong in Vietnam has faced these Hmong missionaries with the dilemma of how to accomplish their religious mission, which is to help the Hmong convert so as to make a radical break with the past, on the one hand, and to carry out their message about the preservation of Hmong identity on the other. It appears that there are impulses to both recapture a lost past and modernize and improve it.

In the ethnic and transnational dimensions of Hmong conversion, different forms of media and the continued importance of kinship and ethnic relationships both at local and transnational levels have bound overseas Hmong missionaries together with their Vietnamese Hmong fellows in a "single field of social relation" (Basch et al. 1994: 5). Ethnic ties were one of the most important motivations for overseas Hmong to carry out missionary work in Vietnam and are also the primary factors that explain why evangelism carried out by Hmong missionaries was so readily accepted by so many Hmong people in the country.

Missionary zeal is the result of an incomplete conversion from the Hmong traditional religion to Christianity and at the same time from being Hmong refugees to becoming Hmong Americans. The incompleteness of both conversions is explainable by the binary logics of American assimilation and minority identity politics. Becoming a missionary, for many Hmong Americans, is one of the solutions to the contradictions they experience in their lives. Evangelism to their Asian Hmong ethnic fellows is an act of paying one's dues to one's kinsmen elsewhere as well as an act of remitting modernity. This remittance of faith and remittance of modernity is, nonetheless, double edged. Not only did it transform Hmong society in Vietnam via massive conversion, and by doing so it effectively causes the disappearance of traditional culture for which American Hmong have a longing.

CHAPTER FOUR

MILLENARIANISM
AND CONVERSION

C ư Seo Lử, in his late forties when we first met in 2005, was one of the first converts and church leaders in Phong Hải. The cadres at both the provincial and commune Mass Mobilization Committee (Ban Dân Vận) labeled him a hard-headed "leading element" (*đối tượng cầm đầu*) who needed to be watched closely. This label originated two decades before when Lử, amidst tremendous hardship caused by his family's resettlement in Phong Hải, had been involved in a millenarian movement. When the end-of-the-world prophecy failed as had happened so many times before, some followers tried to resume life as before but Lử, among many others, continued his quest for truth. This quest eventually led him to the Evangelical Church in Hanoi, which provided him with instructions on church leadership; he formed a church community soon thereafter.

Lử's journey from millenarianism to Protestantism has been shared by many Hmong people in Vietnam during the last few decades. Millenarianism, a perennial historical tendency in Hmong society, can be transformed into Christian hope. Hmong traditions have played an important role in fostering acceptance of end-of-the-world Protestantism conceptions, and, in turn, instead of absorbing Hmong millenarianism, Protestantism has played a big role in reviving it. Some Hmong have continued their quest, and millenarian episodes continue to erupt. This is partly because of the Hmong's awareness of Protestantism's end-of-the-world message and not in spite of it.

Although Protestantism for Hmong converts represents a form of modernity, conversion to the religion does not mean an instant embrace of modernity or a radical change to another life. Most Hmong converts have gone through a slow process of experimentation and negotiation with another way of life. The

New Way, or Christianity, is not simply a better way, but rather a different one with both new possibilities and new problems. Most serious among the latter is the Vietnamese state's perception of the Hmong's messianic aspirations and the policies devised to curb them.

A DISENCHANTED MILLENARIAN DREAM

On an early spring day in 1990, while touring a weekend market in Bắc Hà, a neighboring district, Lử heard a rumor that was already widespread in the region and had begun with Hmong people who listened to the FEBC broadcasting. The rumor warned about the coming of Vang Tsu who, as Lử knew, was the Hmong mythical King Fua Tais under a different name. As a child, Lử had learned by heart all the stories about Fua Tais, how powerful and benevolent he is, and that he promised to return when the world was to be destroyed to save only those who worshiped him. The rumor had more effect on Lử than on people like Grandpa Ceem and his villagers in Hua Tra. Lử immediately decided to return home. His family had just prepared two pieces of uphill land for growing dry rice (*lúa nương*). The seedlings subsidized by the local government were ready for sowing. When Lử came home, he ordered all farming activities to be stopped and had the seedlings cooked for dinner.

In the following weeks, Lử and others visited other different Hmong communities around Phong Hải and asked for more information. To their surprise, many people had heard the rumor and some could describe in stunning details what would happen when Vang Tsu arrived. Two families in Ải Nam, the neighboring hamlet, claimed to have heard from the radio that Vang Tsu would be arriving in the early morning of April 15, 1990, which was Easter Sunday. It was then approximately the middle of March. April 15 came, but Vang Tsu was nowhere to be seen.

Meanwhile, a man from Hà Giang passed by the village and told them that they had to go to Nghĩa Lộ, a district in Yên Bái, where there was a Catholic church built in the French colonial period, to put their names on the list of people who would wished to go with Vang Tsu. Anyone who did not register himself and his family would be swept away by the sea when Vang Tsu came.[1] Lử and his family had no means to finance a trip to Nghĩa Lộ, and they became desperately convinced that they were all going to die. A cousin of Lử's wife who went to Nghĩa Lộ brought a form back for them, and told them to pray and to buy an expensive package of cigarettes with a golden cover and a picture of a lady wearing a hat on it, probably Hero brand, then recently imported from Thailand and among the most luxurious commodities available in Vietnam in the first few years after Đổi Mới reforms opened the country to the world economy. They were told that Vang Tsu accepted only this kind of cigarette. Lử later recalled this event with a laugh, saying how silly he and everyone else had been buying the expensive cigarettes.

They were told to place the cigarettes next to a column in the house. Not knowing exactly which column and in which direction the package should be placed, they went to Mr. Chou, a skilled shaman, for advice. Mr. Chou guessed that the cigarettes should be next to the roof beam at the right side of the living room where the ancestral spirit (*dab xwm kab*) altar is usually set up. Lử placed the package on a wooden stool that he quickly made for the occasion under the ancestral altar. Meanwhile, the family stopped all of their farming activities and stayed home praying and waiting for Vang Tsu. The small stock of maize and cassava, which they possessed from the previous crop, quickly disappeared.

One day a man named Sùng Seo Páo from Hà Giang came and gave the family more instructions. Sùng Seo Páo told them that they should only wear clothes made of hemp, a mark of authentic Hmong culture, and should throw away any polyester garments. He explained plastic clothes would burn when Vang Tsu came and took them flying to heaven. A few weeks later, Sùng Seo Páo returned with another man and told them that every month they had to sacrifice a goat for Vang Tsu. After the sacrifice, they could cook the meat of the goat for a feast. During this ritual, they had to hang two pieces of Hmong hemp clothing—one in front of the house and one in the back—similar to a shamanic ritual that Lử's family had conducted when someone was seriously ill.

Nearly a year passed. There was still no sign of Vang Tsu. Meanwhile men from different regions passed through Lử's village, leaving different sets of instructions. Those instructions became less and less clear and made Lử and his people increasingly restless and distressed, especially when the food was gone and no more edible roots could be found in the forest. By January of 1991, like many others, Lử's family had no choice but to go back to tilling their land to prepare for the next crop. A Kinh family near the market sold Lử and others like him money for the the seedlings and pesticides on credit at extremely high price. That spring, policemen in every district of Lào Cai arrested Hmong men who were active in spreading the rumors about Vang Tsu. In some districts, Hmong politicians suggested parading the arrested men around to demonstrate to Hmong villagers that the rumors they spread were false and had been fed to them by foreign reactionaries—more specifically, American-supported and Manila-based individuals—who wanted to destroy the social stability of Vietnam.

Rumors continued, though not quite as loudly and publicly. Hmong men still traveled around talking about the possible coming of Vang Tsu, hemp clothes were still being sought—by believers, here and there goats were still being sacrificed; and there were still people enthusiastic enough to attend "flying classes" which resulted in two deaths in Bản Phiệt, a commune not far from Phong Hải. Lử, after finishing the second grass clearing of his cornfield, continued traveling in search of the truth. By then, most of the people he talked to recommended that he listen to the FEBC radio, which Lử ultimately did after saving enough money to buy a receiver. Villagers would gather at his home to hear broadcasts of prayers and stories about Vang Tsu, whom they took to be a Hmong. Since they thought the radio could teach them that they needed to know, Lử and his friends travelled less to other areas to get updates about what to do to follow Vang Tsu. At the end of 1991, they were surprised to hear the radio voice address them as "our Hmong brothers and sisters in Vietnam" and instruct them to get in touch through an address in Hong Kong. Soon after that, the radio also urged them to look for a church, which was described as a big house with a cross on it. The teacher at the church would instruct them on what to do next. Hmong listeners like Lử set off again, looking for a church. In the region, there were a few Catholic churches that were all led by Kinh priests who, every now and then, took care of Hmong believers, who were the descendants of Hmong who had converted to Catholicism during the French colonial period. After failed efforts to communicate with the priests, Lử and his friends went to visit Catholic Hmong in Sa Pa district and had a very warm reception there. Lử told them what he had heard on the radio. They told him that Vang Tsu could not be the Hmong king but the God that the Kinh people called *Chúa Trời* (Lord of the Sky), who is similar to Yawg Saub in Hmong mythology.[2] He had a son called Jesus who was sent to earth to save humankind from their sins. At the end of their visit, Lử and his friends were lent a copy of the Bible written in Vietnamese. All the answers to their questions, Lử was told, could be found in this book.

Upon returning from Sa Pa, Lử tried to read the book to his family but his ability to read Vietnamese was limited. A few months later Lử went to see Ma Seo Hang, a friend in nearby Sín Chải. The two men compared what they were told by the Catholic Hmong with what the radio told them. They concluded that the teachings were not the same. For example, the priest in Trạm Tấu had said that they had to go to church every day or as often as possible while the radio said that they could stay home and pray to Vang Tsu. While the Hmong Catholics in Sa Pa and Trạm Tấu worshipped Jesus's mother, Mary, the radio did not instruct them to do so. Several years later, it was still not clear to Lử and many of others why they should not worship Mary. Some of them came up with their own reasoning that perhaps Mary was not a virtuous woman as she had conceived Jesus out of wedlock and then used Joseph to support her and her child.

In 1992, the radio started instructing Hmong listeners to get in touch with the Evangelical Church at number 2 Ngo Tram Street in Hanoi. In November of that year, several families in Sảng Pả contributed money so that Lử could buy a train ticket to Hanoi. When he arrived at the church, to his total amazement, he found that there already was a Hmong Committee as well as plenty of books written in the Hmong language about Vang Tsu. Back when Lử went to school in Lùng Sui, he had been taught to read and write the (Green) Hmong script, derived and used by the Vietnamese government since the 1960s. The (White) script in which the Bible was written was totally strange to Lử. He remembered that the radio had mentioned this script and had started teaching listeners how to read it, but he had not paid attention until now. Among the materials that Lử was given to bring back to his village was a small book with instructions on how to read this script.

During the rest of the three days Lử spent at the Evangelical Church, he was instructed on how to conduct different prayers, how to perform other evangelical rituals, and how to burn the ancestor altar. A church member also took Lử out for a city sightseeing tour. The very kind guide also paid for a photo of Lử in front of the Hanoi Opera House. This was the first photo that Lử ever had taken in his life. That photograph, now old and torn, is still proudly displayed hanging from a central crack in a wooden wall of Lử's house.

Back in Phong Hải, Lử was assisted by Ma Seo Hang in organizing a ceremony during which all members of his lineage—adults and children, men and women—knelt down in a circle in the front yard at Lử's house while Lử and Hang stood in the middle and prayed. Then Lử went inside, tore the ancestral spirit (*dab xwm kab*) altar down and took it outside together with the stool that he had made to hold the cigarette package. As Lử started burning these items in the middle of the circle, Hang urged everybody around to go on praying. When the fire died down, the crowd stood up and in excitement, they went from house to house and conducted the same ritual. That day in 1992 was marked as the official conversion of Cư Seo Lử and the other twelve families in his lineage.

LORDS OF THE SKY

As it is clear from Lử's story, a millenarian reaction was triggered in the 1990s by the ambiguous use of the terms *Vang Tsu*, the Christian God, and *Fuab Tais*, the Hmong mythical savior.[3] Generally, millenarian beliefs are an important feature of Chinese religion. They are held by many groups in China and continue to manifest themselves when these groups migrate to Southeast Asia (Tai 1983). One such group is the Hmong, who in China are a part of the larger Miao group. In early modern Chinese history, Miao groups became known for their allegedly persistent tradition of rebellion, which often went hand in hand with millenarianism. However, Robert Jenks (1994: 58–73), who examined the Miao Rebellion that swept Guizhou between 1854 and 1873, points out that although the revolt is labeled a Miao Rebellion, Miao people only composed less than half of the followers. Other followers were Han and members of other ethnic groups. Millenarian folk religion was a much more important factor in the rebellion for other Chinese participants than for the Miao. The tendency in the literature to see especially the Miao as millenarians is incorrect. Rather, millenarianism is a general trait of Chinese popular religion. This is exemplified by all those rebellions that were collectively known as White Lotus Teachings by the Chinese state in reference to the Buddhist idea of the Coming of the Maitreya Buddha (Ter Haar 1992). Millenarian religion, Jenks (1994) argues, offered explanations and justifications that led these non-Miao members to cross ethnic boundaries when participating in the rebellion. But in addition, it provided the organizational framework for the uprising.

Knowledge of the Miao Rebellions comes from historical record compiled by Ming and Qing government officials who were a part of the states' effort to crush them. These records are, therefore, naturally partial and strongly reflect the proclivities and prejudices of non-Miao writers. The Hmong were portrayed as warlike barbarians whose wild nature made them resistant to civilizing projects and whose militant temperament made them akin to a group of incorrigible rebels. There is a tendency among Hmong and non-Hmong writers today to carelessly point to these historical records as evidence of the Hmong's ancestral love of autonomy and to millenarianism as a mechanism to pursue this love (Yang 1993; Halminton-Merrit 1993; Đặng 1998; Vương 2005; Scott 2005). Jenks debunks the assumption—thus far taken for granted and still advocated by scholars like Scott (2005)—that millenarianism is a persistent trait of Hmong culture, which is always connected to a history of resistance against the state or against lowland people.

The Miao Rebellion overlapped with the great Taiping Rebellion. In the aftermath of both events, hundreds of thousands of people of various ethnic backgrounds—among them many Hmong—fled China to the mountainous region of today's northern Vietnam, Laos, and Thailand. The notoriously volatile coalescence of indigenous millenarian belief and Christian millenarianism in the Taiping Rebellion had already set the trend for future revolts in South China regardless of the ethnic background of the rebels. For the Miao group, who stayed in China, early twentieth century reports of the towering figure of Fuab Tais at the center of numerous Miao uprisings began to emerge. These reports started to appear soon after Catholic and Protestant missionaries reached the group (Pollard 1919, 1921). Among those who left for Southeast

Asia, the Lord of the Sky was consistently summoned in various millenarian movements, the most significant of which was the revolt led by Vừ Pá Chay from 1918 to 1921.

Vừ Pá Chay was an orphan in Yunnan province who lived for a period in different places in northern Tonkin, including Lào Cai province, before being adopted into a Hmong family in Laos. In 1918 he had a revelation: the Lord of the Sky called him to lead the Hmong in an uprising against the French who levied intolerable taxes on them. Followers of the revolt believed that the Lord of the Sky would protect them from attacks. Such belief in magical protection and the recklessness with which some of the Hmong fought inspired the French name for the rebellion the War of Fools (*La Guerre des Fous*). What is most significant in this movement is that Vừ Pá Chay's teaching of what he received from the Lord of the Sky during his revelation showed the marked influence of Christianity (Lee 1987; see also Tapp 1989c; Culas 2005; Smalley et al. 1990).

Vừ Pá Chay's was the first of many Hmong messianic movements in Laos that were known as Chao Fa (Lao: "Lord of the Sky" or "God") movements; some of these Chao Fa groups are still active today. As a Hmong revivalist movement that germinated amidst all the suffering sustained by the Hmong in the Lao civil war, Chao Fa advocated the formation of a true Hmong society in anticipation of the return of the legendary Hmong king who would rescue Hmong believers from oppression by other groups.

Not all Chao Fa messianic movements, however, were militant. In some cases, as in the messianic movement that Yang Shong Lue led following previous models, the promotion of literacy was of paramount importance. An illiterate Hmong farmer living near the Vietnamese border with Laos, Mr. Yang Shong Lue, affectionately called the Mother of Writing (Niam Ntawv) by his followers, devised a complete and complex writing system named Pahawh writing, which he claimed to have received from the Lord of the Sky along with other forms of wisdom and morality. Shong Lue's teaching, like Pa Chay's, bore many Christian characteristics and quickly attracted many followers who saw him as a messiah. The Vietnamese communist government however was not comfortable with Shong Lue's tremendous popularity and, suspecting him of association with Vang Pao's military activities, began to suppress his movement. Shong Lue was forced to move to Laos where he attracted more followers. But in Laos, his advocacy of peace made him an enemy of other Hmong groups, including Vang Pao's, who supported the militarization of Hmong society. In 1971 he was assassinated by Vang Pao's associates (Smalley et al. 1990).

However, in the aftermath of the Secret War in Laos and with the increased number of followers who were the remnants of Vang Pao's disintegrated army, Chao Fa became closely associated with armed resistance. Under military guidance and messianic leadership of a man called Yong Youa, the Chao Fa resistance movement attracted many Hmong desperate to stay alive but unwilling to submit to the Pathet Lao government. At its peak, this messianic army was said to have had four hundred to five hundred men operating against the Pathet Lao forces in units of twenty to fifty men. Believing that they were invulnerable and had God's protection, they went to war with strong religious convictions and carrying their own flag (Lee 2008: 4–5). By 1979, many Chao Fa followers were no longer able to stand the shelling and gassing of their strongholds by the Pathet Lao and Vietnamese troops and were forced to flee to Thailand. Yong Youa and other followers continued to roam the thickets of Phu Bia Mountain. In the Thai refugee camps, the Chao Fa movement was once again revitalized by former adherents who escaped from Laos. This group was headed by Pa Kao Her who named his group the Ethnic Liberation Organization of Laos. Following the border war between Vietnam and China in 1979, this organization gained support from the Chinese government, which between 1979 and 1980 supplied them with arms and military training. This support was short-lived as the Chinese shied away from giving aid to Hmong resistance groups in Laos after learning that one of the Chao Fa Hmong's intentions was to recruit large numbers of Hmong in China to fight to make Laos a Hmong nation (Lee 2008: 10). Once they no longer received Chinese support, the Chao Fa in Thailand were forced to depend on donations from Hmong refugees resettled in America and other countries. Meanwhile, Yong Youa and his group continued to live on the run in the Laotian jungle.

In 1998, Yong Youa seems to have pinned his last hope on General Vang Pao's return to the jungle of Laos to help him with the resistance effort. He declared in a video that "I am continuing the fight for you and we are all suffering from your dirty legacy [of cooperating with the American CIA]" (Lee 2008: 5). After its leader, Pa Kao Her, was assassinated in 2003 and his successor Nhia Long Mua died in 2005, the Chao Fa movement in Thailand lost its leadership and support base in the country. Die-hard followers claim that they still have a network of supporters in the diaspora and have been able to maintain direct contact with those inside Laos to keep the fighting going in remote jungles of the Xaisomboun Special Zone.

In Vietnam, from the second decade of the twentieth century on, almost all Hmong political revolts were either initiated by or sustained by messianic beliefs. For example, the movements in 1918 and 1953 in Sa Pa, in Mường Khương in 1938, and in Lai Châu in 1972 were all underpinned by messianic aspirations. From the late 1980s and during the 1990s, various such movements broke out in smaller scale in Lào Cai, Tuyên Quang, and Hà Giang but this time they were connected to Christian evangelism. Once regarded by the French colonial government as rebels, the followers of these messianic movements came to be seen as insurgents by the Việt Minh. This became quite important in the context of the global Cold War and its effects on Southeast Asia. Today Vietnamese communists see Hmong millenarianism as a form of separatist rebellion.

REBELLION AND REVOLUTION

Ironically, despite Chinese, Vietnamese, and Laotian official opposition to Hmong millenarianism, the twentieth century history of nationalism and communism in Asia has a very close relationship with millenarian ideas. Prominent roles were played by Maitreya and Marx, the spiritual and ideological leaders of millenarian movement and the communist movement respectively (Ho Tai 1983; Dubois 2005). The peasants in southern Vietnam in the mid of the twentieth century, for example, were the targets of both Hoa Hao millenarianists and underground communist cadres. In order to build a secular movement out of a sectarian mass-base, communist cadres had to draw from the same source of memberships as the sects with the resulting risk of great ambiguity on the part of the members toward millenarian and revolutionary politics (Tai 1983: 107). Therefore, one of the most vexing problems involved in building a mass-based party in Vietnam and China was finding a way to teach the masses how to distinguish between millenarian and revolutionary action (Tai 1983: 108). For Vietnamese peasants in early twentieth century southern Vietnam, the language of millenarianism was more familiar and easier to accept than Marxist terminology. Similarly, in southern China, Peng Pai, who launched the Hailufeng soviet movement, which was the inspiration for the Nghe Tinh soviet movement in Vietnam, also recognized the power of traditional millenarian language as opposed to new-fangled Marxist terminology (Galbiati 1985; Quinn-Judge 2002).

The Hmong's encounter with communist revolutionaries in the second half of the twenty century shared a number of similarities with those of southern Vietnamese and southern Chinese peasants. As the Việt Minh fought their way to Điện Biên Phủ in the late 1940s and early 1950s, the support of ethnic groups in the Northern Highlands of Vietnam was crucial. In winning this support, mass mobilization campaigns were launched in which Kinh cadres and "enlightened" ethnic minority leaders were sent to the hills and valleys to explain the purpose of the revolution of which the anti-French colonial war was just the beginning. In the mid-twentieth century, each ethnic minority group in the Northern Highlands had a different position toward the French colonial government. To use the French as a common enemy of all ethnic groups for the revolutionary struggle was hardly feasible. In the Hmong case, the task was even more complicated. Virtually half of the Hmong who resided in the Tai federation on the western side of the Red River chose to fight alongside the Việt Minh against the French because they held some animosity towards the Tai rulers supported by the French. The other half of the Hmong, those who resided on the eastern side of the Red River, were left free by the Tai and had been selling their opium to the French. On account of this, they saw the Việt Minh as their enemy. Thus, while military attacks were launched in the eastern side to capture and kill leaders of the Hmong resistance movements armed by the French, Hmong clan leaders and strong men in the western side were courted by the Việt Minh as potential ethnic revolutionary leaders.

The consequence of this double-edged policy was confusion and doubt on both sides. Today a number of Hmong elders I spoke to in Si Ma Cai, the former headquarters of Chau Quan Lo's army in the 1950s, only remembered that Chau Quan Lo was killed by Việt Minh cadres because he was a powerful messiah. At the same time, others told me that they knew of many other Hmong messiahs who were left alone because they encouraged their followers to be receptive to Việt Minh cadres. Acutely aware of the potential political power of Hmong millenarianism, the Vietnamese state did not plan to entirely eliminate these powerful figures but to find a way to exploit them. In the policy for ethnic minority cadres of the 1960s and 1970s, a government document recorded the following recommendation from the central committee: "[M]aybe ethnic leaders should be created to become the 'modern' Mèo kings." The case of Vừ Mi Kế, chairman of Đồng Văn district, Hà Giang, was a good example of this. Being a cadre with enough education to be able to understand the party's guidelines, Vừ was seen as "a respectful Mèo, a real representative of his people."

If the declaration "Mèo people still need to have their king" reflected the Việt Minh ambition to take Hmong millenarianism under the wing of the revolution in the early 1970s, from the end of the decade onward, it became a dreadful reminder to local communist cadres of what danger this tradition entailed. The pre-judgment of Hmong millenarianism that was heavily influenced by the reading of Chinese and French colonial records on Hmong uprisings came to dominate government discourse. A document that recorded a meeting between Lào Cai leaders in 1974 with their superiors from the Supreme Court indiscriminately labeled all Hmong millenarian movements as "Phỉ" (Bandits or Rebels). Similarly, Hmong millenarianism, and its direct connection with the problem of uncontrollable migration of Hmong people, was perceived by Kinh officers as the result of the influence of "Phỉ" Vang Pao.[4] Today, the same construction of Hmong identity continues to dominate the government discourse on this matter, which has also increasingly gained a moralizing undertone. State officials told me that they needed to stay alert to the potential influence of the Chao Fa movement on the Hmong population in Vietnam.

The strong ethnic and kinship ties between Hmong groups in Southwest China and the Southeast Asian Massif and their skillful use of porous international borders to enhance these connections make movements like Chao Fa possible. Such ethnic and transnational networks were at the center of the state's attention paid to the Hmong when Protestant conversions began to occur at the beginning of the 1990s. In 1998, professor Đặng Nghiêm Vạn, the director of the Institute of Religious Studies in Hanoi and a prominent advisor for the Vietnamese government in affairs related to Hmong conversions, made the following observation:

> The element that is exploited by reactionary forces is the millenarian belief, which was and still is strong among the Hmong and can easily be called upon at any time by the head of a clan or head of a village. Their history gives the Hmong an experiential cognition according to which they should never believe in people of another ethnicity. The Han have been their archenemies. The Hmong who do not follow a revolutionary ideology also believe that the French, the Tay, and the Kinh to be enemies who every now and then stand as obstacles in the way of the realization of their historical dream. The Hmong is a powerful ethnic group with firm determination but have constantly suffered the bitter fate of a drifting, unstable, and impecunious life. A noteworthy element is that the religious consciousness of the Hmong is heavy. Despite poverty, stupidity, ignorance, and an unstable life, Hmong people are always motivated by an aspiration to realize for themselves the glory and prosperity which their ancestors had in the past. Being rather continuous and righteous, this aspiration further influences the Hmong religious consciousness. (Đặng 1998: 36, my translation[5])

Aiming to connect traditional millenarianism to current Protestant conversion, Đặng's statement did little to conceal his lack of trust for people of ethnic groups that have "abundant faith in millenarianism with a heavy religious consciousness" (*tâm thức tôn giáo nặng nề*), which is seen as further intensified by their poverty, ignorance, and the instability of their drifting life. Đặng's view is shared by many other scholars and government officials in Vietnam and, in this regard, is not very different from the viewpoint held by Việt Minh leaders over half a century ago.

Communist cadres played an important role in depicting the military dimension of Hmong millenarianism. As a child, Lử recalls that he only knew of Fuab Tais's benevolence and power to protect the Hmong from malevolent forces. Only after he grew old enough to understand what the Kinh cadres of the Stabilizing and Renovating the Highland campaigns said, did Lử begin to learn about Fua Tais' militant power. The cadres often invoked stories about Châu Quán Lồ, the Hmong chief in the Lùng Sui area who, half a century earlier, had claimed to be the reincarnation of Fua Tais to force "innocent" Hmong villagers to join his pro-French army to fight against the Việt Minh and the revolution. Officials always ended their speech with a call for the Hmong not to wait for Fua Tais and to report to the government any "bad elements" and "false prophets" who proclaimed Fua Tais's return.

The main difference between the Hmong converts and the peasants of Hailufeng or the early Hòa Hảo converts was that in the 1920s and 1930s, the Marxist utopia had not yet been established, whereas in today's Vietnam there is a socialist state and still the Hmong remain poor and marginal. Though communism promises paradise on earth, the system has been unable to deliver on its promises for large sections of the population. This is particularly the case among ethnic minorities in the mountainous borderlands. The Vietnamese state had once tried to attract the Hmong by its vision of total change—a millenarian wish no less—but this vision is now blunted by its promotion of market capitalism. On the contrary, Marxist evolutionism that puts the Hmong always behind the Kinh and the state endless attempt to make the Hmong "catch up with their Kinh brothers" have only negatively affected Hmong people. It has never been the Hmong who reaped the profit of High Socialism or of market capitalism of the Đổi Mới era.

Unlike the Hailufeng and Hoa Hao movements, Hmong millenarianism was always presented as an ethnic affair. Thus attempts to absorb it by the Vietnamese state have been seen, both then and now, by Hmong followers as an attack on Hmong ethnicity. This is reinforced by the fact that the liberalization of Vietnam of the last decade has lifted some restrictions on religious practices of the Kinh majority group but has not done the same for the religions of ethnic minorities like the Hmong. Similarly, the neoliberal economy of Vietnam—albeit with a "socialist orientation"—has produced what the Comaroffs (2001) term "millennial capitalism" and "occult economy." While there is something occult in any economic system—Adam Smith speaks about "the hidden hand" of the market—and some elements in the responses to the opening up of the Vietnamese market economy resemble the South African case, it is important to note that the Hmong have transformed their millenarianism quickly into mainstream Protestantism. In fact, they are much less given in to speculation and quick consumerism than their Kinh neighbors.

THE COMING KING AND PROTESTANT MILLENARIANISM

In his recent and impressive work, James Scott (2005) devotes an entire chapter to understanding the role of millenarianism and Christian conversion in the history of the Zomian people's attempts to escape the control of the state authorities, mostly dominated by lowlanders. Based extensively on the example of the Hmong, the Karen, and the Lahu, Scott concludes that "the ubiquity of potentially violent prophetic movements suggest that when 'cornered,' with their normal modes of escape closed to them, they have appropriated enough cosmological architecture to serve as the necessary glue for pan-ethnic rebellions" (2005: 319). Christianity for the Zomians is, in light of this escape scheme, "a powerful alternate, and to some degree oppositional, modernity." As Scott sees it, Christianity brought to hill societies two great advantages: its own millenarian cosmology and its detachment from the lowland states for hill people who might want to maintain their distance (2005: 319). In Scott's view, Christianity in the hills bears on hill-valley relations in two ways. First, it represents a modern identity that confers the "uniqueness and dignity which the wider world . . . refused to acknowledge." (2005: 320) This new identity promises literacy and education, modern medicine, and material prosperity. It has, furthermore, a built-in millenarian cosmology that promises its own version of a conquering king who will destroy the wicked and uplift the virtuous. The eschatological message of scriptural Christianity maps closely enough onto Hmong millenarian beliefs that little adjustment is required. In addition, the presence of Christianity as an institution as well as an ideology ought to be seen as an additional vector and another resource for group formation. It allows a group or a fraction of a group to reposition itself in the ethnic mosaic. Like village fusion and fission or modern techniques of social identity—the political party, the revolutionary cell, or the ethnic movement—Christianity offers a powerful way of creating a place for new elites and an institutional grid for social mobilization. Each of these techniques can be put to the service of maintaining and emphasizing hill-valley distinctions—sometimes a kind of proxy for hill nationalism—or, more rarely, for minimizing them.

James Scott's argument certainly captures some aspect of the relation between Christianity and millenarian tradition in hill societies in general, but the development of this relationship in the Hmong case is far more complex. Instead of being able to replace a millenarian tradition, Christianity continues to spark millenarian interest in certain Hmong communities. In early April 2011, for instance, the Vietnamese government was alarmed about the gathering of thousands of Hmong people from all over the country in the remote Mường Nhé district of Điện Biên province. The majority of the Hmong who came were Christian. Mường Nhé is a district that on the northwest borders Laos's Phong Sa Ly province where the majority of residents are also Hmong and on the southwest borders China's Yunnan province. Given the recent tensions in China-Vietnam relations and the ongoing resistance movement of some Hmong rebels in Laos, the gathering of a massive crowd of Protestant Hmong—estimates range from 5,000 to 11,000—in such a geopolitically sensitive spot was perceived as a serious problem by the Vietnamese government. By mid-May, it turned out that the cause for this unusually large movement was a combination of the May 21 end-of-the-world prophecy promulgated by the American evangelist Harold Camping and the work of a self-proclaimed Hmong messiah from Mường Nhé.

Famous for applying numerology biblical interpretation, Harold Egbert Camping, a California-based radio evangelist, predicted that the end-times would fall on May 21, 2011. This prediction was circulated globally via his Family Radio group. By the end of 2009, the prediction had circulated throughout the Christian Hmong community in the United States and sparked intense discussions. In addition to arranging for Radio Taiwan to broadcast his message to China on AM radio, Mr. Camping also worked with Hmong pastors to spread his end-of-times prophecy in a Hmong language letter.[6] This letter was distributed widely among Christian Hmongs in Vietnam through various channels, including cellular phone messaging.

The spread of Mr. Camping's end-times prediction to the Hmong had a peculiar result. Early in 2011, Christian Hmong in Vietnam began to hear about a Hmong messiah that had emerged in Mường Nhé. This was Zhong Ka Chang, a twenty-five-year-old man born in the Muong Tong commune of Mường Nhé district and who had recently converted to Protestantism. One Hmong man, who followed the messiah and had been arrested and brought back to his village by Lào Cai authorities, said that after receiving a text message about Mr. Camping's prediction from a Hmong friend in Laos (who learned of it from a US relative), Zhong Ka Chang started to receive "signals" from the other world that he had been chosen as the Hmong's messiah. Christian Hmongs throughout around Vietnam circulated stories about the messiah's miraculous powers such as the ability to foretell events and his personal knowledge of individuals he had never met. According to the report of the Black Hmong radio group, belonging to the Far East Broadcasting Company, this messiah proclaimed that at his command an army would rise up out of the dust on the ground, and the rocks on the hills would become weapons, guns, and armaments to destroy his enemies.[7]

This messiah renamed himself as Tu Jeng Cheng, meaning "the important one," a name chosen from apocalyptic literature found in the book of Revelations in the Christian Bible. From Mường Nhé, Tu Jeng Cheng echoed Harold Camping's prediction and summoned his followers to join him to wait for May 21. According to his version of Camping's prediction, however, when the end-time came, it would be the powerful Hmong King who would appear instead of Jesus Christ. Starting in mid-April, Hmong Evangelical leaders from the South reported to FEBC that up to 70 percent of Christian Hmong in the Central Highlands were preparing themselves to move North to join the Messiah. In the previous two decades, approximately 40,000 Hmong people had migrated from the North to the Central Highlands against the state's wishes. The Central Highland Hmong who had relatives in the "affected" areas in the North appeared to be particularly vulnerable and were the ones making the long trip back from the south. In the northern provinces, large numbers of Hmong Evangelicals also signed a paper pledging allegiance to the Messiah. Many of his followers had accordingly sold or rid themselves of their homes, lands and belonging to converge on Mường Nhé and wait together with their messiah for the prophesized event.

Just as with Communism, Protestantism was evidently not able to absorb or contain Hmong millenarianism. In spite of its remarkable success among the Hmong population during the last twenty years, Protestantism was only able to convert roughly one-third of the Hmong population in Vietnam. The growth of this religious minority was at least as much hindered by the ongoing millenarian tendency of many of its members as by the political control of the Vietnamese state. Several house churches in my field sites, for example, were not given legal recognition by local authorities because a number of their inhabitants had been caught participating in "subversive plots."

From its very beginning, the Hmong's conversion movement in Vietnam was suspected by the state of being the root of future separatist movements, especially ones connected with the long-distance nationalist movement headed by General Vang Pao and his exiled government in the United States. In June 2007, Vang Pao was arrested by federal agents in California, over an alleged plot for the overthrow of the Laotian government in order to create a Hmong country for Hmong people on Laotian territory. Earlier that same year, nine Hmong men from Phong Hải were arrested in a border town in Laotian territory. It was said that the Lao army had caught them among the Hmong Chao Fa resistance force. These men were detained in a re-education camp in Thanh Hoa for several months before being sent back to Phong Hải. In early November, the government organized a public gathering of hundreds of representatives of Hmong communities to hear the official statement on these men. Cư Seo Pao, Lử's first cousin, was among these men and he was asked to speak for the group. In his statement, Pao described how he was tricked into going to Laos by a group of

Hmong men—two of them from Sơn La province, one from the Xieng Khoang province of Laos and one from America. These men promised that anyone who went to Laos to work on a rubber plantation would receive an advance payment of seven million Vietnamese *đồng* —roughly $500 in 2007—and once in Laos, his family would receive another seven million.

When they arrived in Laos, instead of working on a plantation as they had been told, the group ended up in a type of military camp where they had to attend ideological training and learn to fight. Pao said that besides Hmong men from Vietnam and Laos, there were also Hmong from China and Thailand who attended the camp. Very soon after his arrival, Pao realized that his life was in danger on two accounts. If he stayed, sooner or later he would be killed in one of the battles that he was training for. If he left, the people running the camp would kill him. He ended his speech by saying that it was to his good fortune that the camp had been raided and that he was arrested by the Laotian army and returned to Vietnam where he was received back with forgiveness and tolerance. He had learned his lesson and urged his fellow Hmong men never to make the same mistake.

Besides drawing more negative attention to the Hmong population in Vietnam, the arrest of these young men was also an unfortunate occurrence for the Protestant Hmong communities. Since all nine men were Protestant converts, their arrest was used as proof by the government of a connection between Protestantism and Hmong separatism. For decades this connection had been articulated by those who stood against conversion. They concocted a pun that goes: "[to] follow Vàng Chứ (Vietnamese pronunciation of Vang Tsu) is to follow Vàng Pao (Vang Pao)." It is important to note that some anti-conversion sentiments in the non-Christian Hmong population came from the negative attention that they, as a part of the Hmong community, had received because of these allegations.

For many Hmong house churches like Tòng Già, the arrest of these young men has damaged their efforts to prove to the government and their non-Christian Hmong fellows that they were a fellowship of apolitical and sincere Protestant believers. Proving that they have nothing to do with politics has been part of the agenda for many church leaders and Protestant Hmong in Vietnam, as they are constantly in contestation with the government and with the non-Christian Hmong. As conversion waxes and wanes, many members of the Hmong Protestant communities in Vietnam are also in contestation with themselves in relation to what being Protestant really means and what "true faith" is. These questions have become more urgent in communities that include members failing to comply with the demands of the new faith; after the emergence of this military plot, which intensified the criticism from non-

Christians. Given that the controlling gaze of the government is constantly lurking above everything, the need to demonstrate one's faith is continuously re-emphasized.

In December 2007, I attended a Hmong wedding in Ải Nam at one of the four state-recognized Hmong house churches. I was warmly welcomed by many people there because of my earlier association with some members of the Ải Nam church. While I was chatting happily with a group of women, a man in his early thirties approached me. Even though he gave me a polite smile, it was clear to me that this was not going to be a friendly chat. Tsab Yaj was the man's name and with the serious face and manner of a policeman he asked me to show him my ID papers as well as a reference letter. He wanted to know where I came from, what kind of work I was doing, and who I worked for. The way he spoke worried me, so I took from my purse a copy of the reference letter from the Lào Cai Provincial People's Committee. I asked him why he wanted to see my papers as he flipped back and forth from one side of the reference letter to the other taking a long time to read and carefully examine it. The paper seemed to convince Tsab of my identity and the smile returned to his face when he introduced himself as the village's policeman (*công an viên*). "We don't want to have reactionaries and bad elements come here to take pictures, film us, or propagate anti-government ideas." I asked him whether any "bad elements" had been to Ải Nam and whether Tsab himself had encountered any of them. Embarrassed, he admitted that he had only heard about "bad elements" but had never met any of them. Pointing to Chinh, the leader of the Tong Gia congregation who had brought me to this wedding, he added: "But sure they come to Tòng Già and Sảng Pả. You can ask him!"

Tsab was one of the most devoted Christians among more than six hundred converts of the Ải Nam hamlet, which is comprised of three villages. For the previous three years, he had been elected local policeman by the villagers and the commune authority. In the church community, he acted as an active leader and organizer of activities. Tsab's cautiousness can be explained in two ways. He wanted to demonstrate to the outside world that, in line with the state, he and his church were cautious and constantly on guard against "bad elements." Against the backdrop of conversion and the politics around it, like many other Christian leaders in communities such as Ải Nam, Tsab wanted outsiders like me to know that his community was a fellowship of sincere believers who did not have and did not want to have anything to do with reactionary activities. My presence in Ải Nam was a good opportunity for him to demonstrate precisely that.

Although Ải Nam is one of the two communities that were given permission to gather for Christian activities, such gatherings were and continue to be closely monitored by local authorities. To be selected is to have the community recognized as a real Christian fellowship and that is a title that the Ải Nam people are proud of and wish to preserve. So it may be understandable that in asserting the nonpolitical character of his Christian community to me and demonstrating it to Chinh, the leader of the Tong Gia congregation, Tsab also asserted to himself the fact that his community wants to assume a politically neutral position. The internal motivation beneath Tsab's actions was more complicated but perhaps also more important than the external one.

But for Hmong conversion, framing the discussion in terms of human rights seems to have more impact because of the strong links between the Hmong in Vietnam and the Hmong in the United States. A few days after the Mường Nhé event became known to the media, there was considerable effort in the Minnesotan Hmong community to mobilize political support for the Hmong "protesters" in Vietnam.[8] Right after the Mường Nhé event became news, a website called www.change.org launched a petition by Hmong activists in the United States calling on the US State Department to speak out about Mường Nhé and what they called a "human rights violation."[9] The petition got 2,233 signatures, four of which were from senators from different states.[10] In studying the impact of missionary encounters between the Hmong in the United States and the Hmong in Vietnam, I find a fairly systematic formation and self-assertion of the American Hmong community's role as guardian of religious freedom and human rights for the Hmong community in Asia. I was told that, in response to a Hmong woman whose family members were victims of religious persecution in Vietnam, a Wisconsin's Hmong missionary made a promise that he and many others in the United States would do their best to influence the Vietnamese government to stop the persecution of the Hmong. In this particular case, the missionary did not follow up on his promise. But in general, perceiving themselves as guardians of the civil rights and religious freedom of the Hmong in Vietnam is another way the American Hmong connect with their Vietnamese Hmong counterparts. The reasons for this self-appointed guardianship are connected to the antagonism between the American Hmong and the Communist Vietnamese state, on the one hand, and the general rhetoric of American Christianity and worldwide religious freedom on the other.

US Hmong often connect their advocacy of human rights for Hmong in Vietnam with their own political agenda of advocacy for a Hmong homeland. Hmong conversion and the Mường Nhé incident are often interpreted as "protest for political freedom" or as a "calling for more autonomy." It is this kind of narrative of advocacy that the Vietnamese government uses as evidence to suppress Hmong conversion. And indeed, because of their voting influence as well as their anti-communist agenda, Hmong advocates often find their voice heard in the American government.

Usually, the Christian networks that advocate Hmong conversion in Vietnam have agreed with the general plea for human rights made by Hmong activists and American political activists. Interestingly, however, in the case of the Mường Nhé event, some Christian missionaries were highly critical of the way human rights advocates and Hmong activists named the event a "protest," and went on "calling for political freedom." Their reaction reflects their genuine concern over the future course of Hmong conversions. Having spent so much effort to get the Vietnamese government to recognize Hmong Christians, after events like Mường Nhé, they are afraid that the government has found reasons to restrict the work of Christian Hmongs again.

On May 17, 2011, a review of the Mường Nhé event was put up on the FEBC Black Hmong Radio Facebook page.[11] With many Hmong Christian contacts inside Vietnam, many of whom happened to be at the event either as bystanders or as followers of the Mường Nhé messiah, the FEBC Black Hmong Radio had access to a number of credible sources. Participants in the Mường Nhé event were considered by FEBC Black Hmong Radio as Christians attracted to "false teachings," which mixed various false beliefs and messiahs into one confused whole, and manipulated by false leaders, who were interested in their own gain. According to the FEBC Black Hmong Radio, this happened because there was still a very limited knowledge of Christian doctrine from lack of sufficient teaching. The FEBC Black Hmong Radio, in all of its reports, persistently condemned the characterization of the event as a protest against the state that called for an autonomous Hmong land. It denied outright the report by the AFP that quoted a foreign diplomat as saying that "Some Hmong have previously called for a Hmong Christian State" and declared its support for the Vietnamese government's position.

The reaction of the FEBC and their associated missionaries reflects their fervent desire to be seen as standing apart from politics. Also, their reaction reflects their stand toward Hmong millenarianism. Although Evangelical Christianity is apocalyptic in nature, it does not recognize Hmong millenarianism. Christianity has been seen by the Vietnamese state as a "protesting force," a foreign religion capable of undermining the state's power. Yet, what we see in the FEBC response to the Mường Nhé event is something entirely opposite. Instead of instigating the Hmong into an anti-state fervor; the FEBC tried to encourage the Hmong to be good citizens of Vietnam. The organization's motivations, however, are mainly to preserve the integrity of its account of Christianity by taming Hmong millenarianism, which has to be turned into a Christian message of hope.

Millenarianism is a common phenomenon in the history of China and Southeast Asia. State authorities in the region interpret it as a form of rebellion to be brought under control. That interpretation is not entirely incorrect since millenarianism often refers to the end of all injustice and the coming of a new era having as one of its effects the rejection of the legitimacy of the current political order. However, to simply reduce millenarianism to political rebellion is only correct when one is "seeing like a state" (Scott 1998). Regardless of what factors are cited to explain the emergence of religious movements, the old and tired "sociological question" (Burridge 1969) remains: why some (parts of) populations convert while others who are in the same boat do not? Burridge warns that one should give full ethnographic accounts rather than premise one's understanding on assumptions about causality.

What is striking in assessing Hmong millenarianism is how much it has in common with both Communism and Christianity. Both of these ideologies promise the coming of a better era and an end of injustice through the destruction of the old society. Neither is able to fulfill that promise especially in the case of marginalized people like the Hmong. Neither can contain and encompass Hmong millenarianism. It is clear that Christianity, while entertaining an intimate relationship with millenarianism, is not able to contain and exhaust the possibilities of Hmong millenarianism. Millenarianism can be "translated" into Christianity since Christianity itself can carry a strong millenarian and, on some occasions, apocalyptic element, but it is not uncommon for something to be lost in this translation. The coming of the Hmong King and the coming of Jesus Christ can be easily conflated. It is ironic that many Christian groups in fact want to subdue this millenarian element of the Hmong and make them obedient lambs in God's kingdom while simultaneously quiet citizens of the state. This element of the Christian missionary work is not recognized by the Vietnamese authorities because of their unchanging view of Christianity as a dangerous "foreign" religion, and of conversion as a danger to Vietnam's sovereignty.

CHAPTER FIVE

NOT BY RICE ALONE

A FTER the burning of ancestral altars led by Cu Seo Lu in 1992, all members of the Cư clan in Phong Hải declared themselves to be Christian. Although this brought them more trouble than they had expected, no Cư I spoke to has ever regretted the decision to convert or his or her determination to remain a Christian.

Wanting to understand why some Hmong chose to become Protestant, I conducted hundreds of interviews between 2004 and 2008, soliciting family histories and narratives of conversion. After the first batch of interviews in winter 2004 and early 2005, it appeared to me that material benefits, spiritual crises, and disappointment with state development policies were commonly cited factors to explain conversion. However, when I returned to the field for a longer period between September 2007 and June 2008, most of the people whom I had interviewed before wanted to offer somewhat different conversion narratives, which complicated my earlier understanding of their motivations. Most interviewees shifted their emphasis from conversion's material benefits to spiritual empowerment and the sense of security that they had gained after becoming Christian. Rather than feeling forced to convert by the fear of having inadequate ritual knowledge of the old way, interviewees characterized conversion as a choice made after weighing the power and efficacy of Christianity versus that of Hmong traditional religion. One thing that interviewees did not change in their narratives was the emphasis on the socioeconomic and political contexts in which their conversion took place. In other words, my informants were painfully and acutely aware of the socioeconomic and political forces that were beyond their control. And they wanted to tell me that conversion to Protestantism was their way of achieving some control, however slippery, over their own lives. Their stories provide a lens through which we can grasp a deeper sense of life in contemporary Vietnam.

The most common explanation my informants gave was that they converted to escape poverty, a condition that was partly due to their costly traditional religious practices. As they put it, whereas traditional Hmong religious practices entail costly and cumbersome ritual procedures, Protestantism requires much simpler rituals and the abolition of animal sacrifice and bride price. More importantly, however, Christianity was understood as able to protect converts from being punished by ancestral and other spirits.

> Twenty years ago, when I was still living in Bac Ha, my father passed away. At that time I could still give him a proper funeral. I planned to do the sacred cow sacrifice ritual (*nyub dab*) for him a few years later when I had more money.[1] But then we had three more children, and the last one was sick all the time. Most of the chickens we raised were used to do the *ua neeb* [shamanic healing] ritual. Once we even had to sacrifice a young buffalo when the spirit tortured him by making him both hot and cold. It even took his soul away sometimes. Lucky the spirits did not ask for a white buffalo because—I remember—there was no white buffalo in the whole region. But my child died anyway. We lost everything, our son and all the money we had saved for doing *nyub dab* for my father. My uncles and brothers constantly asked me to be ready soon to perform the ceremony. So in 1990, when communal cadres told us that the soil in Phong Hải was much richer than in Bắc Hà, that we could grow more maize and rice, we could also join the state-owned tea farm and we could have a regular income in cash—growing opium was not allowed there anymore—we moved. But five years later I still could not do *nyub dab* for my father because we did not have that much more maize to sell and no cash income because we could not speak Vietnamese well enough to work with Kinh people. We could raise barely enough pigs for family use but did not have spare ones to sell because the weather is much hotter here than up there in Bắc Hà. So not only did we get sick more often but so did our pigs. Around that time, I heard from Hmong radio [FEBC] that if I prayed to the Lord about our difficulties, he would protect us so that we would not have to do *nyub dab* and still not suffer any punishment. In 1996, after some considerations, we signed in the form that a friend of my wife gave us to register at the Protestant Church in Hanoi. We have saved more money ever since and did not receive any punishment from the ancestors for not doing *nyub dab* for my father.

But my uncles and their children as well as four brothers of mine who are still in Bắc Hà rarely visit us.[2]

Such pragmatism is common in the history of Hmong encounters with Christianity. Samuel Pollard, a missionary from the Bible Christian China Mission, for instance, noted in 1904 that economic despair in the aftermath of the suppression of the A-Hmao rebellion encouraged this group to convert (Pollard 1919, 1921). Since Pollard, scholars have consistently pointed out that for the Hmong Christianity often seems to have carried with it something of a mass appeal, particularly in situations of severe economic distress. In his account of this process in several Hmong villages, Robert Cooper (1984: 82, 169, 179) states that Christianity appealed to the poor and that the six families who converted to Christianity in the village of Khun Sa were the poorest in the community (Cooper 1984: 77). The attraction to Christian conversion, according to Cooper, was not only about gaining the support and resources which missions and missionaries could provide. Conversion was also a means of escaping costly traditional ritual obligations. Cooper suggests that the poor Hmong of Khun Sa were led to convert because it spared them from paying the bride price and having to provide animals they could not afford for sacrifice in traditional ceremonies (1984: 51). Similarly, many Hmong Christians in the United States point to the economic hardship of resettlement in the United States as well as the cost in time and energy involved in maintaining Hmong traditional practices as reasons why they convert.

The Hmong's pragmatic motivations to convert are not at odds with Protestant conversions in other parts of the world in the last few decades. The converts' economic destitution and the perceived ability of Christianity to address that destitution tend to be among the first explanation for conversions of marginalized ethnic groups in China and Southeast Asia (Cheung 1993; Kammerer 1990; Keyes 1996; Tapp 1989c; Aragon 2000). Charles Keyes (1996), in his overview of Protestantism in Southeast Asia, perceives conversion as a response to either personal or collective crises, which, in Keyes's pessimistic view, is connected to the prevailing crisis of political and religious authority and legitimacy in Southeast Asia (Keyes, Hardacre, and Kendall 1994). He detects crises at multiple levels, in different contexts, and for different groups. These complex and multiple crises require solutions, not just at instrumental—social and economic—levels, but also at a deeper existential level as well. One example of such a crisis concerns tribal groups whose "practice of localized animistic religions is markedly disjunctive with the world in which they now live" (Keyes 1996: 288). Protestant conversion, then, becomes a form of "modernization" through an alliance with a major world religion that is different from the dominant ideology of the nation-state and thus expresses ethnic differentiation without inferiority.

But to say that indigenous people convert to Christianity because their traditional religion is no longer suitable for modern life is to replay the problematic polarization of Christianity as socially and intellectually superior to traditional beliefs: "great tradition" versus "small tradition." Robin Horton (1971) has used such an intellectualist approach to understand what he called "African conversion" in which conversion to a world religion opens up venues for spatial and social mobility. On the one hand, Horton exaggerates the usefulness of world religion; in the case of the Hmong in particular, Protestantism also brings with it a new set of demands that confuse and burden many Hmong converts. On the other hand, as plenty of evidence shows, globalization also helps to propagate traditional religions, which not only continue to thrive but also expand and are able to flourish anew. Laurel Kendall has shown how the global financial crisis actually created new opportunities for shamanism to flourish in Christian Korea (Kendall 2009). While Hmong evangelists penetrate the heartland of Hmong society in Asia, Hmong shamans and ritual specialists from China, Laos, Thailand, and even recently from Nghe An in Vietnam are being flown all over the world to provide services to the Hmong diaspora.[3] To some extent, perhaps thanks to the fact that they dwell in the new context of Christianity, many traditional religious practices are today being redefined and restructured and are gaining new strength to rebound unto the global religious stage. While, for example, Christian missionary expansion on Sumba resulted in spirit worship being redefined as "religion, moving from adhesion to ritual practice to conversion to a rational reflective belief" (Hoskins 1987), Buddhist revival in the former Soviet Buryat has brought Buryatian shamans together to promote their local Tengeri—Tengeri means both sky and is the name of the highest god in the shamanic pantheon in Buryat—to a multinational audience (Quijada 2009).

Although recognizing that the economic motivation of Hmong converts in Thailand may make them appear similar to the "rice-bowl Christians" of other parts of colonial and postcolonial Asia, Tapp (1989b: 70–71) warns against any overestimation of purely economic motives. In most cases of conversion, he asserts, a complex interweaving of indigenous with Christian practices and beliefs appears to have taken place in a way that "material and spiritual benefits and perceived advantages were inextricably mingled" (ibid. 71). Tapp emphasizes that Christianity has achieved much of its success through its promise of education and, above all, its promise of literacy (1989c: 72). He points out that what had attracted the great Hmong crowds to Pollard's missionary station was "not initially economic succor, but a rumor that the missionary had a *book*, or *books*, which was specially meant for the Miao" (ibid. 75). The desire to achieve literacy and to obtain education can be seen as a materialistic motivation (as opposed to, for instance, no longer believing in ancestral spirits). Colonial and postcolonial missionaries commonly built schools and provided free education as a means of attracting converts. Contemporary evangelists offer free English language classes in hopes of gaining converts in non-English speaking societies. For Hmong people, however, the desire for literacy that Pollard and Tapp have noted also reflects the myth about the loss of ancient Hmong writing and thus the historical desire to have their *own writing* back. Instead of thinking about literacy immediately as a tool for economic and political betterment, they long for "the book" that holds sacred power, the power to enlighten them.

So in the case of Hmong conversion in Vietnam, although practical considerations are admittedly involved at various levels of the decision, one should be careful not to overestimate their role. Extra caution in the evaluation of such motives is actually necessary, because they are often used by the Vietnamese authorities to delegitimize conversion. The reasons Hmong people convert can only be understood through the sociopolitical and cultural context of their lives in contemporary Vietnam. The complicated religious trajectories of Mr. Gi, Mr. Chou, and Chinh, Su, and Dung, detailed below, show that conversion is complicated by the dynamic nature of traditional religious practices and culture as well as the transformative element of Christian conversion, which goes beyond the economic need of a person or a community. Rather than explaining exactly why people convert, conversion narratives of Vietnamese Christian Hmongs can be better seen as reflections of the economic, political and social dilemmas Hmong individuals face in Vietnam today.

To some extent, the Vietnamese Communists themselves laid the groundwork for the Hmong abandonment of certain traditions that had been inextricably linked to Hmong identity. The North Vietnamese state inherited the virulent critique of village life that circulated among urban modernizers in the 1920s and 1930s (See, for example, Marr 1981; Hue-Tam Ho Tai 1992; Hy van Luong 1992; Malarney 2002; Ninh 2002). Rural society, according to these critics, was burdened by superstitious beliefs and oppressive, wasteful practices that emphasized social and economic inequalities. Even before launching the Cultural Reform campaign in 1958, the North Vietnamese state sought to combat such beliefs and practices, ranging from costly weddings and funerals, to community festivals. Its agents were deployed to smash idols and ban spirit mediums and fortune-tellers. While religions were protected under the terms of the Constitution, limits were put on the number of Catholic priests or Buddhist monks, and religious property was similarly severely curtailed.

Thus, the abandonment of costly traditions such as bride price was not due to conversion alone, but was facilitated by a long campaign against this practice spearheaded by the socialist government in Vietnam as well as—interestingly—by feminist activists in the United States. The anti-feudal campaign was waged with even greater severity in Hmong villages than in the Kinh villages of the Red River Delta for two reasons: one was the greater perceived backwardness of Hmong culture, and the second was their geopolitically sensitive location in border regions.

Each individual has his or her reasons for converting (or not converting). For older Hmong, these reasons involve abandoning old traditions. For them, conversion is a sometimes painful process. For younger Hmong, looking to the future, reasons include the desire to be part of the global modernity they can perceive through cassette tapes, films, and television programs, but also through the presence of Hmong missionaries from the United States who embody Hmong modern for the marginalized Hmong youth in border areas.

THE PRICE OF A DAUGHTER-IN-LAW

The burning of the ancestor altars by the Cư was not attended by any member of the Sùng lineage. Yet in all Sùng households, it was intensely discussed. In the home of Mr. Gi, discussion centered on what would happen to the families whose ancestor altars were burned. "Their ancestors must have been terribly upset and soon will punish them," Mrs. Gi speculated, while her husband's concern was more about how the Cư's kinsmen back in Lùng Sui were going to take the news of the event. And he was right; on several visits to Lùng Sui, Mr. Gi witnessed how terribly upset the Cư people were after learning of what Lử did. A few months after the event, a baby girl from one of the Cư families died of diarrhea. Her relatives insisted that her death was a prominent sign of retribution by their ancestral spirits for what Lử had done. Soon after that, Lử's paternal uncle and a group of Cư elders were delegated to Lử's house. They demanded that he rebuild the altar then conduct a large ceremony of sacrifice to apologize to the ancestors. After a day of heated debates, the delegation left in anger; Lử and his immediate family are still not welcome in Lùng Sui.

This example of damaged relations among kinsmen made Mr. Gi cautious about conversion. Mrs. Gi, however, grew increasingly interested in joining the newly converted crowd, especially after noticing that no accident or significant mishap occurred to those who burned their ancestral altars. Through a cousin who married a Cư in the village, Mrs. Gi became familiar with Christian stories. In her youth, Mrs. Gi had become so well known in her region for her beauty and her skill in singing the Hmong traditional *kwv txhiaj* that in 1975, at the age of sixteen, she was selected to be one of the representatives of ethnic minority youth to go to Hanoi to attend the military procession (*diễn binh*) to celebrate the reunification of the country. Even though she was still rather fond of *kwv txhiaj*, Mrs. Gi soon began to spend her time humming the Christian hymns that she had memorized from the radio. As Mrs. Gi saw it, she became Christian from that time on.

At first, Mrs. Gi tried to persuade her husband to join her in learning about this new faith. Her persuasion was met with strong resistance, but she never gave up. Mr. Gi was not only concerned about whether it was right to stop worshiping one's ancestors, but he also worried about disapproval from his kinsmen and the local authorities, who had begun to intensify persecution of the new converts. In 1997 there was a turning point. At a wedding in Ải Nam, Mr. and Mrs. Gi met Châu Thị Cu, the bride's younger sister. They liked Cu so much that they immediately thought of a plan for her to marry Chinh, their oldest son who had just reached sixteen and was then studying in secondary school in Bắc Hà. Cu came from a fervent convert family, and her father would only marry her to a Christian Hmong. Apart from this, Cu was the most attractive option that Chinh had in his father's view. Not only was she very good looking, she was known as a girl of good virtue. If Chinh married her, Mr. Gi wouldn't have to pay the very high bride price (*thách cưới*) that was commonly demanded by parents of eligible girls in the area. Moreover, Cu's parents already set aside for her a handsome dowry that included a sow raised for breeding, a pair of chickens, a new bed, a new wardrobe and three pairs of Hmong dresses. Altogether, this was an impressive number of gifts and therefore made Cu a very wealthy bride by Hmong standards.

Yet this marriage would only happen if Chinh's family became Christian. Mrs. Gi, who very much wanted her husband to convert, saw this as a golden opportunity to give him an extra push. Faced with such an irresistible offer, Mr. Gi had to reconsider whether he could sacrifice his faith and ancestor worship for the fate of his son who—depending on his decision—might be able to marry well and live in prosperity. In the end, his love for his son won him over and Mr. Gi agreed to convert. While the family mobilized the help of their relatives to prepare for the wedding, Mrs. Gi brought Mr. Gi to her Christian group every day to learn about Christianity and one week prior to the wedding, the mother-in-law of Cu's sister came with a group of Christian converts from Ải Nam to perform the ritual burning of the ancestor's altar. This was to be the official moment of Mr. Gi's conversion.

Up to this point, Mr. Gi's conversion appeared similar to other Hmong conversions. For instance, Christianity was brought home and quite persistently promoted to Mr. Gi by his wife. From a gender perspective, conversion is seen as a way of empowering women as it seems that conversion is more attractive to women than to men, and in many cases of conversion women play a leading role. Many women explained to me that if they—and ideally their husbands also—became Christian, life would change significantly for them. As a Christian, a Hmong woman does not have to work every day, but can enjoy a Sunday free from any labor. She does not have to spend money hosting rituals and ceremonies, which often involve lots of cooking and cleaning. If her husband is a Christian too, he will give up drinking alcohol. The Christian God also prohibits men from beating women and from having two wives. So Christian Hmong women face less of a risk of domestic violence or having to share their husband with other women.

In any case, the motive behind Mr. Gi's conversion appears purely practical; he converted in order to avoid the high cost of his son's marriage and, indeed, this motive is also rather common. Among the Hmong converts in Vietnam, a demand for bride price is forbidden. I was told by many young Hmong men that they were grateful to the Lord because he taught the parents of their wives not to ask for a high bride price. Hmong men of limited resources often consider conversion to avoid having to pay the bride price that is still asked by non-Christian parents. They must also add the high cost of a wedding in traditional style, which normally requires a lot of alcoholic drinks, because non-Christian guests drink copiously while the Protestants do not.

The payment of a bride price can be a real financial burden. In the past, the price could come to a hundred kilograms of pig and chicken, hundreds of liters of rice wine, several kilograms of opium, and up to seventy Indochinese silver coins. In 2008, in Lào Cai I witnessed a wedding in which the groom's family brought two big pigs—more than 100 kilograms each—two cages with at least a dozen chickens, 100 kilograms of sticky rice, 200 liters of rice wine, and twenty million *đồng* —about $1,300. In the Hmong diaspora, in addition to the cost of the wedding, the bride price may reach phenomenal amounts: from $5,000 to $50,000 in the United States, or from 3,000 euros to 15,000 euros in France in 2005 (Kaoly Yang 2005).

However, the payment of a bride price has come under attack both in the Hmong diaspora and in Vietnam. In the United States, in 2006, a heated debate concerning the practice of asking and paying a bride price took place across the Hmong community, from California to the Midwest. Those advocating abolishing the practice argued that bride price, or at least the two elements —the "wedding price" and the "price of the bride's head"—carry the negative connotation of selling and buying an object and thus force the commoditization of marriage. It was also argued that the practice amounted to sanctioning domestic violence against women as the husband and his family could take the bride price as the mechanism by which they had appropriated the woman. These views were fiercely challenged by advocates of the payment of bride price who pointed to the practice as being a pillar of Hmong traditional culture. Their argument was that the practice works as a kind of insurance of a marriage in that—after the transaction—the working of a marriage became the concern not just of the couple but also of the two clans involved. When a marriage fell apart because of the husband's fault, the wife could return to her clan without having to reimburse the husband's family. If it was the fault of the wife, the husband could demand the money back. It was also noted that the escalating bride price had become a negative element could eventually push young people away from the Hmong tradition and also broadened antagonisms within the Hmong community. The debate was reflected not only in Hmong media but also leaked to national English outlets, which presented negative portraits of the Hmong culture, its community, and its practices. In online forums, the debate deepened the religious and class conflicts among the Hmong themselves as critics tended to be Christian or educated Hmong. Their criticism, however, was met with fierce counter attacks by advocates who accused the critics of practicing cultural genocide and "white-washing." To minimize these frictions, members of a national Hmong council representing eighteen clans met in Fresno in July 2005. The clan council—calling itself United Hmong International Inc.—capped the "gift-price" at $5,000 plus another $800 for other wedding expenses such as food, drinks, and the reception. The cap was published in the first-ever *Hmong Traditional Culture Procedural Guide*, containing a code of conduct. The thirty-one-page manual was drafted by clan leaders with the help of two Fresno lawyers; it was unveiled in booklet form at a gathering of five hundred Hmong leaders who were supposed to disseminate it to the different Hmong communities across America.[4] Yet, such intervention only further intensified debates about Hmong bride price, even among those who advocated it. According to them, the value of a human being is different from individual to individual. As one Hmong man explained to a journalist in California, if their daughter is a good person, is well educated, and conforms to rules, some parents ask for more than $10,000. If you have a daughter who belongs to a gang, you will get nothing.

When Protestantism arrived to the Hmong regions in Vietnam, bride price became one of the first practices to be abolished. However, Protestantism was not and is still not the only force against this practice, which has been under attack for more than half a century by socialist agents. The payment of bride price was one of the first items to be abolished during various socialist campaigns in Hmong areas in the 1960s. For example in *The A Phus* (Vợ Chồng A Phủ), a popular 1961 movie about Hmong society, the custom was singled out as the main cause of Hmong suffering. In the film, the father of My—the female protagonist—is an orphan and thus too poor to pay for his wife's price. He has to borrow money from a landlord, the head of his village, who represents the feudal authority collaborating with the French colonialists. The man imposes upon My's father an impossibly high interest rate that he and his wife spend their life trying to settle. In the story, the debt is still outstanding even after My's mother is dead. In order to pay off her parent's debt, My must become the slave wife of the landlord's cruel son and lives a miserable life. Eventually she runs off with A Phù—also an orphan and slave of the landlord—to join the Việt Minh revolution. The movie summarizes neatly the Kinh Vietnamese socialist agents' criticism of bride price as a feudal and backward custom which makes women into objects and enslaves them. It is also presented as a system through which the feudal and colonial powers have continued to exploit poor Hmong people.

Although the loud and clear message of the movie that revolutionary socialism is the only way to close the door to a miserable past and open the door to a happy future by abolishing the payment of bride prices—the custom continues mostly uninterrupted today. Attacks on the payment of bride price has raised the awareness of Hmong people—especially those that work for the government like Mr. Gi—of the Kinh's prejudice against them. After his de-conversion, Mr. Gi continued to have positive thoughts about Protestantism's prohibition of the Hmong bride price. He disagreed with his Kinh colleagues and non-Christian relatives who denounced his in-laws for tricking him into conversion by using bride price exemption. In his articulation of why he thought that the bride price custom should be abolished he deployed a strikingly similar reasoning to that of his peers in the United States. Instead of presenting his decision to convert as a pragmatic calculation of gain and cost; Mr. Gi framed his decision to convert as resulting from a certain negative understanding of the practice of paying a bride price that he learned from socialism. Only when the happiness of his family became the cost of his de-conversion from Protestantism did Mr. Gi begin to feel that he had paid too high a price, not for his daughter-in-law, but for becoming Protestant in the first place.

SHAMANISM AND THE NEW SOCIALIST PERSON

Since the 1950s, cultural campaigns have been carried out in Vietnam to eradicate religious and popular practices deemed backward, superstitious, wasteful, or promoting inequality. While these campaigns were carried out throughout North Vietnam and all northern Vietnamese were affected (Kim Ninh 2002; Malarney 2002), ethnic minorities were particularly affected. During the Renovating the Highland campaign not only Kinh cadres but also hundreds or even thousands of young Hmong men and women were mobilized and trained to roam villages and regions to carry out "small revolutions." They were tasked with getting rid of old customs; backward, primitive or unhygienic practices; and superstitions. The shamans, seen as fake healers and wicked spiritual leaders in feudal Hmong society, were accused of cooperating with the "ruling class" to exploit the poor Hmong masses and came under heavy attack as well. Although some contested the claims made in official reports that the revolution had successfully "civilized" the Hmong and rid them of their—false—enchantment tradition,[5] these campaigns did significant damage to Hmong society. Conversion to Protestantism is partly a result of the destruction of Hmong traditions during this period.

In the mid-1960s, as a young man in his twenties, Mr. Chou had "followed the call of the Party" (*đi theo tiếng gọi của Đảng*) and left his home in the care of his young wife while he joined Kinh cadres and many other "enlightened" (*được giác ngộ*) Hmong comrades to carry out "small revolutions" in his native region, Lùng Sui. He was educated about the "superstitious" nature of shamanism, and he himself had participated in the arrests of a number of Hmong shamans. His active participation in this "cultural revolution" brought him to several "learn to love the Party" (*cảm tình Đảng*)[6] training courses, and he was given a salaried job as a purchasing staff member in the Bắc Hà district food distribution store.[7]

Everything was going well for him for more than a decade but then suddenly he fell ill. For more than two years he was in a half-dead-half-alive state. In spite of countless remedies, both traditional herbal and modern medicine, to which Mr. Chou had much better access than other ordinary Hmong at the time thanks to his position as a government employee, his health did not improve. According to Hmong tradition, if someone suffers an incurable illness for a long time, he or she may be "chosen" to be a shaman. Shamans are ordinary people who are endowed with capacities to render themselves ritually into the supernatural world to deal with supernatural entities in order to cure their patients. A ritual line ties the shaman to the supernatural. Hmong mythology has it that Siv Yis, the first Hmong shaman and the celestial master of shamans, sends the chosen person auxiliary spirits associated with an "incurable illness" to force him or her into becoming a shaman. Among these spirits, there are often—but not always—spirits connected to an ancestor of the future shaman, generally a paternal grandfather who had himself been a shaman (Culas 2004: 106).

Most Hmong people who are chosen to become shamans refuse to be initiated. Among the Hmong, one does not choose to become a shaman but one allows—not without difficulty—one's selection by the auxiliary spirits, which is considered the only way to remove the supernatural illness (Culas 2004: 123, and from my interviews). For Mr. Chou and his family becoming a shaman was a misfortune. For one thing, a considerable amount of wealth and time was lost in the rituals to initiate him. After initiation, he was almost constantly occupied in giving service to Hmong families who were too poor to compensate him adequately. Very soon his initiation as a shaman came to the attention of the local authorities. Mr. Chou recalled that it was embarrassing enough to face other shamans whom he had denounced earlier but facing his former colleagues, the very same cadres with whom he had been working at the Board of Mass Culture and Grassroots Propaganda (Ban Văn hóa Quần chúng và Thông tin Cơ sở) in Lùng Sui, was even worse. It was humiliating. Frequently, they called him up and criticized him for "conducting superstitious rituals to deceive and exploit the masses." This accusation was heartrending for Mr. Chou. He wished they would understand that nothing had changed in his intention to be a good "new socialist man." He just could not refuse to be a shaman, at least if he wanted to remain in good health. No matter how Mr. Chou tried to conciliate his colleagues, his application for Party membership was turned down. His services at the food distribution store were also no longer needed.

Worst of all, although as a shaman Mr. Chou seemed to be able to save a number of patients, he failed to save his own son. Despite spending a fortune in countless chickens, two pigs and even a white buffalo for sacrifice to the spirits, his son still died after a short illness. Upon this heartbreaking episode, Mr. Chou threw away his shamanic gear and went to see his former colleagues at the Committee for Culture of the Mass and Information at the Grassroots Level and submitted himself to their "re-education" program. Villagers gradually stopped seeking his services because he always responded to their requests by giving the same lecture that he received during the re-education program, but the spirits persisted. He did his best to ignore most of their calls but each time he believed that the spirits' anger at his refusal had subsided, they made themselves felt again by making him so sick that his family had no other choice but to invite another shaman to conduct a ritual for him. Although he always felt better after each of these ceremonies, Mr. Chou was determined not to become a shaman again.

This explains why in the early 1990s, when Mrs. Chou received the shamanic "calling" through a constant and severe stomach pain, the family fervently refused to initiate her. At that time they had newly resettled in Phong Hải and were facing many difficulties, as did everybody else. Various traditional herbal treatments were used to deal with Mrs. Chou's illness and numerous shamanic healing ceremonies (ua neeb) were conducted. Several visits were also made to the district clinic; none resulted in any improvement to her health. By this time, Vang Tsu's healing power was already known to Hmong people in the area. In

1992, after about a year of suffering her stomach ailment, Mrs. Chou decided to follow a group of Vang Tsu worshipers from Ái Nam who regularly came to her house to pray for her. They also instructed her and Mr. Chou to listen to the radio, and the couple was immediately attracted to the broadcasts. Nearly a year after they started listening to the radio and receiving the prayers of the group, Mrs. Chou was fully recovered and Mr. Chou had become deeply convinced of Vang Tsu's way. In November 1993, after the harvest, they took down their family altar with the help of Cư Seo Lử and other Vang Tsu followers. Mr. and Mrs. Chou and everyone in their household were from then on recognized as Vang Tsu's worshipers. The local government officially counted them as Protestant converts.

Although conversion from shamanism to Christianity is common in the history of Christianization in Hmong society and in other marginal societies in Southeast Asia (Vang 1998; Walker 2003), many Protestant missionaries I interviewed see the turnaround of local shamans whom they call witch doctors, as a particular triumph. Mr. Chou's rejection of shamanism not only resulted from his own ill-fated experience as a shaman but also from what he knew of the aggressive attacks from the state on this spiritual practice. Hmong shamanism and healing practices are particularly vulnerable to socialist campaigns but are also intricately connected to every aspect of Hmong society. Religious rituals are the heart and soul of communal festivals, yet various cultural rituals and festivals and communal feasts (*noj xjong* or *noj tshab*) have long been prohibited because they are seen as superstitious practices hazardous to social stability (Trần 1996: 174–78). The Hmong have traditionally celebrated the New Year throughout the entire month of December. This lengthy celebration was prohibited and reduced to three days owing to the fact that to "eat the New Year" for the entire month created too much space for "superstitious" practices and was wasteful in terms of time, money, and labor. Reduction of the New Year celebration further contributed to the disappearance of various cultural festivals as well as of the knowledge of how to organize them. Those that resisted such measures were severely punished.

Rambo (2000: 11–12) points out that controlling the lives of ethnic minorities has become increasingly "extra-local" as decisions about economic, agricultural, social, and cultural matters have been taken over by the government's programs and cadres. Conversion to Protestantism is, to some extent, the paradoxical result of the anti-superstition campaigns of the Vietnamese state. Through these programs, the Hmong were confronted with the Kinh's view of their way of life as backward, their religion as superstitious, and their behavior as improper. The internalization of these prejudices has done irreparable damage to the Hmong's self-esteem and to their trust in the Kinh-dominated state.

The government's attacks on their traditional religion and healing beliefs led to "disenchantment"—in the Weberian sense—of the Hmong traditional world. These programs became indirect but important causes of conversion.

THE ASPIRATIONS OF THE YOUNG

If for older converts like Mr. Chou, the difficulty of holding on to old ways made them opt for Christianity, for young people it is aspiration for a different life, fueled by the desire for education and images of life in other countries. Unlike other more powerful groups who are able to influence to some extent the course of their life, the Hmong continue to suffer the frustration of unobtainable opportunities. One cause of such frustration has been ironically their experience with education, which the state sees as a major incentive to bind people to its development program and its ideology. Yet, it is through education that Hmong youth become aware of discrimination. This is illustrated in many of the stories told to me by Hmong youngsters I encountered in Vietnam. Dung's husband, Su, and his brother are two good examples. Of nearly 3,000 Hmong people in Phong Hải, Su is one of only two high school graduates. This low graduation rate is common for the Hmong population of Vietnam—Christian and non-Christian alike—owing to the poor conditions of schooling in the community. Hmong parents' inability to invest in their children's education and the state's insufficient efforts to provide lessons in Hmong language in the first few years of school are the main reasons for poor performance. What is less common in Su's case is that he was denied further education opportunities after graduation. According to the Vietnamese ethnic minority development policy, Hmong students have the right to government-sponsored higher education. Yet, when Su applied to the Lào Cai College of Pedagogy using the quota from Phong Hải commune, local cadres told him that he not only had to renounce the Christian faith, but that he also had to persuade his brother Chinh to reconvert to their ancestral worship. Only then would he be admitted to a government-sponsored vocational school; after he graduated, he would get a job in the Phong Hải commune administration. While Su was ready to recant Christianity, a faith that was chosen by his parents when he was barely five years old, it was impossible to talk Chinh, his brother, out of it. So Su ended up staying home. Su blamed Christianity for this double discrimination until quite soon thereafter when he became drawn into various Church activities. His fluency in Vietnamese and his education earned him great respect from his Christian fellows, and he soon rose to second place in the leadership of his house church group—just after his brother Chinh. Two years later he got married and almost forgot that once he had once dreamed of pursuing higher education.

Su's brother, Chinh, is only five years older than Su but his deep commitment to Christianity was cemented in an adventure that he embarked upon in 2000. Chinh was disappointed with education earlier than Su, and he dropped out the last year of high school. Six years of schooling and living in the dormitory had lessened Chinh's farming skills, and he had difficulty adjusting back to the life of an ordinary Hmong farmer. Yet, more importantly, he believed that because he was educated he should be able to obtain a paid job in the city, or at least should be recruited by the local government for an administrative job in the commune. To Chinh's disappointment, however hard he tried, there was simply no job available to him. This frustrated him especially when he saw that most Phong Hải teenagers from Kinh ethnic backgrounds, even those with less education, were either admitted to vocational training or received a paid job in the city. Even a crippled young man who lived half a kilometer away from Chinh's house could be an apprentice at a motor garage in Lào Cai City. After this he returned to Phong Hải and opened his own car-washing shop.

In 2000, a year after he got married, Chinh's parents only had a small piece of land for him to farm. While his young family had very few options available for earning a decent living, some people came to Phong Hải announcing that they were representatives of a big company in Hồ Chí Minh City that had many well-paying jobs. Anyone who wanted to work for this company had to pay a five-million- *đồng* recruitment fee. It could have been because Chinh strongly desired to be recruited by this company or because he wanted to go to Ho Chi Minh City, that he persuaded his parents and his young wife to borrow five million *đồng* for him so that he could join these men. Yet when he arrived in Ho Chi Minh City, the organization turned out to be a "ghost company" (*công ty ma*). The recruitment men disappeared as soon as they arrived in the city, leaving Chinh and five other Phong Hải men behind at the Ho Chi Minh central train station.

Desperate and scared, it took Chinh a while to remember that before he left, his brother-in-law had given him the address of a Hmong woman who lived in the city. Chinh's brother-in-law had never met her but had been given her address by a Hmong missionary from the United States whom he had met on one of his trips to Hanoi to fetch religious materials. Chinh used the last money he had to get a motorbike taxi to take him to this address. Although this woman could not do anything to help him get his money back from the men who cheated him, she found a solution to his desperate situation. She lent him some money and sent him to Đắc Lắc, a province in the Central Highland where many Hmong people from the Northern Highland had recently migrated. In Đắc Lắc, Chinh was hired by several Hmong families to work on their cassava farms, which was quite profitable at the time. A few months later,

Chinh had earned enough money to buy a bus ticket and several gifts and he returned to Phong Hải.

Before going south, Chinh was a Hmong youngster who grew up in a Christian household in a half converted village and who assumed a rather nonchalant attitude toward the new religion. At the same time, he was too young to be absorbed into the world of the old beliefs. After coming back, his attitude had changed. During his stay in the Central Highland, like most Hmong people there, Chinh was invited by a local Ede community to join their church gatherings and Bible classes. Some members of Ede groups had been converted by American Protestant missionaries during the Vietnam War, and, like many other Central Highlanders, they had experienced a massive Christian revival which had started in the late 1980s (Salemink 2003, 2007). Joining the Ede house church not only helped Chinh to win the support of the locals for his daily needs, but also through the Ede Christian community Chinh learned the organizational and political skills which were needed to run a Christian house church in the politically repressive context of Vietnam.

Today in Phong Hải as well as in other Hmong communities I have visited, the dynamism of the church is visibly traceable to church leaders, who are, like Su and Chinh, often among the most educated in their communities. These men and women are fluent in Vietnamese and they have mastered the Hmong Romanized Phonetic Alphabet script in which the Bible and all Hmong religious materials are written. More importantly, many of them have shared the same experience of rising expectation and subsequent disappointment, which made them aware of their marginal position in Vietnamese society. The discrimination by the Vietnamese state against Christian Hmong has ironically driven more Hmong youngsters to Christianity and gives force to the dynamic growth of the Hmong church of today. As illustrated in the stories of Su and Chinh, Christianity provides a way to bring to an end their endless waiting. Through the New Way, Hmong youngsters learn of new possibilities and develop new aspirations.

THE DESIRABLE LIFE

Conversion to Christianity also relates to a mediated imagination of belonging to a transnational Christian community. The sociocultural imaginary of what a desirable life is for Hmong youngsters does not only come from encounters with Hmong missionaries from the United States, but also largely from Hmong media productions in Thailand and the United States. While the Hmong in the United States become increasingly interested in the Hmong in Vietnam, the Hmong in Vietnam are even more curious about the life of the Hmong in the United States. When the two missionaries Pao and Fu came to Cardamom Hill they were peppered with questions about the lives of the Hmong in America. Young girls thought that in all Hmong weddings in America the bride wears a white gown, and young boys thought that all Hmong Americans drive cars and live in three-story houses. This knowledge was fed to them by various media channels that have recently become widely available in Vietnam.

In the late 1980s, Grandpa Ceem was the only Hmong for miles around to own a radio, but today many Hmong families who live in the highland own satellite dishes. Via satellite, they receive about thirteen television channels; eight are broadcast around the clock and four others are evangelical broadcasting stations. In some of the most remote Hmong villages in Vietnam, I found Hmong families enjoying these programs notwithstanding obvious linguistic barriers. For example, at a Hmong wedding in a very remote village in 2007, though my mobile phone had no reception, the old and worn Chinese television in my host's living room was showing a film of the Reverend Billy Graham speaking at the "Classical Billy Graham Lecture" in Minneapolis-Saint Paul in 1961. While a small crowd of adults had their eyes glued to the screen—probably unaware of what Rev. Graham's speech was about—a larger crowd of children was laughing and wriggling about with the swinging rhythm of the hymns.

More popular than these satellite television programs are Hmong religious movies and hymnal music DVDs which are made by Hmong and feature famous and attractive Hmong actors and actresses. Hmong people in Vietnam told me that they admired the looks, attire, and alluring voices of the actors, and the fact that Hmong people acted in and produced the movies made them proud to be Hmong. These programs were also quite popular with non-Christian Hmong, many of whom told me that they watched them regularly, especially when there was nothing else to watch. Since 2004, the Lào Cai provincial media station has introduced an hour-long Hmong television program consisting mainly of policy announcements, agricultural and cultural news, and ethnic minorities' music performances either by amateur artists or by the Lào Cai Dance and Cultural Performance Troup. Besides being very short and broadcast only in the evening, the show's broadcasting station had a rather weak signal that could not reach remote areas in the province or villages nestled behind rocky mountains. Also, despite the fact that it was in the Hmong language, this government television program was reportedly "rather boring to watch" (*tsi lom zeem*). It is the alternative to these government media materials that help Hmong audiences in Vietnam better picture the life of the Hmong in the United States, and ultimately provides materials for them to imagine the kind of life that might be possible in the distant future.

While films that portray a desirable future were highly popular, my Hmong informants were also captivated by films that depict themes from Hmong history, mythology, and folklore. *The Bloody Drum*; *Tracing the Bloody Path: Hmong History in China*; *Hmong General Vang Pao and the Secret War in Laos 1960–1975*; *Lady Yua Pa and Orphan Jao Cua*; and *The Love Story of Nung Phai and Ger* are good examples of this type of film. Prasit Leepreecha (2008) observes that these movies have captured the hearts of many Hmong in Thailand, Laos, and China. These films have also become popular with the Hmong in Vietnam since pirated copies began to be smuggled in from China and Laos roughly around 2004. Leepreecha (2008) has also confirmed the critical role of media technology in reproducing Hmong ethnic identity on a transnational scale, ranging from print—journals and other publications—to the Internet to music cassettes. From my observations in Vietnam, it is evident that media products are having a profound impact on the transformation of the identity of the Hmong by connecting the local community with an imagined global Hmong that is thought to share the same imagination, memory, and history. *The Love Story of Nung Phai and Ger* (Nuj Nplhaib thiab Ntxawm)—a movie re-enactment of a Hmong folklore story—was so popular with the Vietnamese Hmong audience that roughly a year after it was released, I encountered seventeen baby boys named Nung Phai in the Mường Khương district alone. My sources often quoted details in the films to explain certain Hmong customs or traditional beliefs. The story told in *The Blood Drum* (Vaj Hmoob Roj Ntsha Ntxaum Nruas), a film about a battle between the Miao in Guizhou, which ends with the loss of the Hmong leader's life and the survivors fleeing southward, was quoted by a middle-aged Hmong man who claimed that all Hmong people had suffered injustices throughout history (Mường Khương December 2007). He especially stressed the brutal images of the battle in the movie as if they were visual evidence of what happened in the historical past to Hmong people. He insisted that all Hmong people in the world today know this historical event just like he knew about it even before watching the movie.

Media practices, as Louisa Schein aptly points out, "have become pivotal in securing, and even generating, Hmong transnationality" (2002: 229). "Hmong could be seen to be making space for their very particularized narratives, ones that [they] enunciate their own cultural memories, war genealogies, sentiments of loss, and struggles of resettlement" (ibid. 241). Similarly, Lee (1996: 1) maintains that "these moving video images and new singing voices constitute a form of cultural reinvention that connects the Hmong together as a global community, and brings them a new changing identity, a new level of transnational group consciousness both in the diaspora and in the homeland." An illuminating example of this kind of power of Hmong media is the documentary *Tracing the Bloody Path: Hmong History in China* (Taug Txoj Lw Ntshav) and its popularity with Hmong people in Asia. Produced by Mr. Yue Pheng Xiong, the owner of the Hmong ABC store in Saint Paul, Minnesota, the documentary begins with an introduction by the producer, standing in front of his bookshelves, with an open book in his hand: "I am a Hmong among the White people. I wonder where I come from and what is my history? The only one thing I have learned from my parents is that I was born in Laos and migrated to the US, but our ancestors originally came from China. I then traveled to trace my own origin in China, as told by my ancestors." He then presents locations that represent the history of the Hmong in China, which he has recorded on video. One place is the presumed graveyard of Chiyou (Txiv Yawg), believed to be the first leader or king of the Hmong at a location west of Beijing. The highlight of the film is the erecting of a large statue of Zhang Xiong Meng, a great Miao leader in Guizhou, whom the narrator describes as "one of the great former leaders of the Hmong people, who fought against the Chinese, in China." According to Hmong villagers in Thailand and Vietnam, the content of these two films was entirely new to them. The film, a juxtaposition of events and information about Miao groups in China, has created new images of Hmong history for viewers around the world.

In Vietnam, the reception of this documentary led to a political drama in early 2008. After watching it, some Hmong people—both Christian and non-Christian—interpreted the message of the producer as a call to join a separatist movement to go to China and reestablish the Hmong nation. Some people in the areas bordering Laos even went so far as to identify the producer as one of the leaders of the millenarian-cum-resistance movement Chao Fa. This rumor soon came to the ears of the police and extra security measures were put in place in various Hmong areas. Arrests were made in Phong Hải, although those that were arrested were released shortly afterward. Sua was called by the police who—according to him—sought his advice. At the police station, Sua was shown a photo of the documentary producer posing with two other Hmong men, who were among those arrested in Phong Hải. In fact, as most Hmong house churches are on high alert for such rumors, knowing the potential harm they can do, Sua was already informed about this rumor and the events around it. He had already been shown this very photo by his fellow church leaders, but he had never met the producer.

As he knew that I had done fieldwork in the United States, Sua thought I could give him information about the producer. He said it was important for him and his church to know whether the man was a member of the Chao Fa movement. If he was, Sua said, he would do his best to stop local Hmong people from watching this documentary. Although I knew of the producer, I had no answer for Sua. Later in 2008, I went to St. Paul and visited the Hmong ABC store. I spoke to Mr. Yue Pheng Xiong who maintained that he has never visited Hmong people in Vietnam.

†

Hmong people converted to Christianity and remained determined to stay on the Christian path for various reasons. Despite the rhetoric of the Communist Party, Hmong attempts to escape poverty through education and mobility have not only been impeded by the hegemonic prevalence of Kinh language and culture, but also are hindered by their choice of Christian faith. After conversion, Hmong are considered to be not only backwards and exotic, but also a threat to the state. After more than a half a century, the Vietnamese state has implemented a number of social engineering programs that have had significant but contradictory impact on the Hmong. The anti-superstition campaigns have, to some extent, paved the way for conversion to Christianity. Moreover, through them, the Hmong have become fully aware of the racist views that the Kinh majority holds.

Hmong converts make sense of their community, locality, and identity especially in the context of material and moral challenges of globalization. Conversion and the subsequent formation of a Protestant Hmong subjectivity are products of the interplay of the global and the local and are shaped by the competing global forces of communism and Protestantism. Although these forces are at loggerheads, they share some important characteristics. Communism and Protestantism share an ideal of equality as well as of salvation. Communism and Protestantism are both discourses of modernity in the view of the Hmong. The important difference is that the Communist Party has captured the Vietnamese state, and since the collapse of the Comintern works within the confines of the nation-state, while Christianity is a transnational movement that is independent of the state. Within the communist nation-state, the Hmong have little chance for upward mobility and this is at least one of the reasons why transnational Christianity, with its capacity to transcend national boundaries, is seen as capable of providing new opportunities. Whatever the similarities and differences between communism and Protestantism may be, of significance here is what the Hmong make of each.

Despite all the difficulties faced by Hmong Christians in Vietnam, the Hmong continue to convert in considerable numbers. Their challenge remains on how to establish a community of believers amid the adverse circumstances in Vietnam today.

STATE, CHURCH,
AND COMMUNITY

Although large numbers of Hmong had converted to Christianity since Grandpa Ceem first heard FEBC broadcasts on his radio in the late 1980s, it was two decades later that converts began to establish formal communities of believers to sustain one another in their new faith. This slow pace must be seen in the context of state policies and the reactions of nonconverts, which, in turn, were shaped by these state policies. At the same time, transnational forces have both hindered and promoted the growth of institutionalized Protestantism among the Hmong. On the one hand, involvement by diasporic Hmong and their advocates especially in the United States has reinforced the state's suspicion about the possible association of Protestantism with American imperialism; on the other hand, the state's desire for acceptance by the international community at key moments in its strategy of economic development has forced it to relax some of its more repressive measures against Hmong Protestants.

A church building process, according to Weberian sociologists, roughly begins with the *routinization* of charismatic authority so that the sect can be transformed into a community of believers with a church-like structure (Weber 1947: 358–73). The sect-to-church theory (Berger 1954a, 1954b) specifically argues that a sect characterized by a high intensity of worship and some tension with the surrounding society may eventually reconcile itself to prevailing social conditions and become more churchlike. This development depends on many factors, such as the changing social characteristics of the sect's members, especially the possibility of upward mobility, the succession of generations, and the increase in the size of the group and the impact of the state's policy toward the sect.

According to the Weberian model, the starting moment of the Hmong's church building process should have occurred right after the first millenarian response to the Far East Broadcasting Company's program ebbed in the early 1990s, giving way to Christian conversion. However, only in the mid-2000s did Protestant Hmong in Vietnam begin to focus on building their community of believers. The constant surveillance and pressure put on the Christian Hmong community by the Vietnamese state forced groups of converts to largely operate underground and in secrecy. As a result of their secrecy and isolation, these converts continued to receive inadequate doctrinal training and ecclesiastical instruction from missionaries and established Protestant churches. This created a fertile condition for misunderstanding and misinterpretation leading to disagreement about doctrine and in turn preventing many converts from coming together in larger church communities.

STATE POLICIES AND STATE PERSPECTIVES

The authorities' opposition to Hmong conversion is not inconsistent with the general religious policy in Vietnam. Although the constitution states that all Vietnamese citizens have the right to freedom to believe and adhere to different religion, in reality, like elsewhere in the communist world, the Vietnamese state has condemned religion as the "opium of the people" and popular ritual practices as "superstition." Like the Confucian officials of precolonial Vietnam, Communist leaders consider that the state has the right to monitor and guide religious life. During the Ly dynasty (1010–1225), exams were held to gauge the doctrinal knowledge of Buddhist monks; those who failed were defrocked and returned to the ranks of peasants who were liable for taxes, military service, and corvée labor. The Confucianizing emperor Lê Thánh Tông limited the number of pagodas and Taoist temples that could be built, the number of monks that could join monasteries, and the amount of land that monasteries could own. Periodic purges of sects that were considered heretical and superstitious were also conducted. Today, the state continues to arrogate to itself the right to supervise religion and demands that believers acknowledge the right of the state to do so. Thus, the Unified Buddhist Church, which was created in South Vietnam in the aftermath of the Buddhist crisis of 1963 and does not acknowledge the authority of the state to regulate its size and activities, is banned.[1]

The other major world religion in Vietnam, Roman Catholicism, has had an even more difficult history of relations with the state. Introduced in the sixteenth century, by the end of the eighteenth century it had the largest number of faithful in Asia outside of the Philippines. Although Catholics had previously suffered repression by the imperial state and harassment by non-Catholic villagers, especially after the Papal Bull of 1742 forbade Catholics to engage in ancestor worship, it was in the nineteenth century that they became the target of violent persecution under Emperor Minh Mạng (1820–40) both on account of Catholicism heterodox (i.e., non-Confucian) nature and its foreign origins and associations. When the French used the pretext of coming to the rescue of persecuted Catholics to conquer Vietnam, the association between Catholicism and French colonialism was sealed in the popular mind. This belief was particular strong among anticolonial activists although the overwhelming majority of Catholics did not side with the French (Keith 2012). After the Việt Minh came to power in 1945, it followed for a time a live and let live attitude toward Catholic villages. However, in the 1950s, as the Communist state sought to penetrate villages and substitute its Party branches for old elites and revolutionize rural life, Catholics resisted having their parish priests replaced by Party cadres. Friction between Catholics and communists led to a massive exodus, estimated at 700,000 of northern Catholics to South Vietnam following the Geneva Agreement of 1954. There remained, however, about the same number of Catholics in the North. In 1955, a Liaison Committee of Patriotic and Peace-Loving Catholics was set up by the state to win over and control them. The church was allowed to retain its link with the Vatican, unlike in the PRC, but most of its traditional activities were banned, priests and nuns were required to devote part of their time to agricultural labor, and church property was confiscated. Today, although not officially regulated in laws, Catholics are forbidden to join the police force and professional military.

Introduced into Vietnam in 1911 by missionaries of the Christian and Missionary Alliance (C&MA), Evangelism was not supported by the French colonial authorities. Only in 1927 was the Vietnamese Protestant church established under the name of the Vietnamese General Confederation of Evangelical Churches. In 1945, it was renamed the Northern Vietnamese Evangelical Church, and since then it has generally not had an easy relationship with the communist government. When the Vietnam War began, Protestantism was perceived as no more than camouflage for American imperialism. As the war escalated, missionaries from a number of American-based churches were supported by the American Army to proselytize in South Vietnam. They successfully converted members of the Ede, Jarai, Churu, Koho, and Lat, some of the groups that make up Vietnam's Montagnard population. Many Protestant converts were also soldiers recruited by the American Special Forces. After the war ended and American missionaries left, Protestantism continued to growth at dramatic rate in the Central Highlands, a development seen by Salemink (2000: 140) as a "conspicuous act of covert resistance" of Vietnam Central Highlanders against the colonization of the region by the Vietnamese state and Kinh immigrants. Since many new converts have been members of the separatist United Front for the Liberation of Oppressed Races (FULRO),[2] the Vietnamese authorities have had one more reason to believe that the American government continue to use Protestantism to lure Vietnamese ethnic minorities out of the national fold in order to sabotage the country's independence and unification.

In the thick of late Cold War politics, the reception of Protestant messages, broadcasted by an American-based radio ministry from the Philippines, and the conversions of Hmong people have seemed to confirm the authorities' opinion about the Hmong's inclination toward foreign power. On May 9, 2011, only five days after news of the millenarian gathering of—mostly—Christian Hmong in Mường Nhé appeared on the BBC and other international media outlets, the Vietnamese government-controlled presses began to discuss the event. Instead of addressing what actually happened, a series of articles published by major government agencies focused on condemning Protestant conversion, which they said was flawed as it was rooted in "material allurement." An article in the national newspaper *Pháp Luật* (Laws) was titled "'Vàng Chứ religion' and poverty: a dull-witted indoctrination."[3] The article condemned "Vàng Chứ-ism," or Christianity, for luring the Hmong by the "false promise" of "material enrichment without labor" and "curing illness without modern medicine." The article lamented: "being lured and indoctrinated, dim-witted Hmong wasted three days a week to attend prayer gatherings instead of working on their farms." It also pointed out that in these gatherings, despite their miserable poverty; the faithful emptied their pockets to support their religion, believing that Vàng Chứ (God) would reward them tenfold. Hmong women especially, the article stressed, "ragged and strenuous, soon after waking up they leave for the corn fields, to return only way after dark, so late that they hardly have time to rub their feet together before falling asleep. Such strenuous life prompted them to follow the Vàng Chứ religion as soon as they heard of its promise." Conversion to Vàng Chứ religion, the article concludes, leads to the destruction of Hmong traditional culture and ethnic solidarity, the further impoverishment of deprived Hmong, and an increase in social ills.

This article is but one of numerous examples showing that although more than two decades have passed since Protestant conversion began among the Hmong in Vietnam, it continues to be viewed as a serious social problem. State-employed analysts adopt an explanatory model of "internal stress" versus "external inducement" to determine the cause of conversion. According to this model, the "internal stress" is constituted by the Hmong's economic deprivation (*nghèo đói*), their lack of education, the "backwardness" (*lạc hậu*) of their culture, and the superstitious (*mê tín dị đoan*) nature of their worldview. This was combined with various elements of "external inducement," namely "material allurement" that Christian missionaries allegedly presented to the Hmong. These incentives came either in the form of cash given in exchange for conversion or as the false promise of future prosperity following conversion. Conversion, in short, results from and continues to be influenced by the Hmong's material impoverishment and their vulnerability to the false promises of bad elements, namely, Christian missionaries.[4]

Based on this assessment of the causes of conversion, the Vietnamese authorities designed and implemented various official laws and secret policies to deal with the phenomenon. When conversion was reported for the first time in 1991, local authorities resorted to persecution and denial of the existence of Protestants among the Hmong. For years, Hmong Christians have been sending petitions to Vietnam's authorities asking for the freedom to follow Christianity based on the constitutional guarantees of religious freedom. Often, however, their requests meet with official rejection. The government has even forced Hmong Christians to participate in the destruction of their own homes if they have refused to recant their faith. While failing to stop Hmong conversion, such harsh measures have produced an outcry by international human right activists. The situation has been further complicated by the fact that, since 1986, the communist regime has been in a transitional phase in which market economy and economic globalization have become central to its functioning. As such, it was very sensitive to the attention paid by the international community to Hmong conversion, for instance by the global Christian networks which have nurtured a very close relationship with international human right advocacy groups.

Since 1998, following advice from a special action committee composed of government policy-makers and state-employed intellectuals, the state has implemented a new set of directives to handle Hmong conversions. In essence, these policies, which continued to strongly oppose conversion, provided guidance in how to achieve this aim within the rule of law. In 2000, the Vietnamese central government secretly launched a comprehensive national plan coded 184 to deal with Christian movements in the country, but the harshest measures were directed at the Hmong and a number of ethnic groups in the Central Highlands who had also become active Christians in recent years. The plan was, simply, to force them to abandon the Christian faith.

A top-secret government document written in July 2001 concerning the anti-Christian campaign in Bảo Thắng and Bắc Hà districts in Lào Cai provides further details on how the plan was carried out at local levels.[5] The document established that a special bureaucratic infrastructure had been operating to "deal severely with anyone who has illegal beliefs," to "restrict to the lowest possible limit any prayer meetings," and to "stop any new manifestations of religion which recently appeared illegally." The local authorities decided that the Evangelical Christian movement was illegal for the Hmong because the religion had only recently come to the region. The bulletin instructed officials not to allow the spread of Christianity from the Hmong to other minority groups and to "step by step, reduce the number of villages, families, and individuals who follow Christianity illegally." The method was to organize seminars for Christians during which they were urged "to sign pledges to follow their traditional customs and beliefs and to resist the useless, socially deplorable, outdated, backward, and confused people who follow Christianity illegally." The Christian Hmong were to be educated "to tell right from wrong so that, of their own volition, they [would] abandon their religion."

Until the end of 2004, not only did the Vietnamese state continue to deny the legitimacy of conversion by claiming that it was motivated by Hmong desire for economic betterment. Hmong converts were seen as people without agency who had been duped by foreign agents into converting. In order to fence off the Hmong from the influences of the state's perceived adversaries—the missionaries—a collection of booklets were published and distributed to local authorities to use as propaganda. One such booklet, titled *Don't Follow Bad Elements* (Đừng Theo Kẻ Xấu) guides officials at the grassroots level through a set of questions and answers to impart stern warnings to the Hmong about the "deceitfulness" of illegal proselytizers, who are commonly and conveniently called the "bad element" (*kẻ xấu*). Here are some examples:

> (Q2): "Illegal proselytizers said Protestant followers do not need to work but still have food to eat. Is that true?"
>
> (Q3): "Illegal proselytizers said one only needs to read the Bible and praise God every day and God will give him or her many material goods. Is that correct?"
>
> (Q9): "There are many bad elements who sneakily and under the pretext of charity come to give our compatriots some small useless things in order to propagate, lure, and trick them to follow the illegal religion. Are these acts right or wrong?"
>
> (Q17): "There are people who said the Hmong people are hungry and poor, and if they want to be rich they need to follow God so that God will help them. Is this correct?"

While it is quite unlikely that any Hmong person would approach a government authority figure to ask such questions, these questions are phrased in such a way that Protestant missionaries are portrayed as "malicious liars" and "bad elements." Moreover, the questions, supposedly raised by Hmong people themselves, are phrased in the most simplistic and simple-minded way and tell us more about the way the Kinh-dominated government contemptuously perceives the Hmong as naïve, gullible people. The answers are given in strong, patronizing language denouncing the deceitfulness of all such promises, and at the same time they warn people of the "spitefulness and cunning" of missionaries and "bad elements."

In late 2004 and early 2005, significant changes began to occur in the government's policies toward Hmong conversion. Until then, the Vietnamese government was still denying outright that there were Hmong Protestant Christians in the Northern Highlands. Yet under heavy international pressure—especially after the United State's designation of Vietnam as a "Country of Particular Concern"—the central government set out new plans to improve what international human rights advocates saw as the country's dismal religious liberty record. This change in intention came at the same time that Vietnam actively lobbied for admission to the World Trade Organization. In 2004, the government promulgated the Ordinance on Belief and Religion (*Pháp lệnh Tín ngưỡng, Tôn giáo*) to provide the basic legal framework for policies on religion in Vietnam. Soon after that, the Prime Minister issued Guideline No. 1 Regarding Protestantism (*Chỉ thị số 01 của Thủ tướng Chính phủ về một số Công tác đối với đạo Tin Lành*) on February 4, 2005, and the central government issued Decree 22 on March 1, 2005, which specifically instructed government authorities at all levels to implement the norms to manage Protestant Christianity. Specifically for the Hmong conversion, Guideline No.1 was interpreted and implemented through the "Internal Training Document on Dealing with the Hmong Christian Movement in the Northwest Province." This document was released in May 2006 and was made available to Hmong Christians in August of that year. It retains the old notion that Protestantism is part of the scheme of a "peaceful evolution" of the American empire and its unnamed allies, whose goal is to fight against the revolution. However, in a departure from previous stances, the document allows that, for some Hmong and other ethnic minorities, there is a legitimate need for religion. Therefore, some may be officially registered and permitted to undertake religious activities. Theoretically, in a system that previously denied the existence of Hmong Protestants, this is certainly a step forward. Yet, in practice, it is an uncomfortable development whereby the government unilaterally, subjectively, and arbitrarily decides which Hmong Christians have a genuine need for religion, and will be allowed to practice it under strict rules, and which Hmong must be "mobilized and persuaded to return to their traditional beliefs."

Beginning in mid-2006, government authorities in all Northern Highland provinces sent out work teams to conduct a thorough inspection to identify

Christians. All the personnel on these work teams were non-Christian, and practically all of them were agents of Plan 184 implemented in 1998 to aggressively eradicate Protestantism among ethnic minorities. These agents were known to be hostile to converts. Hmong converts were individually interviewed by work teams, which must have been a rather uncomfortable experience for them. The interviewers included police and other officials from the central government, the province, and the district. The interviewees themselves may have been previously beaten in raids or may have seen their leaders hauled off, mistreated, or jailed. Many Hmong interviewees, especially the women, spoke limited Vietnamese. How they were expected to pass these oral tests in an unfamiliar language and designed by government authorities with their own standards for weeding out Christianity is unclear.

The results of these inspections classified Christian Hmong into three categories. *Category one* designated Christians who seemed to know their faith by practicing it for at least twenty years and had a need for communal worship activities. These were eligible for registration. *Category two* designated those who called themselves Christians but were not knowledgeable about their faith and met irregularly. These were to be encouraged to return to their old ways but if they insisted on remaining Christian, they would be allowed to worship alone in the confines of their own homes without teachers or other Christians. *Category three* included the new Christians, those who had converted within the past five years and who were now the largest group of Christian Hmong in Vietnam. They were given no choice but to be "mobilized and persuaded to return to their traditional beliefs."

After identification, the plan's next big step was to register house churches. This was a lengthy process, which prompted numerous complaints even from the churches that were allowed to register. A registered church was and still is subject to strict government surveillance, which includes visits by officials that often made parishioners nervous. In many places, before each church gathering, the leaders were made to read the list of Christians registered in the location, and those not on the list were sent away. Today in some locations no one under fourteen years of age is allowed to participate in services. The reasoning is that "the government allows Hmong people to practice Christianity but should not obstruct education and the schooling of Hmong children."[6] At the time of registration, if the church leaders fail to mention all activities, even informal ones such as functions for children, young people, and women, these activities will no longer be allowed. In one location, authorities allowed only twenty-five of the thirty-five registered families to attend services, saying that those who were refused did not have local family registration. The reason for this was that they had married someone who was not from the locality. In some places, officials refused to allow the church's chosen leader to continue in his role and insisted that someone else be chosen in a process under their supervision. Officials sometimes insist that a worship program must follow exactly what is written and in that order. Nothing can be omitted or changed. Many church leaders and churchgoers told me that, compared to the current situation, their church life was easier when they were still "illegal" Christians.

THE UNCONVERTED BROTHERS

It is common that when a new religion is introduced in a community, the converts and the unconverted continue to cohabit at least for a while. In the Hmong case, the continued cohabitation of Christian and non-Christian Hmong in many areas has had a direct influence on the routinization of Christian practices for the converts. Although more than two decades after their conversion the majority of Hmong converts are determined to remain Christian, some continue to slide back into old practices, lapse into millenarianism, or de-convert altogether, as did my host, Mr. Gi. Also, as shown in the outbreak of millenarian fervor in Mường Nhé in 2011, the arrival of Christianity and global connectivity provided by modern technology and media, has exposed the Hmong in Vietnam to Christian end-of-the-world theology and re-invigorated traditional Hmong millenarianism. Such millenarian outbreaks draw unfavorable attention; this can hinder the earnest efforts of Christian Hmong to routinize their faith in their own way. In the process of establishing their church and their new community, Hmong converts in Vietnam try to connect to the world outside Vietnam. These attempts, however, have brought Hmong converts into deeper conflict with both the Vietnamese state and with the Northern Evangelical Church of Vietnam, the official patron of Hmong churches. The transnational dimension of Hmong conversion is perceived by the state authority as politically subversive and by the Northern Evangelical Church of Vietnam as a challenge to its organizational hierarchy and potentially heterodoxical. Thus, while Christianity does provide possible solutions to the marginality of the Hmong converts, it does not simply end it. On the contrary, being a Hmong Christian has meant being seen as a target of suspicion by the state and as practicing a deviant form of faith by other ecclesiastical organizations.

Social and family conflicts continue to occur not only between the converts and the non-converts but also between the converts themselves. Although Christianity provides alternative linguistic and ritual instruments for elucidating conflict, conversion remains a divisive force. While Hmong converts continued to yearn for a social space, a virtual community in which they can place themselves at the center, political tension and scriptural misunderstandings due to lack of proper ecclesiastical training deprive them of a clear knowledge of how to organize their community. The making of a Christian Hmong community thus has become an arduous process in which converts have had to navigate various contentions with Vietnamese state authorities, with their non-Christian Hmong fellows, and even with their own supporters, the missionaries.

The Vietnamese state's anti-conversion policies and propaganda play a crucial role in influencing the attitudes of the unconverted towards those who convert, further intensifying the conflicts between the two groups. A case I happened to witness shows how literally the non-converted Hmong interpret and follow state instructions on how to curb conversion. One sunny day in late November 2004, while I was visiting Windy Plateau, I encountered a crowd of nearly one hundred Hmong people marching toward the office of a local commune's People Committee building. Near the front of the crowd was a buffalo-drawn wooden cart in which sat a man whose hands had been tied behind his back. As the crowd drew closer to the People Committee's building, people became more and more excited. The wooden cart stopped at the front yard of the building. Several young men came forward and dragged the bruised man out from the cart. They made him kneel down on the yard, and people quickly encircled him, I found myself standing close to the innermost circle along with my Hmong assistant. A man who looked like a local official wormed his way through the crowd and halted right in front of us. Pointing his finger to the kneeling man, he shouted in Hmong "Talk! Confess your lies." No response. The man shouted again several times and many others joined him. Still, there was no response. Keeping his eyes tightly shut, the kneeling man lowered his bruised face. His body trembled. Drops of sweat rolled down his temples. It was almost midday. The sun began to burn, but because of the plateau's altitude the air was still cold. When the shouting died down a bit, an older man nearby pointed his finger at the kneeling man and said "Yesterday he said 'Vang Tsu is very powerful. He can protect anyone who follows him.' Let's tie him tighter and see how his God can help him." The suggestion was followed right away; two young men came with another rope and tightened it around the man's arms closer to his elbows. The man bit his lower lip but as the robe reached his elbows, his arms became seriously twisted; he let out a scream. Tears ran down his cheeks as he cried out "I confess. I confess. I lied."

As I gathered from my assistant's translation of the trembling confession, from members of the crowd, and from other local people, the kneeling man, whom I shall call Giang Seo Lử, was a Christian Hmong from Sơn La province. He had come to Windy Plateau the day before and lodged with a Giang family in the commune. From the moment he arrived, he talked to the family about Vang Tsu and why they should all follow Vang Tsu's way. Believing that the family was open to listening to him, Giang Seo Lử urged them to call on other families. He also suggested that his host kill a chicken for dinner. The family complied, but wasn't happy. Next morning, his host secretly sent his son to the commune's security officials who quickly came to arrest Giang Seo Lử. At first, they just kept him in the house of his host and challenged the veracity of his claims about the New Way, or Christianity. When Giang Seo Lử refused to back down and insisted on how powerful his Christian brothers and sisters were, not only in Vietnam but also abroad, he began to irritate the security officials, who started to beat him up. It was at that point that the head of the commune—the one who would later make his way through the crowd and demand that Giang Seo Lử confess—arrived and immediately stopped the beating. He then ordered the group to bring Giang Seo Lử to the People Committee's office so that he could confess his lies in public. The head of the commune had been trained to extract public confessions as a strategy to prevent further conversion. It is unclear what level of government authority was responsible for detailing how to carry out such public confession. But it is clear that what happened at the scene I witnessed in Windy Plateau was a startling enactment of the propaganda that the central government had published and distributed to local administrations.

In spite of the rapid growth of Christianization among the Hmong, two-thirds of this ethnic group—roughly seven hundred thousand Hmong—remain unconverted. What happened in Windy Plateau might be extreme, but the unconverted share a strong resentment toward Christianity and toward those who have converted. This disapproval is partly the result of political pressure from the authorities and the unwelcome heightened scrutiny that converts bring to their locality. The messianic character of Hmong Christianity not only causes anxiety within the Hmong community, but also intensifies outside political pressure upon both the converted and unconverted Hmong. In many cases, condemnation only becomes significant when the unconverted are made responsible for the behavior of their converted family members or kinsmen.

The majority of non-Christian Hmong also perceive conversion as an act of betrayal or apostasy. First, they denounce the converts' repudiation of ancestral worship and spirit offering. This comportment is thought to be morally wrong with serious consequences not only for the converts themselves but also for the rest of the community. This would be the revenge and punishment from spirits and ancestors. Even though I tried to remain neutral when I was with unconverted Hmong, I was inundated with criticism about the strange and alien behavior of their polluted cousins and neighbors who sang their wishes to Jesus Christ. A Hmong man said to me: "I am so worried for those who worship the 'western ghost' [Ma Tây]. They must be out of their minds to be able to burn their ancestral altars. They are insulting the people who gave birth to them. I ask you, who are closer to you: your parents or people you've never met? Who is more important? Your parents, right? So your parents' spirit must be closer to you and therefore can protect you better than the spirit of western people who live so far away." A seventy-year-old man whose sons converted ten years ago worried: "I often cannot sleep because I am scared. Many times when I have dreamt about my parents and grandparents who constantly confront me [and ask me] if I die who will worship them? I am also worried for myself. If I die, my sons will not do Ma khô for me and I will not be able to enter the village of ancestors. I will have to wander without knowing where to go."

Apart from these issues, many unconverted Hmong express their concerns about other factors affected by these conversions. Conversion will damage the solidarity of the group and make Hmong culture and identity disappear. Similar to what Ovesen (1995) observed of the Laotian Christian Hmong in his village study, what is felt by the non-Christian majority to be much more serious is the refusal of the Christian converts to participate in the common ritual obligations towards relatives particularly in connection with funerals. For the Hmong, it is very important to provide for deceased relatives to ensure their safe passage to and reception in "the village of the ancestors," for which the sacrifice of a number of farm animals is necessary. Such animal sacrifice is not tolerated by Christians, which means that many elder people whose sons have converted or whose daughters have married Christians are both resentful and more than a little concerned about their posthumous fate. The practice of animal sacrifice is deprecated by Christians as sinful, irrational, and wasteful. Moreover, Christian Hmong refuse to participate in ritual ceremonies because they do not want to risk having to eat sacrificial meat and food, which they are prohibited from doing.

For most of the converts, there is a strong tendency to radically break away from their pre-Protestant life; this has as an unintended consequence their separation from the groups to which they once belonged. One of my sources, a young non-Christian Hmong, told me that he was willing to be my guide and interpreter in his home village but not in the neighboring one. This was not because of the inconvenience of distance—the two villages are separated from each other by only a twenty-meter wide road but belong to two different administrative units—but because of subjacent antagonism. "I can't even come close to these guys—the Christian Hmong—not to mention talking to them. They don't want to talk to us. If they talk, they call us 'the long tails' [bọn dài đuôi]." This is a mocking term developed since Protestantism was introduced to the Hmong. The Protestant Hmong ridicule the

CHAPTER SIX

non-Christian Hmong still dragging behind them the long tail of traditional burden. I observed in several communes young Hmong Protestants who refuse to pursue or marry a non-Protestant partner. Some explained that this was because "they [the non-Christian Hmong villagers] laughed at us and ridiculed us as 'Hmong with wings.' They often provoked us by shouting to their friends in our presence 'look! look! They are going on flights!' or saying 'why don't you stay home and eat your Lord's words instead of coming here to work in the field?'" The ridicule about "wings" and "flying" is a way to shame Christian Hmong for early conversion practices when converts followed all kinds of millenarian practices. The ridicule directed at the way that Christians approach work on the field is a way for non-Christians to refute the idea that for a Christian, only God's words—the Bible and FEBC teachings—are enough to make him happy and satisfied.

RITUAL COMPETITIONS

Although the process of selective legalization of Hmong house churches began in 2005, the Vietnamese government has essentially continued to disapprove of Hmong Protestantism. Yet, under the watchful eyes of the international community and of human right advocates, government officials could no longer ban further conversions and persecute members of underground Hmong house churches or churches not yet recognized by the state authorities. Under the new conditions, state-directed "anti-conversion" policies began to take a cultural turn. Instead of open restrictions, the state gave active support to the unconverted Hmong in their fervent resistance to the conversion of their ethnic fellows. Such support has taken the form of encouraging and promoting the revival of what they see as traditional Hmong religion to turn it into a bulwark against Protestantism. Since 2005, government authorities have sponsored traditional Hmong calendric rituals and festivals. By doing so, the government has hoped to kill two birds with one stone. On the one hand, they can prevent further conversion and, on the other, they can potentially pull back converted Hmong to their "good and beautiful" cultural roots. This sponsorship has the added benefit of helping to enrich the range of cultural commodities for the growing ethno-tourism market.

This was, however, a contradictory and ironic maneuver. Social engineering programs have long fought against Hmong traditions that the state has perceived as superstitious, anti-modern, anti-socialist and, sometimes, potentially riotous. Even during the transition to market economy and economic globalization, which began after the economic reforms of 1986, elements of Hmong religion and culture continued to be written off as the causes for the perceived sluggishness of the Hmong and for their incapacity to adopt an ethos suitable for a market economy and capitalist modes of production. Only after a massive number of Hmong people converted to Protestantism did the government see the need to revive Hmong traditional culture urgently, if still selectively (*khôi phục có trọn lọc*). Following the growth of the tourism industry, Hmong traditional practices such as communal festivals, bullfights, and weekly market gatherings were recognized as potentially profitable and were cautiously encouraged.

What do Hmong people, Christian and non-Christian, make of this new policy development? Converts, initiated into Protestantism in secret and living their faith underground for such a long time, have had a fragmented understanding of what it is to be a Protestant. The loosening of state control has accelerated their search for authentic ways of being Christians while also intensifying confrontation with their non-Christian Hmong fellows. This process has ranged from the internalization of doctrinal and catechetical knowledge to the formation of a new morality by changing discourses and practices that govern faith-based behaviors such as sexual manners and standards of propriety. Ritual competitions, often newly invented, have become arenas for showing the identity differences of converts and non-converts alike. For non-converts, not only has their resistance to Christianity been redefined as "the battle" against Christianity, but traditional beliefs and practices have become rearticulated in order to gain new strength to rebound in the national and global religious stage. The new form of consciousness of the non-Christian Hmong, however, is also a cause for concern for the Vietnamese state.

†

The invention of tradition is a well-known phenomenon in processes of cultural change and modernization (Hobsbawm and Ranger 1996), but the circumstances in which it takes place in Vietnam today is quite special. On the one hand, we have the Vietnamese Communist state that is forced by international trade negotiations to give more freedom to Christians. The process of selecting "well-established" house churches for legal status has set in motion the increased public presence of house churches that wish to be recognized. The public performances by these Christian converts have drawn the attention of their non-converted fellow Hmong who have responded with their own performances of "traditional religion." These "traditional" responses have been actively supported by the Vietnamese government as providing an obstacle against further conversion. The Vietnamese cadres, however, want to distinguish between the religious and the cultural aspects of Hmong ritual revival.

As such, they continue their efforts against "superstition" and in favor of secularization, while supporting Hmong ritual performances. The distinction that they make between culture and religion is not made, however, by Hmong themselves who stage these performances precisely to show the power of their religious traditions against Christianity. The contradictions shown in these performances (that are connected to globalization via foreign tourism and global Christianity) are a perfect illustration of the tensions inherent in the Christian conversion of the Hmong.

Social conflict and division, however, are not intended either by the converts or the non-converts. This is, rather, the product of the dilemma that both groups are facing. Continuing a strong tradition of ethnic belonging and identity, the converts believe that Christianity is the methodological answer to the Hmong's current problems and that conversion will help them gain a powerful spiritual resource, which will enhance and strengthen the unity of the Hmong community. The unconverted Hmong, however, do not share this view even if they share the ideal of a strong and unified Hmong people. The commitment to traditional Hmong belief and practices—not to mention the pressure exercised by the government in discriminating against Protestant Hmong—makes it difficult for some to associate practically and spiritually with the Protestant members of the community.

Yet, a total break between the converts and the non-converts is impossible, as most of the Hmong still need to rely on clan-based relationships as a strategy for social survival. In the current situation, although solidarity can in general be expected from fellow clansmen, substantial assistance in economic and social matters requires the presence of blood relations. It is to the relatives from his or her lineage that a Hmong will primarily turn for economic help, practical assistance, and consolation. If a man wishes to move his household to another location, he will almost invariably have relatives there who should be prepared to sponsor his entry into the new location by giving him land, loaning him rice or money, and helping him to build his house. The importance of relatives also applies to spiritual matters. Ovesen (1995) observes, "[a] Hmong can only be really happy when he is together with his relatives, since such close contacts represent emotional assurance, social support, spiritual comfort as well as the greatest possible economic security" (22–23).

This explains why when a portion of the Hmong community decides to choose a different faith, a dilemma emerges for both groups. For those who remain unconverted, the conversion of their relatives and acquaintances can signal the need for changes in their social and cultural life even if Christianity itself is not seen as the solution. For the converted, unsolvable conflicts with non-Christian Hmong—sometimes as close kin as father or wife—make difficulties that much harder to resolve and give rise to a number of tensions. For these tensions, there is no foreseeable end in sight. For those who converted, the divisions and conflicts with their unconverted next of kin are the most painful consequences of the process. These are the wedges that have the highest potential of undoing conversion as in the case of Mr. Gi.

CHAPTER SEVEN

TRANSFORMATION OF
MORALITY AND SUBJECTIVITY

I N the 1985 documentary *Between Two Worlds: The Hmong Shaman in America*, a bald-headed American Mormon missionary in a slick grey suit and his nervously cheerful Hmong assistant arrive in the living room of a Hmong immigrant family newly resettled in suburban Chicago. After giving out candies to the children, who are practically the only members of the family to extend any sign of welcome to them, the missionary has his assistant explain the purpose of their visit: "I come here today to tell you the good news about our Lord, Jesus Christ who died on the cross for our sins." The room remains silent after the assistant has finished his translation, so the missionary continues. "You," he says, pointing his finger at several adult members of the family, who have kept their distance from him, "and me, we are sinners. We have done things wrong that we deserve to die and go to hell for, because we have done things wrong." "I don't know anything," says Mr. Thao, the head of the family, who is also a shaman. Quite clearly he wants to avoid further discussion, but he feels the need to maintain some of the politeness that a Hmong head-of-household is supposed to have, even to unwanted guests. His wife's disagreement is, however, clearly expressed as she shouts to the translating assistant: "Oh you silly, you haven't sinned at all. You must tell the missionary that you haven't sinned at all." Mr. Thao returns to the conversation, as if to rescue the missionary from discomfort, "I haven't sinned at all, so I don't know. In my life, I have never seen or heard anything about sin." However, this answer is quickly taken by the missionary as an invitation to explain further about sin. He presses on: "We are all on the same boat, in the same place. Every one of us has done things wrong. I wish I had a Bible in his [Hmong] language, but, hmm. . . . The Bible is God's word, and it said [pointing his finger to an open page of a pocket-

139

size Bible] Jesus died for our sin [reading slowly and punctuating every single word], everybody's sin. The whole world sinned."

This scene is a perfect illustration of the persistent rejection by many Hmong of the notion of "sin." Rejection of the idea that they are sinful is common among those who resist conversion in the diaspora; and that was exactly the reaction of Hmong converts in the early stages of their contact with evangelical Protestantism despite of the vigor with which many of them embraced this new religion. Nearly two decades later, however, more and more Christian converts are starting to speak of themselves as sinners in typical Christian fashion. Issues of Christian morality—its demands, the difficulty of meeting those demands, and the consequences of not doing so—have become consuming topics of daily conversation not only among the converts but also among the unconverted in Phong Hải. While converts are preoccupied with their own sinfulness or, more precisely, with figuring out what their own sinfulness amounts to, the unconverted are much more certain that their converted fellows are still doing things wrong despite their conversion. Arguments and disputes occur quite frequently over the claim of moral success or failure in this divided community.

Conversion is a cultural project that entails the multifaceted transformation of a person's patterns of behavior, ways of thinking, and ways of speaking. It is the transformation of moral consciousness. Given that the change from the "traditional" Hmong moral system to the new "Hmong Christian morality" is taking place at this very moment, even Hmong converts and non-converts in Vietnam are unclear as to what "Hmong Christian morality" is supposed to be. For Hmong converts to Protestantism, it also entails rethinking their commitment to some key aspects of their tradition. But what this tradition actually entails is also subjected to interpretation. Over the last half-century, Hmong notions of their own traditions have been influenced by generalized Kinh prejudices about them and other ethnic minorities and by the Vietnamese state's attempts to both incorporate them into the larger (Kinh) polity and simultaneously to construct the "New Socialist Person." That these attempts have been largely unsuccessful especially among ethnic minorities does not diminish their ability to reshape normative beliefs if not necessarily behavior. Recently, further confusion about what is old and what is new has been created by the state's efforts to restore and revalorize certain aspects of Hmong "tradition" as a bulwark against the advances of Protestantism.

Additionally, as Protestant conversions occur in an intricate web of social and kinship relations, the transition from one system of morality to the other becomes a highly interactive and, often, divisive force which also has a great impact on the understanding of what "traditional Hmong morality" is. To understand what conversion entails for both Hmong converts and non-converts, I draw on Nicholas Tapp's (2002) work on Hmong morality, on Foucault's (1983) late work on the genealogy of ethics, and on Robbins's (2004) comparative work on Christian conversion and moral torment among the Urapmin, of Papua New Guinea. Building on that theoretical and comparative literature I will focus on a central part of moral transformation: sexuality, courtship, and marriage.

TECHNOLOGY OF THE SOUL: CONVERSION AND THE TRANSFORMATION OF MORALITY

To understand change in Hmong moral reasoning in Thailand, Nicholas Tapp (2002) mobilizes Marshall Sahlin's conceptualization of concentric spheres of influence and obligation spanning from the most personal domain of one's lineage group to increasingly more distant spheres of affines, non-Hmong peoples, jungles and wilderness, and heaven and earth. Different moralities apply to people or things in different spheres. Actions that are strictly forbidden when dealing with relatives are less offensive when acted on individuals or objects that are more socially distant from oneself.

Using this traditional morality as a baseline, Tapp contends that as the Hmong have become ensconced in the ways of urban life—both from urban migration and from urbanizing ways of life permeating village life—the traditional basis for distinguishing moral conduct has dissolved. More particularly, the hierarchy of family, lineage, village, co-ethnics, etc., has become irrelevant in the new urban economy and interpersonal relations. He argues that the changing socioeconomic base to which urban Hmong have had to adapt has led to new behaviors—for example, competition with close kin through market activity—that previously would have only been acceptable if enacted towards socially distant others. Previously, the subsistence-based economy encouraged a type of morality in which close kin and affine clung together. This new context has led the Hmong to universalize moral behaviors for socially distant others to close kin as well, and, indeed, to all human beings:

> Returning to the original model of a relative tribal morality, it would seem reasonable to conclude that what will have occurred under the impact of urbanization, is a kind of gigantic stretching of the traditional boundaries of the Hmong moral universe, in which the boundaries between the self, community, and the world have been exploded, and the relative basis of traditional Hmong morality therefore having largely collapsed. Behavior which was traditionally seen as only appropriate to

MORALITY AND SUBJECTIVITY

141

those beyond the pale of the social system has now been universalized, and it is this kind of behavior we would consider as immoral. (Tapp 2002: 100)

Tapp provides an understanding of a particular type of change in morality that one might expect when a contextual "traditional" morality is displaced by a more universalizing urban ethos. His argument that a significant change in the global consciousness of the Hmong as a group took place as a result of increased encounters with other kinds of people and particularly the overseas—diasporic—Hmong, is especially relevant here.

According to Foucault, all moralities are composed of two elements: codes of conducts and "forms of subjectification." As Foucault construes them, moral codes are straightforward in nature: they are simply lists of prescribed and prohibited behaviors. The forms of subjectification are more complex. Elsewhere he refers to what he intends by this term as "ethics," or most revealingly as one's "relation to oneself" (Foucault 1997: 226; Davidson 1986: 229). The domain of ethics, taken in this sense, has to do with how "one ought to form oneself as an ethical subject" in relation to the moral code under which one lives (Foucault 1990: 26). After all, ethics or *rapport à soi* is concerned with the way the individual is supposed to constitute himself as a moral subject of his own action. We constitute ourselves as subjects acting on others—as agents, that is, not as patients.

One domain of his projected genealogy of ethics is the power that individuals exercise. Another is an account of "ourselves" in relation to truth through which we constitute ourselves as subjects to knowledge. Again, it is we who are doing *it*; we are not having *it* done to us. In Foucault's account, it is not the rules of the code that are central to ethics but rather the spirit in which they are observed and the kind of effort required to make oneself an observant person.

Foucault's conception of morality has been used intensively by Joel Robbins in his attempt to understand the process of *Becoming Sinners* (2004) that the Urapmin in Papua New Guinea are engaged in. Urapmin Christianization is intriguing because of the vigor with which they embrace the new religion. Unlike other instances of conversion, Robbins notes that the Urapmin were neither under intensive missionary pressure nor subjected to severe socioeconomic dislocation. Importantly, the author claims, Urapmin Christianity was adopted as a "meaningful system in its own right" (2004: 3) and hence it would be misguided to understand it as syncretized or hybridized, as more conventional approaches of conversion to Christianity would have it. At the same time, the speed with which it was taken up allowed for two simultaneous if contradictory cultural logics that interacted with the Urapmin notion of what constitutes a moral person. Exploring the mechanisms and processes through which a "two-sided culture" develops, leads to "a theory of culture change that can explain both how people are able to quickly grasp the logic of the new without sacrificing the coherence of what came before" (2004: 4). Robbins argues that structuralist historical concepts of cultural change, which have traditionally emphasized changes in cultural categories—*assimilation*—or changes in the relations that exist between cultural categories—transformation—can also accommodate what he calls "adoption" (2004: 11). Adoption in this sense is defined as adding new cultural elements without linking them to pre-existing cultural categories.

Where adoption becomes problematic for the Urapmin is in the struggle over paramount values associated with traditional Urapmin life versus Christianity. The former is characterized by relationalism, in that relationships and the maintenance of them define sociality while Christianity is associated with individualism. It is in the focus on values and the struggles over them that Robbins shows the twists and turns of Urapmin morality. The Urapmin's "engagement with moral debates over what defines a good person provides a window through which they can see the contradictions with which they have to live" (Robbins 2004: 14). The major contradiction that defines Urapmin lives is the need to balance their own laws. Does one pursue a life based on relationalism through which one's will must be exerted to create and maintain social relations? Or does one follow a path of Christian individualism under which the will must be subsumed and social relations wither as a result? These are difficult choices and create a situation in which the Urapmin find themselves becoming sinners, unable to strike a balance between willfulness and lawfulness.

Whereas there are only a few aspects of the Urapmin Christianization that are similar to the Christianization of the Hmong in Vietnam, it is still a useful case for comparative purposes. Like the Urapmin, the Hmong are strong believers in millennialism and hundreds of thousands of them came to embrace Christianity enthusiastically, rapidly, and with strong determination even under threat of harsh persecution by the state. Today, the number of Hmong converts in Vietnam continues to grow even without intensive missionary contact. While most Urapmin have converted to Christianity—perhaps thanks to the small size of their population, 390 people in total, as reported by Robbins (2006)—fewer than 300,000 Hmong in Vietnam, or about one-third of the population, have converted to Christianity. While in some way, the Hmong converts today are going through a "revival," which focuses on human sinfulness similar to the Urapmin's "second-stage conversion," this "revival" among the Hmong does not entail a charismatic development. While it does emphasize the strict abandonment of traditional religion for Christianity, it is not clear whether it is driven by a constant sense of millennial expectation as in the case of the Urapmin.

One special aspect of the Hmong conversion is that—at least in the view of the converts—it comes from a strong ethnic motivation. Unlike the Urapmin, the Hmong are a minority group in a nation-state overwhelmingly dominated by a Kinh majority. Therefore not only their relation to Christianity is important but also their relation to the cultural values of the Kinh. Having internalized the idea of being a marginal group, Hmong converts see Christianity as an answer not only for each individual convert, but also for the Hmong group as a whole in their common quest for empowerment and modernity. This special feature perhaps explains why, despite their active search for moral propriety, which is mainly a task of the individual's consciousness, they cannot easily let go of what they perceive to be the requirements of community life. Their criticism of "improper" conduct, to which they themselves were committed prior to conversion, and which is still the behavior of their non-Christian interlocutors and of the "not-yet-qualified" Christians among them, largely reflects a "constructive" spirit. That is to say the condemnation of such behavior helps to strengthen Hmong morally and spiritually. This may also explain why in the case of the Hmong in Thailand, as observed by Jacob Hickman (2007), the differences between those who proclaimed themselves to be "Christian" and those who called themselves "traditional" were not very significant. For example, the self-proclaimed Christians do not demonstrate an orthodox acceptance of Christian theology. In his observation, many Hmong families in Thailand and the United States participate actively in both Christian and animist communities and rituals without a strong conviction that either is better or cosmologically more appropriate than the other. In such cases, one might expect community-oriented discourse to prevail given that people in these situations commit themselves to the religious communities but not necessarily to the spiritual ideologies.

Yet, since Christianization is supposed to address the Hmong aspiration for empowerment and modernity, the fact that only one-third of Hmong in Vietnam have converted has caused dissension within the Hmong community at large, within clans and villages, and within individual families such as that of my host, Mr. Gi. Hmong people, in Vietnam and elsewhere, converts and non-converted alike, frequently talk about the tension that arises regularly within families and communities regarding conversion to Christianity from "traditional" shamanism. The unconverted complain about the ways that the new belief-system undercuts familial cohesion—for example, many Christians are forbidden to attend shaman ceremonies or *huplig* (soul calling) rituals—and causes the development of new moral beliefs that are incompatible with the old ways, such as a rejection of polygyny. The converted, on the other hand, complain about the burden of living the old life—for example, the heavy ritual duties involved in life prior to conversion. At moments of tension with their unconverted fellows, these complaints often include criticism of moral codes and bodily behaviors that are prescribed or proscribed by traditional morality.

The Christian Hmong in Vietnam, it seems, are currently being torn between their commitment to the Hmong ethnic group as a whole and having to assert the legitimate existence of their religious community, legally, socially, and morally. Although "traditional" discourses already contain rich beliefs regarding the welfare of the soul, currently Hmong converts and those who have helped to convert them such as converted family members and missionaries focus on building another strong Christian soul. In the context of Christian conversion, this can be interpreted as a soul that can be controlled and dominated and that is created largely by the methods of control and domination. The process of "soul formation" is the moment of active transition from an "old" to a "new" morality, a new self and a new subjectivity. At the moment of trying to create a new moral system, not only are new assumptions created and old assumptions transformed, but Hmong converts are also actively creating and making explicit new assumptions that will eventually become unexamined assumptions. They have much discursive work still to do in order to assume a different self, a different moral system, and a new way of representing themselves in a language that is more explicit than the one they used before. But in order to assert the possible existence of such a new self and its corresponding new morality—presumably a better one—Hmong converts point the finger at what they see as representations of the "old self," "old morality," and the "bad guys," who often turn out to be either their unconverted Hmong fellows or those "badly behaved Christians" among themselves. In so doing, they adopt familiar stereotypes long used by the majority of the Vietnamese, the Kinh, to describe the Hmong.

The need to point the finger at the "bad guys" is also due to recent political changes that are influencing the course of Christianization among the Hmong in Vietnam. Since 2005, after the implementation of Guideline No. 1 through which the state allowed a small and select number of Hmong house churches to register their members, the relatively freer political control seems to have made both missionaries and Christian converts switch strategies. If before 2005, the priority was to *expand* their base through evangelization—evangelism was strictly an underground activity—now the strategy has become to *internalize* the new faith. Before this, being courageous in undertaking secret evangelical missions and enduring political persecutions were virtually enough to assert the authenticity of one's conversion and sense of loyalty. Presently, these acts are simply not enough. Many Hmong converts, especially the young, face difficulties in defining to their non-Christian interlocutors and, more importantly, to themselves what being a Protestant actually means.

The Hmong Christian body in Vietnam has grown fast, but, as an FEBC missionary told me, as individuals, people grow "spiritually" at different rates; some never "grow up" to be mature Christians. Part of the problem is the manner in which they were converted—via radio teaching, secret house churches, and Bible gatherings. Owing to heavy political persecution, very little or no guidance by on-site missionaries was available. In fact, as many missionaries admitted, it would be completely normal under these circumstances, for "cults" or "sects" to spring up where anyone with a strong personality articulates his or her own variation of Christianity and gains a following. Often those who had been designated "church leaders," however well meaning, were themselves "immature" in the Christian path.

SEXUALITY AS SINFUL

In discourses about Christian morality that have recently emerged and circulate in Phong Hải and other Hmong areas, sex, sexuality, and gender form a topic that is most frequently deployed to show what has changed and what should change after conversion. It is on the human body that the effects of various technologies of power can most easily be observed (Foucault 1977, 1978, 1984, 1990). The body is the very site of history (Csordas 1994). The discourses on morality increasingly seem to be sites of negotiation and contestation of the Christian configuration of subjectivity.

Hmong customs have been the subject of attempts by both the Vietnamese Socialist state and Protestant missionaries to reform and regulate them and they are the frequent focus of Hmong converts' discussions of sin. These attempts are in turn shaped by popular images of the Hmong among Kinh Vietnamese as exotic and erotic others and the common contrasting of Hmong "barbarism" with Kinh Confucian "civilization." During colonial times, Meo (Hmong) women were said to go bare-breasted though most available photographs depict them as covered from head to toe by colorfully embroidered clothes. This imagined semi-nudity, combined with courtship mores of permissible premarital sexual play, signified an unconstrained and perhaps too seductive sexuality

The way Hmong converts are led to recognize their moral obligations is very similar to what Foucault calls "the mode of subjectification" (1997: 264; 1990: 27). It happens on the basis of both religious law (Giáo Luật) promulgated by the Northern Evangelical Church of Vietnam (NECVN) and on the convert's own incomplete understanding of fragmented Christian teachings from radio broadcasts, missionaries, or the NECVN. Although most Vietnamese Protestants, including Hmong, recognize the Ten Commandments, and an increasing number of them could cite them in their own words, it is the religious laws that they obey (Hội Thánh Tin Lành Việt Nam Miền Bắc 2004). In this translation by the NECVN, the Ten Commandments somehow become Eighteen Commandments. Divided into six chapters, the Giáo Luật of the Northern Evangelical Church of Vietnam is an interpretation of Christian morality through the lens of (Kinh) Confucian and socialist morality. Article 3 in chapter III, for example, stipulates "unfilial" sin. As sexual sinfulness is an important concern of Confucian morality, article 4 instructs in detail on what constitutes sexual sinfulness: adultery, sexual deviancy (tà dâm) such as polygyny, marrying a married woman, marrying a married man,[1] divorce without reason, incest, and sodomy. Article 7 designates "coercive marriage" as a particularly heavy sin. This is because, explained a Vietnamese pastor, in the beginning when American missionaries came to proselytize in Vietnam, they noticed the sinful practice of many Vietnamese parents of forcing their children, especially their daughters, into marriage that would yield economic benefit for the parents. Today, the pastor insisted, this article is still an important regulation, especially when it comes to the case of an ethnic minority like the Hmong, whose former culture tolerated coercive marriage, parents selling their daughters for a high bride price, and marriage by capture.

When I interviewed Hmong church leaders, there were many Christian terms that they could not say in Hmong, or more precisely that they preferred to say in Vietnamese. Sometimes this was because church leaders had been trained by the Hanoi-based NECVN in Vietnamese. More importantly, the words (and concepts) did not exist in Hmong. When Hmong people converted to Christianity, they were forced to struggle with the meaning of many, to them utterly new, Christian concepts. This is clear when it comes to understanding and translating terms and concepts of a sexual nature, a heavily tabooed topic in Hmong society, for which Hmong people habitually use euphemisms. For example, sex or having sex is commonly referred to as "doing it" (ua nawv) or "the way of girl and boy" (kev nkauj kev nraug). When these euphemisms are adopted to translate Christian concepts, misunderstanding and ambiguity arise. For example, to address "illicit sexual relations," some missionaries use the phrase kev plees kev yi; the word plees is sometimes understood as "brazen, impudent, shameless" in the phrase ua plees ua yi (a mischievous way of wooing a young girl). This term, however, is also commonly used in a variety of other contexts that are not sexual in nature, such as parents calling their naughty children plees or naughty folksongs, which are classified as plees kwv txhiaj. By using kev plees kev yi to indicate "illicit sexual relations," the missionaries forced strict ideas of sexual propriety upon a frequently used and very often playful but non-sexual expression. Similarly, the phrase *kev nkauj kev nraug* is used in several Bible translations to mean "illicit sexual relations." However, since the word *nkauj* refers to an unmarried woman and *nraug* refers to an unmarried man, this expression generally refers to courting activities which are, in Hmong culture, not to be talked about—hence the use of the euphemism—but are accepted as a necessary part of the process preceding marriage. By using this phrase to indicate "illicit sexual relations," Protestant missionaries have changed common language practices to impose Christian moral categories that dictate opposition to premarital sex.

Changing nomenclature is not only the way missionaries accentuate Christian moral categories. The discovery of "sin" is an ongoing project in which Protestant Hmong examine their own thinking and debated with non-Christians about key features of Hmong "traditional" morality such as courtship and pre-marital sex, marriage by capture; bride-price, promiscuity and polygyny.

COURTSHIP, CAPTURE, AND MARRIAGE

Unlike many societies, including that of the Kinh Vietnamese, where premarital sex is strongly discouraged, the Hmong allow their youngsters a certain degree of sexual freedom but also channel their sexuality by promoting early marriage. Courting usually starts early in Hmong "traditional" society, and as far as I observed, it is the same among Hmong Christian communities. Whenever there is a sign that "the fruit is ripe," a metaphor for sexual maturation of boys and girls—such as the start of menstruation—courting can start. Interestingly, in a culture that is as highly patriarchal in structure as the Hmong's, a woman's body before marriage—her virginity, to be precise—is not an object of control or of safeguard. It is not treated as a symbol for the integrity of the power of men who are responsible for her—her father or brothers—as is the case in many other cultures such as Muslim, Confucian-based, or Catholic cultures. Although there are many cultural expectations and regulations that discourage too much sexual engagement amongst youngsters, Hmong youths are still in control of their own sexuality.

Hmong youth do not date, but court each other instead. A courting ritual typically proceeds like this: when a Hmong young man finds the girl of his dreams, he will find out about her village and her house. Then at night he will go there, stands outside the wall where the girl sleeps inside, and softly sings songs in which he introduces himself and tells her how much he longs for her and then will ask for her permission to enter the house. If the girl disagrees, he should withdraw. If she shows a sign of approval, he will enter the house quietly by climbing over the sidewall, which Hmong house architecture allows for. The couple's courting, which includes extensive conversation, has to be kept secret from other members of the family. Luckily for them, most of the time, Hmong people in the villages go to bed very early—around seven or eight at night. Once the boy is inside, he will be allowed to sit on the girl's bed—which nowadays is normally surrounded by curtains or a bamboo fence. The two of them will then talk and exchange whatever they have, need, want, or desire to exchange. Understandably, in such a situation, when the "smell of the ripe fruit" becomes "irresistible," sexual intercourse ultimately occurs. Or using the words of my Hmong girlfriends, it is difficult for "it" not to happen when you wear a skirt.

The length of the courting nights varies, depending on the situation. Usually the boy leaves after midnight. However, there are quite a few cases in which the boy has forgotten to leave after "courting" his girlfriend and ended up in an embarrassing situation when the family awoke the next morning. Hmong people do wake up very early. An old acquaintance of mine had experienced it once when he was sixteen. It was a very cold night in late December in the icy Mường Khương plateau, when he went to "visit" his girlfriend, who later became his wife. He said that because it was so cold outside and he was so tired and the bed was so warm, he forgot to get up and leave. Next morning he was woken up by the noise of the mill grinding corn. The open space above the side wall of the house where he had climbed the night before was right above the fire, already lit by the mother and now surrounded by the girl's father and siblings. Too embarrassed, he tossed a blanket over his head and rushed out of the door, passing her family members, whose mouths dropped open in surprise. They very quickly came to their senses and burst out laughing. Almost fifty years later, he could still remember them laughing at him.

Once the courting has gone on long enough—from a few days to a few months as the case may be—the girl may agree to marry the young man; he will then have to ask permission for the marriage from his parents. This is necessary because his parents or guardians have to help pay part or all of the bride price and the wedding costs. If the girl consents to the marriage, her parent's permission does not have to be obtained beforehand. A mediator is used to negotiate with the girl's parents only when she herself has not agreed to the marriage or when the prospective spouses do not know each other well enough. Today, parents are reluctant to force their daughters and will try first to use persuasion because they generally wish to avoid being blamed should the marriage prove unsuccessful. The groom and his relatives are also apt to treat the bride and her parents with respect if the latter do not consent to her marriage too readily (Lee 1988).

If a girl is willing to marry, the man will take her to his home quietly and then send a messenger to inform her parents. If the man does not live too far away, the girl's mother may go there to claim her back and may even be violent with her and her intended husband to show her displeasure. This verbal and physical abuse has to be accepted without retaliation. This ceremonial aspect must be performed even when the girl's parents approve of her match. This is done in order to demonstrate their reluctance in handing over their daughter so that her husband will take better care of her, knowing how highly they value her. The man and his relatives will, on their part, lavish promises or money and gifts on the mother and in the end, she will return home without her daughter to wait for the day when the marriage will be celebrated.

Dương Bích Hạnh (2006) described how young Hmong girls who lived on their own and worked as tour guides negotiated their newly earned freedom and became very good at having fun. In contrast, I found a kind of asceticism that young Hmong converts to Protestantism are imposing on themselves. While traditional Hmong society has great flexibility in its moral code regarding sexuality, in converting to Christianity, sex becomes one of the behaviors that need to be regulated. House-churches have started preaching proper behavior for youngsters regarding "romantic conducts." Even courting in the dark or out in the open, outside or inside the house is now rearticulated as either proper or improper behavior. Virginity, which was not an important aspect of virtue in traditional society, has become one. Many male youngsters in the Christian Hmong community in Lào Cai told me that today when searching for potential partners, they have to make their behavior "transparent" and trustworthy. As some put it, dating a girl in the "new way," one must "stay on the main road instead of wandering off into the bush." In this metaphor, the bush hints at what they take to be the dating practices of the past when young boys and girls sneaked into bushy areas to seek privacy for sexual encounters. The new main road—out in the light—is also a metaphor. According to a church leader in Khe Den, the proper place for girls and boys to "speak about love" is in the house of the girl, under the light and under the observant eyes of her relatives. If youngsters do not obey this rule, members of the house church community to which the girl belongs will do their best to assure that no "impropriety" occurs. For example, any boy from outside the village has to show the head of the house church his ID and the number on his motorbike's license plate (Of course, very soon, people discovered that there were some boys who used fake IDs and borrowed motorbike plates).

An alternative procedure to open courtship, and one of the most interesting customs of the Hmong (but shared by many other societies), is "marriage by capture," or marriage orchestrated by kidnapping the bride-to-be. It has been the subject of much cultural misunderstanding leading in some cases to criminal prosecution of Hmongs in the United States, and forms the topic of much discussion among Hmong converts. Originally, marriage by capture was a cultural custom reserved for a man with an impaired chance of securing a wife owing to poverty, illness, or unacceptable social standing (Lee 1988). Nowadays, this custom is still practiced in many Hmong communities but less often for this reason.

In this procedure, the man and a handful of male relatives "abduct" the girl at a pre-arranged place, often with her full knowledge and consent. The girl is supposed to scream for help and her mother shall come to her rescue, brandishing a stick and shouting verbal abuse at the groom. If her daughter indicates that she is unwilling to be carried off for marriage, the mother will rain blows upon her abductors and ask for her release. But if the girl shows willingness to go with the men, as Lee (1988) humorously describes, the mother's blows will be directed towards her daughter for being too eager to get married.

At this stage of the marriage process, no male relatives of the girl are involved in her so-called rescue from her husband-to-be and his helpers. They have no role to play until the wedding when they take full charge of all negotiations and tasks related to it. Abduction is still deemed preferable to elopement even when the girl has no objection to marrying her boyfriend because elopement is seen as worthy only of those girls without self-esteem or respect for their own families. In Lee's (1988) observation, abduction is also regarded as a face-saving protection for both the girl and her family should the marriage fail, as she will then be able to say that she was uncertain about the prospect all along, and her family, too, can claim that they were not responsible for the failure. Once the "abduction" or elopement has occurred, the young man's parents send a message to the girl's relatives asking for a convenient date to celebrate the wedding. The wedding itself is a costly procedure, consisting of the bride price, fines, and miscellaneous expenses for pigs, food, and alcohol.

The custom of marriage by capture has given rise to a great deal of discussion and opprobrium in which Protestant morality in many ways converges with Confucian and Socialist morality. For instance, In "Vợ Chồng A Phủ," a famous short story written by the revolutionary writer Tô Hoài in 1953 and made into a movie in 1961, marriage by capture is portrayed as the cause of suffering of Hmong women and poor Hmong parents at the hand of cruel, greedy, and exploitative Hmong rulers, backed by the French colonial power. Similarly, Hmong converts in Laos, Thailand, and America were told by Protestant missionaries that the payment of a bride price by a groom's family to the bride's parents, arranged marriages, bride kidnapping, and the tradition of girls marrying within a year or two after reaching puberty are frowned upon and deemed uncivilized by the Church.

There are salient parallels between the use of the term to refer to these marriage practices by the Hmong in Vietnam and the Hmong in America. In Hmong, this custom is called *mus haiv/yuav pus/poj* (literally, "go take a wife"). The Vietnamese term for this custom is *cướp vợ* ("to rob a wife")—this Kinh term is strongly rejected by Hmong speakers. Many of my informants argued that when a boy abducts a girl to make her his wife, she is unmarried thus is no one else's wife. Therefore he cannot be accused of "robbing." You can only be accused of being a "robber" if the object "robbed" belongs to someone else. Recently, due to an increased awareness of the sensitivity of the term *cướp vợ*, cadres in Lào Cai have suggested using the term *bắt vợ* (to seize or to catch a wife) or *dắt vợ* (to lead a wife). In the United States, the term *kidnapping* is used but it has met with a lot of objections as this custom has come under heavy attack by the Christian Hmong populations and under legal scrutiny by American authorities. Recently, many Hmong prefer the characterization "marriage by capture" to name this cultural practice. In 2010, a pastor from the St. Paul Baptist Church started a discussion about "Bride Kidnapping" on the Hmong Online Bible Forum, pointing out that in Judges 21:8–25, which is the story of the tribe of Benjamin, there is scriptural reference to marriage by "kidnapping." In the forum, the pastor raised the following question: "How does the story of the tribe of Benjamin relate to the Hmong practice of 'bride kidnapping'? This has happened in the Hmong community before, even in the US, where Hmong young men 'kidnap' brides at the annual New Year festival (or another time). Does the Biblical story validate these kidnapping? How does the Biblical story connect Hmong culture with ancient Jewish culture? Are these cultures related in a deep way?"

Among the five responses to this posting, the first and the fourth raised doubts about the use of the term *kidnapping*, the violence of the practice, and any similarity between ancient Jewish and Hmong cultures. The first response, however, noted that "currently [English] does not have a better word for the tradition" and said that he or she had come to accept that kidnapping is the correct terminology for the practice. The second responder called for awareness of what is entailed in these kidnappings. "I'm not sure Hmong-American guys do it, but definitely in the old country these women are kidnapped, taken to the guy's house, raped, and then the girl's family finds out about it late. . . . So I would say that maybe 'kidnapping' might not really be the issue but the "raping' itself." This accusation of rape and sexual abuse is also common in the Kinh Vietnamese understanding of this particular Hmong cultural mechanism. The third response expressed a strong feminist resentment toward the inequality of women both in Hmong and Christian culture. The last response appeared to be from a non-Christian Hmong who denounces God for allowing the practice of bride kidnapping according to the Biblical passage. On the contrary, the responder noted, in Hmong culture there is no kidnapping but only a symbolic performance by a boy and girl who are willing to marry each other.

The questions raised as well as the responses to it reflect the complications that are bound to emerge with the need for translation and awareness of traditional Hmong cultural customs while Christianization process is advancing in the Hmong community in the United States. In starting the discussion, the pastor hoped to raise awareness in this online community about Biblical references to an important cultural practice of his people. In some sense, this is very similar to attempts to indigenize Christianity as practiced by the Lees and other missionaries. Although it is clearly still being practiced in the United States, marriage by capture has come under strong attack by both Christian and feminist Hmong. Media portrayals of this custom commonly imply that rape and sexual abuse are involved. The second responder's statement that it is in the "old country" that this practice has led to rape, abuse, and a ruined future for the women is not, in my view, simply an ignorant remark about cultural practices in Hmong traditional society, but an intentional Christian condemnation of the "old" way, the old country—Laos and other Hmong communities in Asia—and thus a positive appraisal of the new way and the new country, the United States.

Throughout my fieldwork in Vietnam, I was consistently told by non-Christian Hmong that there is no rape or sexual abuse in these marriage practices. It was also said that if a girl doesn't agree, nobody could force her. Many of my sources, both converts and non-converts, assured me that there is strictly no sexual contact between the kidnapper and the kidnapped during the three days after the event takes place. As soon as the girl is brought to her husband's home, a female member of the boy's family will be assigned to be with her for literally twenty-four hours a day. This is done for two reasons: first, to prevent her from escaping, and second, to bear witness that her abductor is not taking sexual advantage of her. If the boy has either an older or younger sister, this person will be the guardian. If he doesn't, someone from the extended family will be chosen for this task. Having this guardian and her word of guarantee, the boy and his family can later avoid being condemned for abusing the girl if the abduction does not lead to marriage, in which case they would have to set her free. However, if all goes well and a wedding takes place, the word of the guardian is still important for it shows the girl's relatives how well the boy's family has treated their daughter.

This is an interesting detail because no restrictions are set out for youngsters during the courting period. Yet as soon as the boy makes the decision and chooses a girl to marry, restrictions are imposed. It seems that sex before marriage is invisible or takes place away from the public imaginary and therefore restrictions to regulate it are not really there. But as soon as one moves into the domain of formal relations, as soon as marriage appears in the horizon, sex becomes a visible part of the public imaginary. It is *ua nav ua txiv* (do wife and husband). It is also judged as either proper or improper. Doing "it" during the courtship and on the fourth day after the kidnapping—if the girl agrees to get married—is proper, for now it is sex between husband and wife. However, "doing it" between the moment the girl is taken home and before the fourth night is considered improper.

The decline of marriage by capture is associated, according to Lee (1988), with an increased focus by Hmong parents on their children's wishes rather than their own. Love as a basis for marriage has become popularized by the Thai soap operas that circulate widely in the Northern Highlands. Today, parents leave it to their sons and daughters to choose their own marriage partners so long as they are of acceptable personal and social standing. Parents will interfere mainly when a son or daughter decides to marry someone who is considered a risk such as an opium addict, a person of loose character or lazy disposition, a married man, a widowed or divorced woman, a spinster, or a man whose male relatives have the reputation of being violent with their wives.

Article 7 of the Ten Commandments, which states that children are free to choose their marriage partners, is often preached in house church meetings.[2] Today the youngsters in the house church in Phong Hải readily declare how free they are to date and choose their own future husbands and wives. More than that, some of them emphasize the importance of "romantic love" to a satisfactory marriage. In the Sin Then church, couples were asked before their weddings how they had "dated" each other and whether they, especially the girl, experienced true love, respect, and romantic affection from the boy. If the answer was yes and examples of such experiences were offered, the church would proceed with wedding preparations and the head pastor would bless them. If their answer was not sufficiently convincing for the "committee," then the couple was advised to think about postponing their wedding to have more time for their "romantic love to grow."

The idea of romantic love is also well promoted in various types of Hmong media, which results in images of what a satisfied and desirable marriage life should be like. This is the case of the iconography of a happy couple in the popular video clip "The Road of Love" (Txoj Kev Hlub). According to Su, one of my sources and a good friend, what makes her generation different from previous ones is that in the past, Hmong children were betrothed soon after they were born. Hmong youngsters in her parents' or grandparents' generations grew up knowing that their parents had already promised them to someone, and they had no say in their marital future. This can no longer be done, since young people nowadays want to choose their own partner. If one's parents are too rigid in forcing their marriage, they will likely face fierce resistance. In some cases this kind of confrontation has resulted in suicide. Most of these victims have been girls who kill themselves by eating the poisonous leaves of heart-break grass (*lá ngón*). Su herself was able to name four girlfriends who died in protest of their parent's decisions. Gong, a newly converted young man, cited cases of young girls who secretly joined his Bible study group because their parents were not yet Christian. Some of these girls threatened to kill themselves to make their parents change their minds and allow them to find a partner of their own choice. This, according to Gong, is a clear way to ask their parents to accept their new choices, which include Christianity and its permitted codes of conduct regarding sexual behavior.

Freedom to marry for love, however, is no guarantee of happiness. Because of potential religious conflicts within households and between families, the common practice is for Christians to marry other Christians and for non-Christians to marry non-Christians. Any non-Christian who wishes to marry a Christian is compelled to convert to Christianity at the time of marriage. There were only a few exceptions to this general pattern among my sources and these exceptions were said to often lead to disastrous conflicts.

The eldest daughter of Cư Seo Lử (chapter 3) is one such example. Nearly eighteen, she insisted on getting married to "the love of her life," a non-Christian Hmong from a nearby village. At first, Lử and his wife strongly opposed the marriage, partly because they had heard of the boy's violent temper and partly because he was non-Christian. Yet, after two suicidal threats by the daughter and the boy's promise to consider conversion, they eventually gave in. After all, as the "new Hmong," they were supposed to support their daughter's "free will" and her "freedom" to choose her life partner. Three months after the wedding, their daughter came home black and blue from being beaten by her husband. In her version of the story, her husband was persuaded by his parents to turn violent on her. When she got married, her family did not demand any bride price. For this reason alone, if she did not return to her husband, Lử would not have to return any money to the in-laws. Yet, a month after returning home, it became clear that she was pregnant, and soon after that her husband, who had come regularly to ask her to return home with him, mobilized the elders of his clan to talk to Lử. The request to have her return soon became a demand. Although a Christian, Lử generally obeyed the rule about relations between clans rather strictly. According to this rule, his daughter was no longer a part of his clan; after the wedding she had become a member and in a way an asset of her husband's clan. This membership was then cemented with her pregnancy. Lử, therefore, should do his best to put her back in her proper place—in her husband's family. At first, seeing his daughter's physical suffering, Lử refused to let her go. When her pregnancy became visible, he changed his mind and persuaded her to give her marriage a second chance. Less than a week after the girl left with her husband, Lử was asked by a relative to come to fetch her from the commune clinic, where she had been revived from a coma, which was the result of her husband's beating. She had a miscarriage.

When Lử told me of this tragedy, his daughter was already permanently installed back in his house. Although she slowly recovered from the emotional trauma, her marital future was uncertain. It was clear to many people in the commune that the husband of this poor girl was a bad and abusive man, so I was surprised when Lử told me that his daughter's tragedy was partly his own fault and he had a lot of regrets. He felt that he should not have bought into this whole "freedom" thing and allowed her to marry a non-Christian boy in the first place. He also regretted having made her return to her husband because he had felt the pressure to obey traditional norms regarding clan relationships. Although the church generally frowns upon divorce, a victim of an abusive relationship like Lử's daughter has the sympathy of the church community should she decide to leave her husband. All in all, Lử insisted that it was his uncertainty about God's teaching and his own self-interest that led to his daughter's suffering.

POLYGYNY

While Hmong sexuality is celebrated in popular media and in the emerging travel economy, it continues to be a target of regulation by state development policies. Educational and propaganda campaigns focus on targeting underage marriage practices. Women's unions in the mountain provinces are active in family planning campaigns and family planning and women's development campaigns, which include education on the use of contraceptive methods and the prevention of domestic violence against women. While failing to achieve the aim of regulating Hmong reproductive practices, these programs are successful in making the Hmong conscious of how the majority of society perceives their sexual practices and culture.

In the daily narratives contained in the *Giáo Luật*, polygyny and monogamy are discussed in the light of classification of what are proper and normal types of marriages. In accordance with the saying: "if you convert to Christianity, your husband doesn't want to marry a second wife" (*yog tias nej lawv kev tshiab es yog nes tus txiv tsi mus yuav niam ob /niam yau*), some Hmong women have converted and encouraged their husbands to convert to Christianity as well, with the hope that their husbands would not marry a second wife or go "idling" (*mus ua si*) and engage in extramarital sexual relationships.

The proscription of polygyny weighs on the conscience of many male converts. Polygyny was prohibited by the state as early as 1950 but continues to be practiced by the Hmong, attracting fierce criticism. In a program to evaluate and nominate a "cultural village," many villages in Bắc Hà, which are majority Hmong, failed to qualify owing to too many cases of polygyny. The converts' worry is often due to the unclear sense of whether polygyny is really a sin, how serious it may be in the eyes of God, and what will happen if this sin was committed before one became a Christian. In September 2009, the FEBC received a letter from a Hmong convert in Vietnamese: "Dear Mrs. John, I want to let you know that I became Christian through your programs. In my village I am the first person to become Christian. I tell others about God and ten families follow Christ with me. One thing that bothers me the most is that I have two wives. I am sorry that I did not know God before I did the wrong thing. Also I am the one that leads the believers. What should I do? Please pray for me to be strong in the Lord."[3]

Mrs. John, the widow of famed pastor John Lee replied with a sort of absolution. "It is okay to have two wives because at first he did not know God. After he has two wives let him love both of them and support them, but he can't be the leader in the church. In Hmong tradition they have two wives and they live in the same house. They don't have a problem as long as the husband loves both of them equally." According to Jim Bowman, the president of the FEBC, that was a good answer: "It is a good balance of respecting the individual's circumstances, culture, and the Bible at the same time. Clearly, the Christian traditional view (supported by most civil laws in the world) is that a marriage should consist of just two people. Mrs. John demonstrates in her answer that a Christian should only marry one person, but that since he got his two wives prior to being a Christian and since Hmong tradition sees nothing wrong with it, he should just continue as is and treat both wives as a good Christian husband should."[4]

TECHNOLOGY OF THE SELF

Because of their fragmented understanding of Christian morality, the kind of "self-forming activity" that many Hmong converts in Vietnam follow is performed through what Foucault (1988) calls "technology of the self." According to Foucault this refers to what people are: "to do, either to moderate our acts, or to decipher what we are, or to eradicate our desire, or to use our sexual desire in order to obtain certain aims like having children, and so on" (Foucault 1983). In examining the historic vilification of erotic dreams within European history, Foucault (1978, 1985, 1986) maintains that sexuality increasingly becomes a site of "subjectification" (*assujettissement*) in the West. This neologism is meant to express the fact that sexual desire becomes the indicator of truth about one's self and thus a fundamental element in the constitution of one's subjectivity. At the same time this sexuality is also a conduit for subjugation by social forces such as the church or medical science, which instructed how desire should be regulated. In volumes two and three of *The History of Sexuality*, Foucault frequently considered the evidence of dreams—particularly erotic dreams—and the challenges they posed to images of self-control in antiquity.

The question of "free will," according to Webb Keane (2007) has been an especially fertile subject for Protestants. In Weber's interpretation of Puritan Protestantism, it is precisely in choosing to control sexual and other impulses that one can aspire to receive some indirect confirmation of belonging among the "elected." That one has really converted has to be shown not only to oneself but also to one's community by the apt control of one's impulses. But one has to determine first what is to be controlled. In other words, first, one needs to know whether one is sinning. Second, one has to determine what constitutes the successful control of one's sinful nature, which cannot be done by the individual him or herself alone. This task has to be undertaken and finally confirmed by the community of believers.

Lust is one of the emotions in which self-control must be exercised. Trang, a young church leader, encountered a girl who was attracted to him. After the church hour was over, she approached him. Trang lectured the girl about the wrongness of her lustful thoughts even though she did not explicitly act on her feelings. The fact that such thoughts existed should force her to question the "quality of her soul." He advised her to pray more and promised to pray with her. In his recollection of the event, Trang told me that he also questioned his own thoughts; he realized that he was also partly sinful because he did pay attention to her physical appearance and to her lust for him, and, to some extent, he showed his own desire for her even though he recognized it soon enough to prevent anything sinful from happening between them. Trang believed that if he were a good Christian and knew God purely in his heart, he would not have had these thoughts in the first place.

For Hmong converts in Vietnam, public confessions are commonly used as a way of demonstrating one's recognition of God's righteousness and one's willingness to improve oneself in order to "deserve" God. If we accept that conversion makes itself visible in the changes in the mode of speech and styles of reasoning, we can see how conversion also provides rhetorical tools to help the convert define what it is to be Christian and to separate him or her from the traditional Hmong. Over the five years in which I conducted research, I observed that public confessions have become increasingly longer and include everything from admissions of how miserable the confessor was before knowing God to descriptions of what kind of sin he or she still committed. These acts of self-inculpation have as their function the reasoning and backdrop against which the converts would ask God for forgiveness and continued love.

Because many converts still cohabitate with non-Christian Hmong, conflicts occur and finger-pointing becomes a common way that Christian Hmong note examples of "sinful behavior." I was given much anecdotal evidence intended to show how sexually misbehaved non-Christian Hmong men are. One of the rumors was that twenty kilometers from our village, many girls were impregnated by a number of *hlauj kawg* (old goats) who went around using sweet words to get into their beds at night without any intention of marrying them. Zoo, my Hmong sister-in-law, told me how such stories scared her before she was married. At some point, she was so scared that she decided to wear pants at night instead of wearing skirts like Hmong girls usually do. When a girl in the neighboring village was impregnated, both Zoo and her cousin tied their own legs together before they went to sleep.

In my commune, Lia, a stunningly beautiful sixteen-year-old girl, was the object of affection and pursuit by many suitors and was the victim of several abduction attempts before she was married. The most serious one took place one early evening while she was walking home from her brother's house. She was stopped by a Hmong teenager and a group of his friends. They dragged her to his house, which was not very far away. She did not like that boy—because he was too small, she told me later—but the kidnapping had roused the attention of the public. Her parents, brothers, and several male cousins soon appeared outside the boy's house just when his mother and his uncle finished the ritual of circling a chicken above her head. Having more manpower, her family managed to take her home. Yet her abductor and his family did not give up. The next day they sent a representative to talk to her parents about a wedding. They threatened Lia's parents saying that if the boy was not allowed to marry her, his family would conduct a shamanic ritual to harm her, for her spirit was already submitted to their clan's spirits. But the girl's family was Christian; so her mother responded that her God was stronger than their spirits. She invited them to go ahead and arrange such a ritual since she and her daughter were not afraid. Relationships between the two families and between the two clans were permanently damaged even after Lia and her former suitor married other people and started their own families.

Newly learned objections to marriage by capture and the Christian condemnation of "improper behaviors," such as premarital sex or illicit sexual relations, have informed the unfolding Christian Hmong's "technology of the self." At the same time, I saw no distress in Christian Hmong youngsters that actively sought to uphold a sense of propriety, nor did I see unhappiness when such attempts failed. I learned of numerous cases in which things went wrong and people felt that they had behaved improperly; but, in many of those cases, the ones who had lost their way had productive means of dealing with their failures. They took ownership of their actions, and these events often ended up being seen as important steps in their maturity in the Christian faith. A young church leader explained to me that his own adultery was the way in which God tested him: "I know God put me on trial. He tested me. He called me to go to do his work [Hmong people call evangelism doing 'God's work'] and along the way he planted many beautiful, attractive women. God made me speak very well and charm them. Only if I had been strong in my faith, I would have been able to realize that that was a test. Now, I know that God truly wants me. He wants me to be strong in my faith. I failed his first test but he forgave me and accepted me again."

Converts aim for purity and righteousness, and the proof of one's spiritual maturity, in turn, earns the convert recognition from the church community. Most church leaders or upcoming church leaders work hard to show their moral righteousness. For young people, self-discipline can be rewarded with recognition by their newly formed church community. For those who are getting married, the reward can be a wedding that is fully recognized by the Church. Many house churches have started to refuse to conduct marriage services for those who are very young or those who have engaged in premarital sex. There are rules about how many hymns can be cut out of the wedding ceremony if improper sexual behavior is suspected. The number of hymns is an index of one's righteousness and the direct index of how closely one's life aligns with the commandments of God. To some extent, similar regulations are applied in the Hmong CMA church in the United States. If a couple elopes, the church will refuse to conduct the wedding ceremony, and the couple will not be prayed for or blessed by the church community.

†

To become Christian is to adopt a new morality. It is not easy to construct the "old" morality because moral choices are now subject to intense internal debate among non-converts and converts. This makes it inevitable that "old" customs are now ideologically defended against their detractors, while conversion to new moral ways is often said to fall short of the ideal. Since marriage and procreation are the mainstays of society and in the Hmong case of the relations between clans, much of the debate on morality focuses on sexuality. Hmong traditional ways of life were already changing without the influence of Christianity because of urbanization and the penetration of urban forms of life in the Thai countryside. In the Vietnamese case, change occurred as a consequence of relentless campaigns by the Vietnamese state to incorporate ethnic minorities into the greater Kinh dominated polity and to construct "the New Socialist Person" in pre–Đổi Mới times, and to encourage ethno-tourism and market reforms in the post–Đổi Mới era. However, the strict teachings of Protestantism about proper sexuality have taken these transformations much further (and in some cases, as in the stricter regulation of premarital sex, in the opposite direction to those occurring in Kinh society). Soul searching, introspection, and the conception of sin seem to be some of the most important aspects of the Protestant contribution. These are essential to the transformation from a relational worldview, in which the relations between clans are paramount, to a more individualizing worldview that focuses on the individual and the immediate family. This change however also has brought with it irreconcilable divisions between those who have embraced the New Way and those who haven't.

The changes in sexual mores that have taken place among the Hmong must also be seen in the context of the eroticizing gaze of the Other, which is stimulated by tourism and exoticism. This is a phenomenon that is prevalent in the hill regions of Southeast Asia and China for which a substantial literature is available (Diamond 1988; Schein 1997). The debate about morality between converts and non-converts is not, therefore, merely religious, but plays itself out against a long-established background of civilizational discourse.

The discovery of sin involves the internalization of church teachings, and the debates surrounding the meanings of these teachings between converts and non-converts and among converts themselves as they grapple with unfamiliar ideas and ideals.

CONCLUSION

RELIGIOUS conversion is a phenomenon that cannot be reduced to a general narrative of world-historical change. Contrary to Weber's prediction of the "disenchantment" that societies would experience as they launched themselves into the modern world, religious conversion is in fact part of the rapid and comprehensive transformation toward "a post-traditional order" (Giddens 1991:20) that many parts of the world like Asia, Africa, Latin America, underwent in the last century and continue to experience. Unsurprisingly, conversion to world religions is a theme that has inspired a vast and fast growing body of scholarship.

This book presents the case of the Hmong conversion to Protestantism not just to add another entry to a vast literature, but to explore the perspective of a group situated at the margins of the modernization process, focusing on ethnic relations that are central to a postcolonial, multi-ethnic society. The introduction of Protestantism to the Hmong and the choice to accept or to resist this world religion by members of this marginal ethnic group shed light on a number of theoretical and empirical issues beyond the fields of religious conversion studies or Hmong or Vietnamese studies.

The Hmong conversion to Protestantism is by and large a story of how an indigenous community experiences religious and social changes in late twentieth-century socialist modernity. This marginal group living literally at the geographical margin of Vietnamese society provides an example of how margins and marginality can be sites in which the instability of social categories and the unpredictability of both state discourse and the responses to it are evident. Analyses of the Hmong's struggle to position themselves in the history of modern Vietnam and of how conversion to Protestantism testifies to this lasting struggle help us understand better the relation between shifting social dimensions of space and time in a postcolonial society and the choice that indigenous people make in their religious life. The Hmong's situation is largely characterized by marginality and precariousness, as communist authorities and Christian missionaries agree that they are "backward," that their culture is "irrational," and that they have to be converted to modernity, either in the form of socialism or Protestantism. The testimony of Hmong individuals, however, demonstrates that in the Hmong's perspective, they are coeval with their Kinh neighbors, with communist authorities in Vietnam, with Christian missionaries, with their American neighbors, and with us as anthropological interpreters of their lives. They cannot be understood in the worn metaphors of continuity and change, of tradition and modernity. Like everyone else they need to make sense of the world they live in and must make their own moral choices about what it means to be a good person. As a society they do not have a singular ontology or morality, but a lively inner debate about what paths to choose, what ways to adopt or reject. No doubt these choices are constrained by historical forces beyond their control, but nevertheless they are choices that are not easily captured in opposing categories like modernity versus non-modernity. Every choice has unintended consequences and inner contradictions.

The choice of Christianity entails an embrace of the modern values of education and individual salvation, while at the same time it is accompanied by a belief in a millenarian change that seems to connect very well to traditional beliefs about the return of the Hmong King. Therefore, at one level the opposition is not between a "traditional Hmong culture" and modern Christianity or modern Communism, but between different forms of millenarianism. This is quite different from the way "the old" and "the new" have been conceptualized in the moral choices that are made by the Christian Urapmin of New Guinea, as studied by Joel Robbins. A crucial difference between the Urapmin and the Hmong is that of numbers, not only of total populations, but also in that Hmong converts are a minority of the total Hmong population whereas all Urapmin converted. Another important difference is that the Hmong are surrounded by a Kinh majority and are in constant interaction with their Kinh neighbors. In Robbins' presentation of the Urapmin case, there seems to be a clear distinction between two cultures in the domain of moral choices, but this is not at all the case for the Hmong. What is important to them is the wish to continue family and kinship ties while making different moral choices. The struggle is not between different cultures but between husbands and wives, fathers and sons, brothers and cousins, and between different families in a single village.

While the Hmong are coeval, their choices relate to a number of different understandings of time and history. The Hmong have adopted a "Chinese" understanding of cyclical destruction and renewal (with Buddhist and Daoist elaborations) that can be clearly witnessed at both Hmong and Kinh New Year celebrations. Likewise Kinh and Hmong (as well as Han Chinese) share a history of millenarian movements. Among the Hmong is found the anticipation of the return of the Hmong King who will unite all Hmong in his kingdom that will be separate from the modern nation-states of Vietnam, Laos, Thailand, and China. Unsurprisingly, authorities in these states find this belief troubling, especially since the Hmong are located in border areas and thus put national sovereignty in question. Millenarian movements have troubled the powers that be in China and neighboring areas for centuries. The Miao rebellion of 1873, which unleashed the migration of Hmong to Laos and Vietnam, followed the largest upheaval of nineteenth century China, the Taiping Tianguo Movement, which combined Christianity and Chinese millenarianism. The "pacification" of ethnic movements by Vietnamese communist authorities only took place in the 1950s, but it was immediately challenged in the American War, which allowed some Hmong groups to side with the Americans during the secret CIA war in Laos, which ultimately lead to their exodus to Thailand and the United States after 1975.

It is the interweaving of millenarianism and political history that is so significant for understanding the Hmong case. As Barend ter Haar (1992) has pointed out, however, the suspicion of the authorities that trouble might be brewing also leads them to proactively repress movements that are entirely peaceful and do not aim to overthrow the government. Followers of some millenarian movements in fact withdraw from social life to wait for the events that in their view are inevitably coming and do not need their active involvement. Ter Haar makes the important point that if we simply accept the representation of such movements by the authorities we will not be able to understand what goes on in them; a point that is as valid for the past as for present-day Vietnam. Whenever a movement with millenarian tendencies occurs in Vietnam this problem of representation is worsened by the war of words between Christian activists in the United States who accuse the Vietnamese government of repressing religious freedom and the Vietnamese authorities who interpret such a movement as rebellious and caused by "the foreign hand."

Hmong millenarianism shows an incredible variety as well as a persistent continuity. Some movements are anti-Christian and anti-foreigner, while others are aligned with Christianity. In the latter case, the Christian message of the Second Coming of Christ is overlaid with references to the return of the Hmong King. In general, it is striking how ritual forms remain more or less the same, while their interpretation changes. This makes it possible to call both Christian and anti-Christian movements millenarian because they share a ritual repertoire and an imaginary about "the things to come." Conversion to Christianity, or the New Way, involves change, yet contradiction lies in the continuity between this "change" and Hmong millenarian tradition. Interestingly, Hmong millenarianism is often related to the command, discovery, or loss of writing, and Christianity—with its emphasis on scripture and literacy—fits this theme very well.

The conversion to Christianity examined here, however, came through the air rather than through writing. Hearing the Hmong language through a medium often controlled by Kinh and others was felt as a liberating, messianic force. It was not the successful agency of missionaries bringing literacy and education that led people to conversion, for no missionaries were involved initially. It was the radio and the wide spectrum of interpretation that it allows for that stirred the Hmong imagination. That this imagination went in many directions is clear from the fact that the message was originally interpreted in traditional messianic ways. Only later were the Hmong specifically led to Christian conversion. The role of the radio in capturing the Hmong imagination reminds one of the uses of this medium by the Pentecostal pastor Oral Roberts in the United States in the 1950s. Listeners were encouraged to lay their hands on the radio to feel the voice of prayer. As Anderson Blanton (2013) observes, "prayer in the age of mechanical reproduction thus marks an inversion of the rite of manual imposition: it is no longer the healer who lays hands upon the sick, but the patient who reaches out to make tactile contact with the apparatus. The radio as point of contact organized a new 'apparatus of belief' that no longer subsisted upon earlier modes of temporal articulation. Instead of articulating belief through the temporal deferrals and delays characteristic of the exchange and circulation of objects in ritual, the radio apparatus produced the sensation of belief through sensory displacements and disjunctures attuned through the medium itself."[1]

The Hmong are perhaps an unprecedented case of conversion by radio broadcasts. In other cases in which radio played a role in mass conversions, it was accompanied by missionary activity. In the Hmong case the voice of the radio was literally disembodied and at first listeners had difficulty figuring out that what they heard related to Christianity (whatever that was, since they had hardly had any experience or knowledge of Christianity) and to missionary activity.

The success of the FEBC in converting the Hmong in Vietnam exemplifies the dialectical, rather than merely instrumental, relationship between religion and media. The FEBC's success in gathering large audiences of listeners, some of whom (like the Hmong in Vietnam) were even unexpected, would not have been possible without the "Good News." Evangelical Protestantism—its scriptural emphasis on the great Commission, its long history of media utilization, and its open and dynamic organizational structure—have helped its modern medium, in this case the transnational radio ministry of the FEBC, to succeed in initiating the conversions of thousands of Hmong in Vietnam and elsewhere in Southeast Asia. It did so by thoroughly indigenizing its entire evangelizing process. Christian messages were translated into the Hmong language and the Hmong medium and broadcast by Hmong broadcasters in a typical Hmong manner. Cultural repertoires such as myths and legends of the Hmong were exploited as being the best way to attract the target audience's attention, a good example of how "religious sensation" (Meyer 2006) can be created via the interaction between media effects and a people's culturally formed sensory regime. Modern media techniques like public relations and audience response were employed to enhance the attractiveness of the program. Last but not least, despite being a media ministry, the FEBC worked in close cooperation with local churches and agencies that act to "ground" the "aired faith" into the Hmong.

The virtuality of Protestant radio messages via radio broadcasting and without the proper context of missionary teachings resulted, in the beginning, in various movements which were strongly flavored by millenarianism. The FEBC, however, is not in favor of millenarianism although it acknowledges that the Bible announces Christ's second coming. Except for the very beginning when FEBC's preachers were allowed to draw on Hmong messianic tradition to attract Hmong listeners, the ministry did its best to disassociate itself from millenarian teachings. This is because while entertaining an intimate relationship with millenarianism, Christianity is not able to contain and exhaust the possibilities of Hmong millenarianism. In fact, during the latest Hmong millenarian uprising in 2011 sparked by Harold Camping's doomsday message (which was spread through his Family Radio group), FEBC's Thailand office broadcast numerous sessions to Hmong listeners in Vietnam in the hope of correcting their misunderstanding. FEBC's Black Hmong Group's postings on Facebook in fact urged Hmong followers of this event to return to their homes and cooperate with the state authorities. Such good will, however, was not recognized by Vietnamese authorities who remained suspicious of the missionaries and blamed them for causing the disruption in the first place.

The complicity of Communist utopianism and millenarian thought has played a role in the story of Hmong conversion to Protestantism in Vietnam. In the case of China Thomas Dubois (2005) has argued that Mao's communist party had little difficulty in eradicating redemptive societies with a millenarian message like the Yiguandao since it also offered an alternative vision of a better life on earth and did so more powerfully and persuasively. Communism does not imply a radical break with the ritual repertoire and visionary language about health and well-being that is available in society, as David Palmer (2007) shows in his study of the participation of the Party in the rise of the Falun Gong. Similarly, in Vietnam among the Kinh there is a striking continuity between the belief in ancestral spirits and the power of the afterlife and the veneration of the dead heroes of the past, including the worship of the spirit of Hồ Chí Minh (Ngo and Tai 2013). While this interweaving of repression of "superstition" according to nineteenth-century Marxist materialism and the acceptance of cultural realities is already the case for dealing with the Kinh majority, the traditions of minorities like the Hmong were always treated with even more care and caution. While the Communist Party definitely wanted to remove the obstacle of magical beliefs and rituals from the social life of the Hmong to enable them to move forward, it considered at the same time that the Hmong were not coeval, but at a different stage of evolutionary development and thus would need more time to come into enlightenment. While this attitude characterized the period until the Đổi Mới era, the "opening up" to the world market produced a relaxation of the "anti-superstition" campaigns among the Kinh and a remarkable reversal of policy in the case of the Hmong. Since the furthering of tourism played an important part in the new economic policy of stimulating consumption, Hmong culture was primed for tourism purposes. This new policy has the added advantage of using the new respectability of Hmong culture as a bulwark against Christian conversion.

While Hmong Protestantism was gradually stabilized thanks to the increase of contacts with and doctrinal education from overseas (Hmong and non-Hmong) missionaries and the building of churches, misunderstandings or deliberate insertion of local socio-cultural preferences continue. Many converted Hmong are on their own in their interpretation of Christian messages and what it means to be Christians Hmong. A notion of sin, relating to practices of—and by the same token relegated to—"the past," has to be produced and dealt with. Christian converts, however, cannot simply abandon the past, since their sense of community and their status as a minority within that community continues to connect them to their Hmong traditions. This problem is reinforced by constant attacks on Hmong "barbarism" by their Kinh neighbors. To an extent the Kinh view of the Hmong parallels Christian morality, but that is exactly what many Hmong, converted and unconverted alike, reject. The contradictions in this situation cause worries, confessions, and troubled soul-searching for many new Christian Hmong people in Vietnam today.

In analyses of communist societies, post-socialist developments are often seen as causes for conversion. It is assumed that people who have lost their belief in Communism have to find another belief (Pelkmans 2009). There is little evidence for this in the Hmong case. It is always questionable whether people really believe in the state ideology or whether such belief is actually necessary for the continuing power of the state. Whatever the dominant ideology, the Kinh majority has maintained a persistent cultural hegemony. This is more important in Hmong conversion than the waxing and waning of Communism. The Vietnamese state does not directly and overtly address the difference between the Kinh majority and ethnic minorities, but it targets ethnic minorities with development programs that are meant to rid the minorities of so-called backward ideas and behaviors. In doing so it produces a plethora of contradictions, the main one being that the ethnic minority's religion is both unrecognized politically but negatively targeted socially. The state neither recognizes the entanglement of culture and religion nor pays attention to the sensitivity of ethnic relations. For a long time the state had made strenuous efforts to eliminate the native religions of minorities; it only now accepts part of these religions as a possible bulwark against foreign conversion.

The Hmong are highly conscious of the biases and prejudices held by the Kinh and perceive clearly the objective elements of their marginalization in the development projects of the state. However, besides this objective marginalization, the subjective element of being constantly seen and portrayed as a backward, stupid people that can be blamed for their own marginality has deep effects on the Hmong. Moreover, by being exposed to ideas and images about the life of their ethnic fellows in America, their subjective marginality has increased. Despite the egalitarian rhetoric of the Communist Party, their attempts to escape poverty are blocked by the hegemony of Kinh language and culture. This is especially true in the field of education. Within the Kinh-dominated nation-state, the Hmong have little chance for upward mobility and this is at least one reason why transnational Christianity, with its capacity to transcend national boundaries, gives them a new opportunity. It is not that marginality causes conversion, but it can be argued that Christianity as the religion of the downtrodden (the religion of the rejected Christ) provides special ways to understand marginality and also offers transnational avenues to escape marginality.

Christianity provides a global community with transnational networks and resources and a field of aspiration that transcends the national boundary. The Hmong are particularly well positioned to make use of these transnational networks and connections because of their history of migration and the maintenance of strong ethnic ties across national borders. It is therefore not only the nation-state that is implicated in the struggle in the Hmong community about conversion and ethnicity, but also the transnational Hmong community, especially the one residing in the United States. The nation-state is not the only available provider of legitimacy and respect; instead, it is contested by a transnational community that has access to international economic and political resources and that cannot be ignored. It is in this heavily politicized atmosphere that brothers, sisters, sons, fathers, husbands, and wives have to find their way in relation to Christian conversion.

Conversion to Christianity is not a singular event, but carries with it a plurality of meanings, in which modernity is perhaps the most embracing and significant. Christianity provides ways of enhancing literacy and self-esteem, as well as understanding suffering and discrimination that play a significant role in a society that is in transition from state socialism and that is affected by various forms of globalization (economic and cultural) and transnationalism. The Hmong are not just a marginal people in a peripheral Asian economy. Their case teaches us that statist analysis of societal transformations miss a large part of the actual story. The rhetoric of development, from either a Communist or a capitalist market perspective, obscures the fact that people have a history and a culture that does not simply "melt away," but informs the choices they make and the options they decline. There is truth to Marx's dictum that "men make their own history, but they do not make it as they please; they do not make it under self-selected circumstances, but under circumstances existing already, given and transmitted from the past. The tradition of all dead generations weighs like a nightmare on the brains of the living." At the same time, ethnography can show that the Hmong are not determined by the weight of their traditions nor by external forces, but have significant agency. Their choices are complicated, unpredictable, and show us the richness of their cultural resources.

The findings of this study challenge the general narratives of development, of communist atheism, and Christian conversion. An ethnographic approach shows social life, as it is lived, not as "data" for generalizable models. Obviously, the case of the Hmong invites comparison with conversion to Christianity and modernity elsewhere in China, in Asia, and in the world, but not as an instance of some universal model of modernization, despite the seemingly indomitable desire of missionaries, communist and some scholars to come to such levels of abstract generality. The power of ethnography is in the richness of its description and analysis which shows not only the "otherness" of other societies, but also their coevalness and their comparability.

NOTES

INTRODUCTION

1   The number of ethnic groups in Vietnam varied according to different national census data gathered in different periods such as 1959; 64, 1973; 59, and 1979; 54. At present, the officially agreed upon number is 54. See appendix I.

2   Keyes 1996; Viswanathan 1998; Gifford 1998; Salemink 2006; Bautista and Lim 2009; Sadan 2013.

3   Interestingly, Vietnamese ethnologists and linguists have justified their decision to work in Sapa by claiming that the Sapa dialect is neutral and more standard than other, more heavily accented, Hmong dialects. But several officials told me that, in fact, Sapa was chosen because it was the most livable place in Lào Cai, having been built as a holiday destination for the French.

4   This is because the script includes a many of the vowels (36 out of 65) and all the consonants (31) of Vietnamese script. While diacritics are used to represent different tones in Vietnamese script, the Vietnamese Hmong script uses seven consonants, which stand at the end of a word to indicate the tone. The script is difficult to learn for both Kinh and Hmong speakers because it requires the learner to have good command of both Hmong and Vietnamese in order to use it. This is one of the reasons why the script has not been more widely used by Hmong speakers, but only by the handful of people, like Mr. Chung, who are also quite fluent in Vietnamese.

CHAPTER 1. THE HMONG OF VIETNAM

1   According to the US Census Bureau, the Hmong population in the United States in 2009 was 236,434 (http://hmongstudies.org/HmongACS2009.pdf). It is estimated that about 15,000 Hmong live in France, 2,190 in Australia, 1,500 in French Guiana, 600 in Canada, 500 in Germany, and couple dozen in Argentina.

2   Tusi is a system of extending central authority's control to areas deem difficult to administer via special appointments of local warlords or chieftains as the powerbrokers. The holders of these appointments assume both official sanction and recognition of local-based power, thus simultaneously represent and potentially resist state power (Davis 2011: 19). The Tusi system appeared during the Han dynasty but become institutionalized during the Ming Dynasty (1368–1628). In the eighteenth century, via the campaign to establish direct rule over local population by replacing local chieftains with mandarins or military leaders appointed by the imperial court known as *gaitu guiliu*, the Qing gradually removed the hereditary position of Tusi in favor of routine bureaucratic officials. In Vietnam, a similar attempt led to rebellions in the 1830s (Vũ 2014).

3   In 1955, following the withdrawal of the French, the DRV created the Thai-Meo [Hmong] Autonomous Zone (Khu tự trị Thái-Mèo). This was changed to Northwest Autonomous Zone (Khu tự trị Tây Bắc) in 1962. This administrative structure was maintained until 1975 following reunification.

4   See the Lào Cai government's webpage, http://laocai.gov.vn/sites/sovhttdl/ lichsulaocai/lichsulaocai/Trang/634051425775520000.aspx (accessed 16/02/2009). From online sources and interviews with former Tieu Phi officials, I was unable to confirm whether 8,788 was the number of *phi* casualties or just the number of *phi* army members that the Việt Minh managed to destroy. Also, "thousand of guns and hundreds of [rounds of] ammunition" may be an exaggerated number.

5   *Ý kiến của Anh Đồng Toà án Nhân dân tối cao về Công tác Phi ở Lào Cai, Gặp lần I* (The opinions of Mr. Đồng from the Supreme Court about the Phi Program in Lào Cai, In the first meeting) recorded by Phạm Xuân Phúc, 29/11/1971, archive 4–2003 at Lào Cai Provincial Archive. In 1971, Mr. Đồng, a representative of the Vietnam Supreme Court, met with the Lào Cai government to reevaluate the Tiểu Phỉ program. Mr. Đồng claimed to have studied the *phi* phenomenon for several decades, during which time he was assigned to Lào Cai on a special mission while he was working in the ethnic minority department within the Supreme Court. In this document, the pejorative term "Mèo" is still used for the Hmong. For consistency, I shall replace the term "Mèo" with Hmong in my own text when referring to Mr. Đồng's words. The term "Mèo" shall only be used in quoted sentences.

6   In the Central Highland, a very similar program, called Building New Economic Zones was implemented after 1975, completely changing the demographic composition of the region and worsening ethnic relations (Salemink 2003a).

7   To a large extent, the same interest is visible across the globe where "farm to table" and "eat local" and other organic food movements are very popular. I want to thank Lillian-Yvonne Bertram for pointing this out to me.

8   Thanh Phúc: "Người Mèo ơn Đảng" [The Mèo are grateful to the Party].

Lyrics in Vietnamese: Đây rừng núi lưng đèo người Mèo ca hát. Sao còn sáng trên trời người Mèo ơn Đảng. Bao đời nay sống nghèo lam lũ. Nay cuộc sống dân Mèo từ đây sáng rồi. Nhớ ơn Đảng đưa tới, ta từ nay ấm no, không bỏ giấy đốt nhà, mà lang thang nghèo suốt đời. Từ nay dân Mèo sống chung, bản Mèo vui trong tiếng khèn, người Mèo ơn Đảng suốt đời.

Lyrics in Hmong: Hmôngz tsâus Đangv: Nor t aox saz ntangr lênhx Hmôngz hu gâux/ u ô changl muôz sâu ntux txax njik ndu tangl/ thâuk ntêx ndu cha txux cêr khử/ uô changl mu ôz sâu ntux tx ax njik ndu tangl/ Ndu tangl zor ndu pêz txix nor tsâu/sur tsi tsê nor lênhx /hmôngz traor uô cêr/ têx Hmôngz uô cê yur kênhx/ lênhx Hmôngz ndu đangv iz cxik.

CHAPTER 2. THE SHORT-WAVED FAITH

1   A US evangelical organization called "Pillar of Fire" applied to the Federal Communications Commission (FCC) for a permit to construct an international shortwave station in May 1938. At the time, frequencies were available on a shared-time basis only, and the organization was not interested in sharing time (Redding 1977).

2   The Vatican Radio, for instance, was the first international religious broadcasting system and its goal was to serve Catholics wherever they might be, but particularly in remote locations. Its program schedule in the way that would help to make up for the absence of a Catholic Church or priest in the region such as focusing on giving instruction on how to conduct a Mass, instead of on biblical teaching and on spreading the good news.

3   FEBC archive, "FEBC Broadcasts Dramatically Changing Worldview of Ethnic Groups," available at www.febc.org/news/271/ (accessed October 12, 2010).

4   FEBC archive, available at www.febc.org/about/timeline.html (accessed October 12, 2010).

5   Ibid.

6   FEBC archive, http://www.febc.org/media/audio/22/world_by_radio_nov_07. pdf (accessed October 12, 2010).

7   FEBC archive, "Listeners Languages," ttp://www.febc.org.au/Listeners/Languages.aspx (accessed October 12, 2010).

8   Author interview with Frank Gray, radio engineer and evangelist in Laos during the 1960s and 1970s, December 2008, Singapore.

9   FEBC archive, www.febc.org (accessed June 27, 2006). Jim Bowman, former president of the FEBC, provided me with a copy of the article (see Nguyễn Xuân Yêm 1991).

10   FEBC archive, www.febc.org (accessed on June 27, 2006).

11   However, there are a few excellent explorations—for example, Laura Kunreuther's (2006) work on radio in Nepal, Debra Spitulnik's (2000, 2002) work on radio in Zambia, Amanda Weidman's (2006) work on voice in South

Indian classical music, and Patrick Eisenlohr's (2009a, b) work on voice and prayers in Hindustan Mauritius.

12 It is fascinating to think about how much Western philosophy, not just Plato but also parts of Hegel and most of Marx, rests on this deep-rooted media ideology whose clearest formulation can be found in Protestantism.

13 One such occasion was at a three-day conference on how to introduce and teach Hmong orthography in primary schools in Lào Cai's remote areas. One local teacher from Bát Xát District, where the majority of Hmong students are White Hmong, raised a question about how he was going to teach his students in Green Hmong. His question received an angry answer from a high-ranking Hmong politician saying that White Hmong is the American Hmong's language.

CHAPTER 3. REMITTANCE OF FAITH AND MODERNITY

1 This war was secret because, according to the 1954 Geneva Accords, Laos had been designated as a neutral territory. However, with the escalation of the Vietnam War in the 1960s, the United States Central Intelligence Agency (CIA) started recruiting men from among Hmong and other hill tribal groups in Laos to rescue American pilots who had to parachute into the Lao jungle after their planes were shot down while bombing the Hồ Chí Minh trail, which was the main supply line for the Vietnamese communist force (Việt Cộng) from North to South Vietnam. The trail ran through some parts of Laotian territory. While the Hmong were told that the Americans would come to their aid should the war go badly, most Americans were not informed about US involvement in Laos until 1970. Americans were mostly unaware of how the Secret War in Laos disrupted the life of the Hmong and many other ethnic minorities in Laos.

2 Other scholars have made this observation as well; see Julian (2003), Schein (2002, 2004), and Lee (1996).

3 Between 1961 and 1975, US airplanes dropped more than two million tons of bombs on northeast Laos, making it the most heavily bombed area in the world (Warner 1975). By 1975, between eighteen thousand and twenty thousand Hmong soldiers died and fifty thousand Hmong civilians died or were wounded (Robinson 1998: 13). The fighting, shelling, and bombing from US planes disrupted village cultural life and sent families fleeing to the jungle. From 1963 to 1973, an estimated one million people were displaced from their homes at least once and, in northeast Laos, half a million people were displaced from two to six times (Weldon 1999: 51, cited in Culhane-Pera et al. 2003: 21). While displacement broke the social base that is indispensable to Hmong traditional religious practice, the sorrow of war made many Hmong villagers turn to Christian missionaries from various denominations working with US AID programs.

4   Conversion in the camps was in fact a very common story not only among the Hmong but also among other Southeast Asian refugees.

5   This is a classic American pattern that has long been discussed by different scholars. See, for example, Herberg 1955, Casanova 2005.

6   In 2008, Minnesotan Hmong publicly celebrated the opening of a new funeral home in Frogtown, Saint Paul, seeing it as a changing of spiritual address as well as a sign of victory for traditional Hmong beliefs. See www.startribune.com/local/stpaul/26126319.html (accessed October 22, 2010).

7   This fact is also shown in many interviews conducted within the framework of the Hmong Oral History Project lead by Dr. Paul Hillmer at Concordia University in Saint Paul, Minnesota. http://www.csp.edu/hmong-oral-history-project/ (accessed March 12, 2015).

8   I want to thank Nick Tapp, a social anthropologist and a well-known Hmong specialist, for his advice on this point (email exchange, July 2009).

9   Author conversation with Nick Tapp, March 2011, Shanghai.

10 Author interview with Dr. Danai, Director of Hmong Overseas Mission in Chiang Mai, April 2008, Chiang Mai.

CHAPTER 4. MILLENARIANISM AND CONVERSION

1   Lử had a moment in which he doubted this information and wondered where the seawater would come from, as they lived on the mountain and were very far from the sea. In fact, no Hmong that he knew had ever seen the sea. However, the messenger was so persuasive that not only was Lử soon convinced, he also dreamed of seeing a large body of seawater coming at him as if it were about to swallow him. What he saw in this dream was very much the same as what he saw during the flood of 1986, one of the Red River's biggest floods.

2   Yawg Saub is a kind figure in Hmong mythology and the creator of mankind and other beings. For more information and analysis of this figure, see Tapp 1989.

3   Fuab Tais (sometimes also pronounced "Huab Tais") means "great ruler, emperor, legendary Hmong King, Lord" (see Heimbach 1969: 56, Lyman 1974: 115). The term is also often used to address a supreme deity named "Fuab Tais Ntuj" or "Lord of the Sky" which Catholic priest Yves Bertrais gave as the equivalent name for the Christian God (Bertrais 1964).

4   Vang Pao was a Laotian Lieutenant General in the Lao Royal Army. During the Vietnam War, he led a Hmong army to fight alongside American soldiers in military operations against the North Vietnamese army in the Lao-Vietnamese border region. Hmong soldiers were also recruited to rescue American pilots who had to parachute into Lao territory during bombing missions along the Ho Chi Minh Trail. At the end of the Vietnam War, Vang Pao was relocated to the United States where he became one of the most prominent leaders of the Hmong refugee population there.

5   *Những vấn đề liên quan đến hiện tượng "Vàng Chứ"* [The Issues Relating to the "Vàng Chứ" Phenomena] is a volume that was marked with the government's *tuyệt mật* (top secret) stamp, but later it was made available to the public at the library of the Institute of Religious Studies. See Đặng Nghiêm Vạn 1998.

6   According to Ms. Georgina Stott, director of the international office of the Far East Broadcasting Company (hereafter FEBC) in Bangkok, this letter was posted on Family Radio's website (http://www.familyradio.com/international/frame/) along with other materials translated into Hmong. This material was removed right after the May 21st event. Dr. Jim Bowman, the former president of FEBC, whose work resulted in the conversion of Hmong people in Vietnam twenty years ago, also told me that because there were no good frequencies available, Radio Taiwan chose to pick one in close proximity to FEBC's station HLAZ in Jeju, South Korea, in order to work with Family Radio. The broadcast from this station interfered with the FEBC's signal. This is contrary to international cooperative practices and procedures. Listeners complained. FEBC asked Mr. Camping to please move his broadcast away from their long-established signal, but he flatly refused. Email exchanges between author and Ms. Georgina Stott, director of FEBC international office, and Dr. Jim Bowman, Bangkok, September 16, 2011.

7   FEBC archives, 2011, "Upcoming Threat to Stability of Hmong Evangelicals." Available at www.facebook.com/pages/FEBC-Black-Hmong-Radio/142609642472349#!/notes/febc-black-hmong-radio/upcoming-threat-to-stability-of-hmong-evangelicals-in-socialist-republic-of-viet/149223311810982 (accessed April 22, 2011).

8   Asian American Press, "Minnesotans Look to Support Hmong in Vietnam," May 10, 2011. Available at: http://aapress.com/ethnicity/vietnamese/minnesotans-look-to-support-hmong-in-vietnam/ (accessed September 22, 2011).

9   https://news.change.org/stories/bruce-thao-and-thousands-more-standing-up-for-the-hmong.

10   Online petition, "Stand up for the rights of Hmong in Vietnam," available at http://www.change.org/petitions/stand-up-for-the-rights-of-hmong-in-vietnam (last accessed December 3, 2015).

11   The review, entitled "Clash of Cults, Orthodox Christians, Ethnic Minorities and Politics in Dien Bien Province," is available at http://www.facebook.com/pages/FEBC-Black-Hmong-Radio/142609642472349#!/notes/febc-black-hmong-radio/clash-of-cults-orthodox-christians-ethnic-minorities-and-politics-in-dien-bien-p/156834844383162 (last accessed December 3, 2015).

CHAPTER 5. NOT BY RICE ALONE

1   In this interview, my informant described in detail how his father's funeral was done properly according to Hmong custom, as best as his family financial

conditions would allow. After a Hmong person passes away, the body is bathed by his or her children or close family members. The corpse is buried during the funeral, which may take place anytime between three to twelve days depending upon when a good burial date can be chosen. During these days, the family performs sacrificial rites by killing animals (cow, pig, goat, or chicken, depending on the family economic situation) and offering food (*laig dab*) to the spirit of the deceased, who is waiting to travel to the ancestors and be reborn. A ritual song called "showing the way" is performed to guide the spirit to the ancestor land and a flute chant call "song of mounting the way" is when the body is brought out to be buried. Within three years following the funeral, a large sacrificial ritual called the "holy-cow ritual" (*nyub dab*) is supposed to be held to appease the spirit. The *nyub dab* ritual can be an expensive event, and it is this ritual that my informant failed to perform for his father.

2   Author interview with Hmong informant, Phong Hải, Vietnam, January 18, 2005.

3   I was told of a Hmong shaman association based in Sacramento, California, whose task is to identify powerful Hmong shamans and herbalists around the world. When possible, the association will facilitate the tours of shamans from Asia in the United States or Australia to conduct rituals for Hmong communities there. When a shaman cannot travel abroad, the association will help Hmong patients from the diaspora to go to Asia and to find the shaman. Even the son of a prominent Hmong scholar in Minnesota had to travel all the way to a remote village in Guizhou to get both spiritual and herbal treatments from a shaman residing there.

4   Stephen Magagnini, "Hmong Marital Traditions Stir Feuds, Controversy," *Sacramento Bee*, December 25, 2006. Available at http://www.deseretnews.com/article/650217876/Hmong-marital-traditions-stir-feuds-controversy.html?pg=all, (last accessed December 3, 2015).

5   This is made abundantly clear in a number of reports produced for internal use and sometimes for the re-evaluation and self-criticism of policy in light of the failure of certain government programs. I must withhold the references to these documents in order to avoid the risk of harming the people who shared them with me. One report names various incidents involving Hmong people, who were seen as being made into the "New Socialist Person" but, in fact, were not. Another report complains that in many places in the Northwest (Lai Châu for example), superstition and cults were returning like "mushrooms after rain." It described one case in which a Hmong nurse, who was in charge of a local modern medicine clinic, often rolled an egg with one hand as a method of divination, while giving the patient an injection with her other hand. In another place, there was only one *y sĩ* (senior nurse, one level lower than a doctor) to struggle against thirty shamans.

6   The translation of the name of this training course is only an approximation. It is a kind of political training, in which course users learn about a selective

history of the Party, its ideology, and its organizational structure. In these courses, people often write criticisms of themselves and others. In order to become a member of the Communist Party, one first has to be selected to join this course. But not everyone who takes this course will necessarily become a Party member.

7   The food distribution store (*cửa hàng lương thực*) was an essential part of the state distribution economy in Vietnam. Run by the state, every town in northern Vietnam had this kind of store. Food produced by cooperative units was sold to the stores, which then distributed goods to consumers who were state employees and even members of the co-ops. Because of the constant lack of food, corruption and unequal distribution, this kind of store and the people who worked in them grew notoriously unpopular. From the beginning, the most difficult task to sustain this kind of store was purchasing food—especially meat—because there were only a few coops that produced meat for consumption. Most of the stock was raised by semi-private households, which were unwilling to sell their pigs and chickens to the stores because of the low purchase price sanctioned by the state. Purchase staff people were thus often recruited among the most respected locals in order to ease these unwanted transactions.

CHAPTER 6. STATE, CHURCH, AND COMMUNITY

1   There exists a rival organization, the Buddhist Sangha of Vietnam, established in 1981, which is part of the Fatherland Front and works closely with state authorities. On July 22, 2003, *Nhan Dân*, the official newspaper of the Vietnamese communist party, openly declared: "Most Venerable Thich Thanh Tu, vice permanent president of the Executive Council of the Vietnam Buddhist Sangha (VBS), has confirmed that VBS has always joined the nation in every step of development. The most venerable condemned linking human rights conditions to non-humanitarian aid to Vietnam, considering it a brazen interference into Vietnam's internal affairs, ignoring international law." The article concludes that the VBS is "a reliable member in the national great unity bloc, acting under the guideline 'Dharma-Nation-Socialism' aimed at contributing to the target of a united and prosperous country of Vietnam." "Vietnam Buddhist Sangha Develops Together with Nation," Nhandan.org.vn, July 22, 2003. Available at http://vietnamembassy-usa.org/news/2003/07/vietnam-buddhist-sangha-develops-together-nation (accessed June 16, 2014).

2   FULRO was an organization set up by members of different ethnic groups living in Vietnam's Central Highlands. Originally a political nationalist movment, it evolved into a fragmented guerrilla group whose objective was autonomy for the Degar tribes, from both South Vietnam and also the Socialist Republic of Vietnam. For more information about FULRO and

Protestantism in the Central Highlands, please see Salemink 2003.

3   Vàng Chứ is the Vietnamese translation of Vang Tsu (or Vaj Tswv in RPA). "'Đạo Vàng Chứ' và sự đói nghèo: Lời truyền mê muộ" ("Vang Tsu religion and poverty: A wicked proselytization) May 9, 2011. Available at http://phap-luattp.vn/20110508110114492poc1015/dao-vang-chu-va-su-doi-ngheo-loi-truyen-me-muoi.htm (accessed June 12, 2012).

4   Vietnamese scholars Đặng (1998), Trần (1996), and Vương (1998), to name but a few, provide analyses of Hmong conversion strikingly similar to the accusations of rice conversion made in the nineteenth century and early literature on Christianization of the non-western world. Rice conversion is commonly associated with the Christianization of non-western societies (Tapp 1989b). Yet rice conversions were also criticized by theologians and missionaries. It is said that rice conversion, and in some cases, salt conversion, accounted for the majority of the early twentieth-century conversions to Catholicism among the Hmong in Northern Indochina as well as in Yunnan, China.

5   Although the document was stamped "top secret," it was copied and distributed widely among local cadres. Protestant authorities also got hold of the document and made its copies available to local Hmong house church leaders who would read the document to prepare for conversations with government authorities. I was given one of such copies by a house church leader in 2005. Later that year, I also found a copy, available for in house reading only at the library of the Institute of Ethnology in Hanoi.

6   Author interview with a cadre in Phong Hải, Christmas, 2007.

CHAPTER 7. TRANSFORMATION OF MORALITY AND SUBJECTIVITY

1   It is unclear whether a "married woman" or "married man" is someone who had previously been married and became a widow or divorcee, or someone who is actually still in a marriage.

2   Author interview with Mr. Xeem, head of the Khe Den church, May 2008, Phong Niên commune, Bảo Thắng district, Lào Cai province.

3   Mr. Q. H. from Vietnam, September 2009, Hmong Letter Index, FEBC.

4   Bowman, FEBC.

CONCLUSION

1   Anderson Blanton, "The Materiality of Prayer: The Radio as Prosthesis of Prayer." Available at http://forums.ssrc.org/ndsp/2013/02/25/the-radio-as-prosthesis-of-prayer/ (last accessed December 5, 2015).

REFERENCES

Anderson, Benedict. 2003 [1983]. *Imagined Communities: Reflections on the Origin and Spread of Nationalism.* Rev. ed. London, New York: Verso.

Appadurai, Arjun. 2006. *Fear of Small Numbers: An Essay on the Geography of Anger.* Durham: Duke University Press.

Aragon, Lorraine. 2000. *Fields of the Lord: Animism, Christian Minorities and State Development in Indonesia.* Honolulu: University of Hawai'i Press.

————. 1996. "Reorganizing the Cosmology: The Reinterpretation of Deities and Religious Practice by Protestants in Central Sulawesi, Indonesia." *Journal of Southeast Asian Studies* 27(2): 350–73.

Asad, Talad. 1992. *Genealogies of Religion: Discipline and Reasons of Power in Christianity and Islam.* Baltimore: Johns Hopkins University Press.

Austin-Broos, Diane. 2003. "The Anthropology of Conversion: An Introduction." In *The Anthropology of Conversion,* ed. Andrew Buckser and Stephen D. Glazier, 1–12. Lanham: Rowman & Littlefield.

Babb, Lawrence A. 1995. "Introduction." In *Media and the Transformation of Religion in South Asia,* ed. Lawrence A. Babb and Susan S. Wadley, 1–18. Philadelphia: University of Pennsylvania Press.

Bainbridge, W.S. 1992. "The Sociology of Conversion." In *Handbook of Religious Conversion,* ed. H. N. Malcony and S. Southard, 178–91. Birmingham: Religious Education Press.

Ban chỉ đạo Tổng điều tra dân số và nhà ở Trung ương [National population and housing census directing committee]. 2010. *Báo cáo kết quả chính thức Tổng điều tra dân số và nhà ở 1/4/2009 Phụ lục II* [Official report of the result of the National Population and Housing Census, January 4, 2009, Appendix 2]. Hà Nội: Nhà xuất bản Thống kê.

Ban Dân tộc, UBND tỉnh Lào Cai [Ethnic Minorities Department, Provincial People Committee, Lào Cai]. 2007. *Báo cáo về sắp xếp dân cư, di dân tự do và tình hình hoạt động của các tôn giáo trên địa bàn tỉnh Lào Cai* [Report on population resettlement, free and spontaneous migration, and the activities of religions within Lào Cai province]. Lào Cai: Ban Dân tộc.

Báo Lai Châu. 2010. "Đấu tranh triệt để tái trồng cây thuốc phiện" [Battling to absolutely stop re-planting opium]. *Laichau Online Newspaper.* Accessed January 14, 2011. http://baolaichau.vn/.

Barker, John. 1993. "We Are Eklesia: Conversion in Uiaku, Papua New Guinea." In *Conversion to Christianity: Historical and Anthropological Perspectives on a Great Transformation*, ed. R. W. Hefner, 199–230. Berkeley: University of California Press.

Barney, George Linwood. 1967. "The Meo of Xieng Khouang Province, Laos." In *Southeast Asian Tribes, Minorities and Nations*, ed. Peter Kunstadter, 271–94. Princeton: Princeton University Press.

———. 1957. *Christianity and Innovation in Meo Culture: a Case Study in Missionization.* MA thesis, University of Minnesota.

Barth, Fredrik. 1969. "Introduction." In *Ethnic Groups and Boundaries*, ed. Fredrik Barth, 9–38. Boston: Little, Brown.

Basch, Linda, Nina Glick Schiller, and Cristina Szanton-Blanc. 1994. *Nations Unbound: Transnational Projects, Post-Colonial Predicaments, and De-Territorialized Nation-States.* Langhorne: Gordon and Breach.

Berger, Peter L. 1990. *The Sacred Canopy: Elements of a Sociological Theory of Religion.* New York: Anchor Books.

———. 1954a. "From Sect to Church: a Sociological Interpretation of the Baha'i Movement." PhD diss., New School of Social Research.

———. 1945b. "The Sociological Study of Sectarianism." *Social Research* 21: 467–85.

Bertrais, Yves. 1978. *The Traditional Marriage among the White Hmong of Thailand and Laos.* Chiangmai: Hmong Center.

———. 1964. *Dictionnaire Hmong-Francais.* Vientiane: Mission Catholique.

Bhabha, Homi K. 1994. *The Location of Culture.* London: Routledge.

Blaettler, Dominic. 2008. "State of Mind: Forest Ownership, the Private Sphere and Governance in Reform-Socialist Transition: A Case Study in the Northern Mountain Region of Vietnam." PhD diss., Oxford University.

Bộ Tư lệnh, Quân khu 2. 1994. *Tây Bắc: Lịch sử Kháng chiến Chống Mỹ, Cứu Nước (1954–1975)* [The Northwest: A history of resistance against the US to save the nation (1954–75)]. Hà Nội: Nhà xuất bản Quân đội.

Bourotte, B. 1943. "Mariages et funérailles chez les Meo blancs de la région de Nong-Het (Tran Ninh)." *Bulletin de l'Institut pour l'Etude de l'Homme* 6: 33–56.

Browne, Donald R. 1982. *International Radio Broadcasting: The Limits of the Limitless Medium.* New York: Preager Publishers.

Brumberg, Joan Jacobs. 1980. *Mission for Life: The Story of the Family of Adoniram Judson, the Dramatic Events of the First American Foreign Mission, and the Course of Evangelical Religion in the Nineteenth Century.* New York: The Free Press.

Buckser, Andrew. 2003. "Social Conversion and Group Definition in Jewish Copenhagen." In *The Anthropology of Religious Conversion*, ed. Andrew Buckser and Stephen D. Glazier, 69–84. Lanham: Rowman & Littlefield.

Buckser, Andrew and Stephen D. Glazier. 2003. "Introduction." In *The Anthropology of Religious Conversion*, ed. Andrew Buckser and Stephen D. Glazier, n.p. Lanham: Rowman & Littlefield.

Burnett, Virginia G. and David Stoll. 1993. *Rethinking Protestantism in Latin America*. Philadelphia: Temple University Press.

Burridge, Kenelm. 1969. *New Heaven, New Earth: A Study of Millenarian Activities*. New York: Schocken Books.

Carruthers, Ashley. 2002. "The Accumulation of National Belonging in Transnational Fields: Ways of Being at Home in Vietnam." *Identities: Global Studies in Culture and Power* 9(4): 423–44.

Casanova, Jose. 2005. "Immigrant Religions in Secular Europe and in Christian America." Paper presented at meeting, "Utopias/Dystopias: Modern Desires and Their Discontents," Utrecht University, October 21.

Castells, Manuel. 1996. *The Rise of the Network Society*, vol. 1: *The Information Age: Economy, Society, and Culture*. 2nd ed. Oxford: Blackwell.

CEMA. 2011. *Vietnam: Image of the Community of 54 Ethnic Groups*. Accessed January 6, 2011. http://cema.gov.vn/modules.php?name=Content&mcid=1128#ixzz1AphjHPeV.

Chan, Sucheng. 1994. *Hmong Means Free*. Philadelphia: Temple University Press.

Chau, Adam Yuet. 2005. "The Politics of Legitimation and the Revival of Popular Religion in Shanbei, North-Central China." *Modern China* 31(2): 236–78.

Cheung, Siu-woo. 1993. "Millenarianism, Christian Movements, and Ethnic Change among the Miao in Southwest China." In *Cultural Encounters on China's Ethnic Frontiers*, ed. Stevan Harrell, 217–47. Seattle: University of Washington Press.

Chinnery, E. W. P. and Haddon, A. C. 1917. "Five New Religious Cults in British New Guinea." *Hibbert Journal* 1: 448–63.

Chu, Julie. 2010. *Cosmologies of Credit: Transnational Mobility and the Politics of Destination in China*. Durham: Duke University Press.

Clifford, James. 2001. "Indigenous Articulations." *The Contemporary Pacific* 13(2): 468–90.

———. 1994. "Diasporas." *Cultural Anthropology* 9(3): 302–38.

Cohen, Robin. 1997. *Global Diasporas: An Introduction*. Seattle: University of Washington Press.

Coleman, Simon. 2003. "Continuous Conversion? The Rhetoric, Practice, and Rhetorical Practice of Charismatic Protestant Conversion." In *The Anthropology of Religious Conversion*, ed. Andrew Buckser and Stephen D. Glazier, 15–27. Lanham: Rowman & Littlefield.

Comaroff, Jean and John Comaroff. 2001. *Millenial Capitalism and the Culture of Neoliberalism*. Durham: Duke University Press.

———. 1991. *Of Revelation and Revolution: Christianity, Colonialism and Consciousness in South Africa*. Vol. 1. Chicago: University of Chicago Press.

Cổng Thông tin Điện tử, sở Văn hóa Thể thao Du lịch Lào Cai [Digital portal of Lào Cai's Department of Culture, Sport, and Tourism]. 2008. "Những học kinh nghiệm trong công tác Tiểu Phỉ ở Lào Cai (1951–1955)" [The experiential lessons from the 'Tiểu Phỉ' mission in Lào Cai (1951–55)]. Accessed January 22, 2011. http://egov.laocai.gov.vn/sites/sovhttdl/lichsulaocai/lichsulaocai/Trang/634051425775520000.aspx.

Cooper, Robert G. 1984. *Resource Scarcity and the Hmong Response: Patterns of Settlement and Economy in Transition*. Singapore: Singapore University Press.

Corlin, Claes. 2004. "Hmong and the Land Question in Vietnam: National Policy and Local Concepts of the Environment." In *The Hmong/Miao in Asia*, ed. Nicholas Tapp, Jean Michaud, Christian Culas, and Gary Yia Lee, 295–320. Chiang Mai: Silkworm Books.

Csordas, Thomas J. 1994. *Embodiment and Experience: the Existential Ground of Culture and Self*. Cambridge: Cambridge University Press.

Cục Văn hóa Thông tin Cơ sở [Ministry department of grassroots-level culture and information]. 2004. *Đừng theo Kẻ xấu* [Don't follow bad elements]. Hà Nội: Nhà xuất bản Văn hóa.

Culas, Christian. 2005. *Le Messianisme hmong aux XIXe et XXe siècles: La dynamique religieuse comme instrument politique, chemins de l'ethnologie*. Paris: CNRS, Fondation de la Maison des sciences de l'homme.

———. 2004. "Innovation and Tradition in Ritual and Cosmology: Hmong Messianism and Shamanism in Southeast Asia." In *The Hmong/Miao in Asia*, ed. Nicholas Tapp, Jean Michaud, Christian Culas, and Gary Yia Lee, 97–126. Chiang Mai: Silkworm Books.

Culas, Christian and Jean Michaud. 1997. "A Contribution to the Study of Hmong (Miao) Migrations and History." *Bijdragen tot de Taal-, Land- en Volkenkunde* 153(2): 211–43.

Culhane-Pera et al. 2003. *Healing by Heart: Clinical and Ethical Case Stories of Hmong Families and Western Providers*. Nashville: Vanderbilt University Press.

Đặng Nghiêm Vạn. 2007. "On Religious Issue." *Religious Studies Review* 1(2): 3–15.

———. 2003. *Lý Luận về Tôn giáo và tình hình tôn giáo ở Việt Nam* [Conceptualization of religion and the development of religions in Vietnam]. Hà Nội: Nhà xuất bản Chính trị Quốc gia.

———. 1998. "Về việc truyền bá đạo Vàng Chứ hay giả Tinh Lành." [About the proselytization of the Vàng Chứ cult or Fake-Protestantism]. In *Những vấn đề liên quan đến hiện tượng "Vàng Chứ"* [The issues relating to the "Vàng Chứ" phenomenon]. Hà Nội: Viện Nghiên cứu Tôn giáo.

Davidson, Arnold I. 1986. "Archaeology, Genealogy, Ethics." In *Foucault: A Critical Reader*, ed. David Couzens Hoy, 235–41. Oxford: Basil Blackwell.

Davis, Bradley C. 2011. "Black Flag Rumors and the Black River Basin: Power-broker and the State in the Tonkin-China Borderland." *Journal of Vietnamese Studies* 6(2): 16–41.

De Koninck, Rodolphe. 1999. *Deforestation in Vietnam*. Ottawa: International Development Research Center.

De Vries, Hent. 2001. "*In Media Res*: Global Religion, Public Spheres, and the Task of Contemporary Comparative Religious Studies." In *Religion and Media*, ed. Hent de Vries and Samuel Weber, 1–42. Stanford: Stanford University Press.

De Vries, Hent and Samuel Weber, eds. 2001. *Religion and Media*. Stanford: Stanford University Press.

De Witte, Marleen. 2010. "Transnational Tradition: The Global Dynamics of 'African Traditional Religion.'" In *Religion Crossing Boundaries: Transnational Religious and Social Dynamics in Africa and the New African Diaspora*, ed. Afe Adogame and Jim Spickard, 253–85. Leiden: Brill.

———. 2003. "Altar Media's Living Word: Televised Charismatic Christianity in Ghana." *Journal of Religion in Africa* 33(2): 172–201.

Di Bella, Maria Pia. 2003. "Conversion and Marginality in Southern Italy." In *The Anthropology of Religious Conversion*, ed. Andrew Buckser and Stephen D. Glazier, 85–95. Lanham: Rowman & Littlefield.

Diamond, Sara. 1989. *Spiritual Warfare: The Politics of the Christian Right*. Cambridge: South End Press.

Donnelly, Nancy D. 1994. *Changing Lives of Refugee Hmong Women*. Seattle: University of Washington Press.

Dubois, Thomas David. 2005. *The Sacred Village: Social Change and Religious Life in Rural North China*. Honolulu: University of Hawai'i Press.

Dương, Bích Hạnh. 2008. "Contesting Marginality: Consumption, Networks, and Everyday Practices among Hmong Girls in Sa Pa, Northwestern Vietnam." *Journal of Vietnamese Studies* 3(3): 231–60.

———. 2006. "The Hmong Girls of Sa Pa: Local Places, Global Trajectories, Hybrid Identities." PhD diss., University of Washington.

Eastern World. 1955a. "The Thai-Meo Region of Tonkin." *Eastern World* (October): 23–24.

———. 1955b. "Minorities under the Viet Minh." *Eastern World* (November): 17–18.

Eickelman, Dale F. and John W. Anderson, eds. 1999. *New Media in the Muslim World: The Emerging Public Sphere*. Bloomington: Indiana University Press.

Eisenlohr, Patrick. 2009a. "What is a Medium? The Anthropology of Media and the Question of Ethnic and Religious Pluralism." Inaugural lecture, Universiteit Utrecht, July.

———. 2009b. "Technologies of the Spirit: Devotional Islam, Sound Reproduction, and the Dialectics of Mediation and Immediacy in Mauritius." *Anthropological Theory* 9(3): 273–96.

Engelke, Matthew and Joel Robbins. 2010. "Introduction." Special Issue, "Global Christianity, Global Critique." *South Atlantic Quarterly* 109(4): 623–31.

Enwall, Joakim. 1995. "Hmong Writing Systems in Vietnam: A Case Study of Vietnam's Minority Language Policy." Working paper, Center for Pacific Asia Studies at Stockholm University, 40.

Eriksen, Thomas Hylland. 1993. *Ethnicity and Nationalism: Anthropological Perspectives*. London: Pluto Press.

Escobar, A. 1995. *Encountering Development: The Making and Unmaking of the Third World.* Princeton: Princeton University Press.

Fabian, J. 1983. *Time and the Other: How Anthropology Makes Its Object.* New York: Columbia University Press.

Fadiman, Ann. 1997. *The Spirit Catches You and You Fall Down: A Hmong Child, Her American Doctors, and The Collision of Two Cultures.* New York: Farrar, Straus and Giroux.

Failler, Philippe Le. 2011. "The Deo Family of Lai Chau: Traditional Power and Unconventional Practices." *Journal of Vietnamese Studies* 6(2): 42–67.

Faruque, Cathleen Jo. 2002. *Migration of Hmong to the Midwestern United States.* Lanham: Rowman & Littlefield.

Festinger, Leon, Henry W. Riecken, and Stanley Schachter. 1956. *When Prophecy Fails: A Social and Psychological Study of a Modern Group that Predicted the End of the World.* Minneapolis: University of Minnesota Press.

Foucault, Michel. 1997. *Ethics: Subjectivity and Truth.* Vol. 1. New York: New Press.

———. 1990. *The Use of Pleasure.* Trans. Robert Hurley. New York: Vintage Books.

———. 1988. "Technologies of the Self." In *Technologies of the Self*, ed. L. H. Martin, H. Gutman, and P. H. Hutton, 16–49. Amherst: University of Massachusetts Press.

———. 1984. "What Is Enlightenment?" In *The Foucault Reader*, ed. Paul Rabinow, 32–50. New York: Pantheon Books.

———. 1983. "On The Geneology of Ethics." In *Michel Foucault: Beyond Structuralism and Hermeneutics*, ed. Hubert L. Dreyfus and Paul Rabinow, 229–52. Chicago: University of Chicago Press.

———. 1978. *The History of Sexuality*, vol. 1: *An Introduction.* Trans. Robert Hurley. New York: Vintage Books.

———. 1977. *Discipline and Punish: The Birth of the Prison.* London: Penguin.

Galbiati, Fernando. 1985. *Peng Pai and the Hai-Lu-Feng Soviet.* Stanford: Stanford University Press.

Geddes, William. 1976. *Migrants of the Mountains: The Cultural Ecology of the Blue Miao (Hmong Njua) of Thailand.* Oxford: The Clarendon Press.

Geertz, Clifford. 1995. *After the Fact: Two Countries, Four Decades, One Anthropologist.* The Jerusalem-Harvard Lectures. Cambridge: Harvard University Press.

———. 1973a. "Religion as a Cultural System." In *The Interpretation of Cultures*, 87–126. New York: Basic Books.

———. 1973b. "Internal Conversion in Contemporary Bali." In *The Interpretation of Cultures*, 170–92. New York: Basic Books.

———. 1973c. "Deep Play: Notes on the Balinese Cockfight." In *The Interpretation of Cultures*, 412–53. New York: Basic Books.

Germani, G. 1980. *Marginality.* New Brunswick: Transaction Books.

Glazer, N. and Moynihan, D. P. 1963. *Beyond the Melting Pot: the Negroes, Puerto Ricans, Jews, Italians and Irish of New York City.* Cambridge: MIT Press.

Government Committee for Religious Affairs [Ban Tôn giáo Chính phủ]. 2006.

Religion and Policies Regarding Religion in Vietnam. Hà Nội: Ban Tôn giáo Chính phủ.

Guest, Kenneth. 2003. *God in Chinatown: Religion and Survival in New York's Evolving Immigrant Community.* New York: New York University Press.

Gusfield, J. R. 1996. *Contested Meanings: the Construction of Alcohol Problems.* Madison: University of Wisconsin Press.

Hackett, Rosaline I. J. 1998. "Charismatic/Pentecostal Appropriation of Media Technologies in Nigeria and Ghana." *Journal of Religion in Africa* 28(3): 258–77.

Hacking, Ian. 1986. "Self-Improvement." In *Foucault: A Critical Reader*, ed. David Couzens Hoy, 235–41. Oxford: Basil Blackwell.

Hamilton-Merritt, Jane. 1993. *Tragic Mountains: The Hmong, the Americans, and the Secret Wars for Laos, 1942–1992.* Bloomington: Indiana University Press.

Handler, Richard. 1988. *Nationalism and the Politics of Culture in Quebec.* Madison: University of Wisconsin Press.

Harding, Sussane Friend. 2000. *The Book of Jerry Falwell: Fundamentalist Language and Politics.* Princeton: Princeton University Press.

Hardy, Andrew. 2003. *Red Hills: Migrants and the State in the Highlands of Vietnam.* Singapore: ISEAS.

Hawwa, Sisthi. 2000. "From Cross to Crescent: Religious Conversion of Filipina Domestic Helpers in Hong Kong." *Islam and Christian-Muslim Relations* 11(3): 347–67.

Hefner, Robert W. 1998. "Multiple Modernities: Christianity, Islam, and Hinduism in a Globalizing Age." *Annual Review of Anthropology* 27: 83–104.

———. 1993. "World Building and the Rationality of Conversion." In *Conversion to Christianity: Historical and Anthropological Perspectives on a Great Transformation*, ed. Robert W. Hefner, 3–44. Berkeley: University of California Press.

Heimback, Earnest E. 1969. *White Meo-English Dictionary.* Data Paper No. 75. Ithaca: Southeast Asia Program, Cornell University Press.

Hein, Jeremy. 2006. *Ethnic Origins: The Adaptation of Cambodian and Hmong Refugees in Four American Cities.* New York: Russell Sage Foundation.

Herberg, Will. 1955. *Protestant, Catholic, Jew: An Essay in American Religious Sociology.* New York: Doubleday.

Herr, Na T. 2008. *Toward a Hmong Contextual Theology.* Accessed September 2, 2009. www.hmongbible.org/blog/ntherr/20101205–411.

Hickey, Gerald. 1993. *Shattered World: Adaptation and Survival among Vietnam's Highland Peoples during the Vietnam War.* Philadelphia: University of Pennsylvania Press.

Hickman, Jacob R. 2007. "The Moral Dimension of the Hmong Refugee Experience in America: A Three Ethics Approach." PhD diss., University of Chicago.

Hirschkind, Charles. 2006. *The Ethical Soundscape: Cassette Sermons and Islamic Counterpublics.* New York: Columbia University Press.

Ho-Tai, Hue Tam. 1983. *Millenarianism and Peasant Politics in Vietnam.* Cambridge: Harvard University Press.

Hobsbawm, Eric. 1996. "Introduction." In *The Invention of Tradition*, ed. Eric Hobsbawm and Terence Ranger, 1–14. Cambridge: Cambridge University Press.

———. 1959. *Primitive Rebels: Studies in Archaic Forms of Social Movement in the 19th and 20th Centuries*. Manchester: Manchester University Press.

Hội thánh Tin lành Việt Nam miền Bắc [Northern Evangelical Church of Vietnam]. 2004. *Nội quy, giáo luật, kỷ luật* [Intramural regulations, religious law, disciplines]. Hà Nội: Hội thánh Tin lành Việt Nam miền Bắc.

Hones, Donald F. 2001. "The Word: Religion and Literacy in the Life of a Hmong American." *Religious Education* 96(4). 489–509.

Hones, Donald F. and Cher Shou Cha. 1999. *Educating New American: Immigrant Lives and Learning*. London: Lawrence Erlbaum Associates.

Horton, Robin. 1971. "African Conversion." *AFRICA: Journal of the International African Institute* 41(2): 85–108.

Hoskins, J. 1987. "Entering the Bitter House: Spirit Worship and Conversion." In *Indonesian Religion in Transition in West Sumba*, ed. R. S. Kipp and S. Rodgers, 136–60. Tuscon: University of Arizona Press.

Hoover, Stewart M. and Knut Lundby. 1997. *Rethinking Media, Religion, and Culture*. Thousand Oaks: SAGE Publications.

Humphrey, Caroline. 2002. "Shamans in the City." In *The Unmaking of Soviet Life: Everyday Economies after Socialism*, 202–21. Ithaca: Cornell University Press.

Iannaccone, Laurence. 1997. "Rational Choice: Framework for the Scientific Study of Religion." In *Rational Choice Theory and Religion: Summary and Assessment*, ed. L. A. Young, 25–42. New York: Routledge.

Jenkz, Robert D. 1994. *Insurgency and Social Disorder in Guizhou: The 'Miao' Rebellion, 1854–1873*. Honolulu: University of Hawai'i Press.

Jeung, Russell. 2005. *Faithful Generations: Race and New Asian American Churches*. New Brunswick: Rutgers University Press.

Jørgensen, Bent D. 2006. "Development and 'The Other Within': The Culturalisation of the Political Economy of Poverty in Northern Uplands of Vietnam." PhD diss., University of Gothenburg.

Julian, Roberta. 2003. "Transnational Identities in the Hmong Diaspora." In *Globalisation, Culture and Inequality in Asia*, ed. Timothy J. Scrase, Todd Joseph, Miles Holden, and Scott Baum, 119–43. Melbourne: Trans Pacific Press.

Kammerer, Cornelia. 1996. "Discarding the Basket: The Reintepretation of Tradition by Akha Christians of Northern Thailand." *Journal of Southeast Asian Studies*, 27 (2): 320–33.

———. 1990. "Customs and Christian Conversion among Akha Highlanders of Burma and Thailand." *American Ethnologist* 17(2): 277–91.

Kaplan, Steve. 1996. *Indigenous Responses to Western Christianity*. New York: New York University Press.

Keane, Webb. 2007. *Christian Moderns: Freedom and Fetish in the Mission Encounter*. Berkeley: University of California Press.

———. 2002. "Sincerity, 'Modernity,' and the Protestants." *Cultural Anthropology*. 17(1): 65–92.

———. 1997. "From Fetishism to Sincerity: On Agency, the Speaking of Subject, and Their Historicity in the Context of Conversion." *Comparative Studies in Society and History* 39: 674–93.

———. 1996. "Materialism, Missionaries, and Modern Subjects in Colonial Indonesia." In *Conversion to Modernities: The Globalization of Christianity*, ed. Peter Van de Veer, 137–70. New York: Routledge.Kendall, Laurel. 2009. *Shamans, Nostalgias, and the IMF: South Korean Popular Religion in Motion*. Honolulu: University of Hawai'i Press.

Keyes, Charles F. 2002. "'The People of Asia': Science and Politics in Ethnic Classification in Thailand, China and Vietnam." *Journal of Asian Studies* 61(4): 1163–203.

———. 1996. "Being Protestant Christian in Southeast Asian Worlds." *Journal of Southeast Asian Studies* 27(2): 280–92.

———. 1987. *Thailand, Buddhist Kingdom as Modern Nation-State*. Boulder: Westview Press.

Keyes, Charles F., Laurel Kendall, and Helen Hardacre. 1994. *Asian Visions of Authority: Religion and the Modern States of East and Southeast Asia*. Honolulu: University of Hawai'i Press.

Kim, N. B. Ninh. 2002. *A World Transformed: The Politics of Culture in Revolutionary Vietnam, 1945–65*. Ann Harbor: University of Michigan Press.

Khổng Diễn. 2002 "Một số vấn đề về dân số với phát triển các dân tộc thiểu số vố miền núi Việt Nam" [Demographic issues and development of ethnic minorities and mountainous regions in Vietnam]. In *Phát triển bền vững miền núi Việt Nam: 10 năm nhìn lại và những vấn đề đặt ra* [Sustainable development in the uplands of Vietnam: A ten-year review of persisting issues]. Hà Nội: Nhà xuất bản Nông nghiệp.

Kue, Naolue Taylor. 2000. *A Hmong Church History*. Thorton: The Hmong District of the Christian and Missionary Alliance.

Kunreuther, Laura. 2006. "Technologies of the Voice: FM Radio, Telephone, and the Nepali Diaspora in Kathmandu." *Cultural Anthropology* 21(3): 323–53.

Kunstadter, Peter. 2004. "Hmong Marriage Patterns in Thailand in Relation to Social Change." In *The Hmong/Miao in Asia*, ed. Nicholas Tapp. Chiang Mai: Silkworm Books.

Lambek, Michael. 2002. "Introduction." In *A Reader in the Anthropology of Religion*, ed. Michael Lambek, 1–18. Oxford: Blackwell Publishing.

Lanternari, Vittorio. 1963. *The Religion of the Oppressed: A Study of Modern Messianic Cults*. Trans. Lisa Sergio. New York: Knopf.

Lê, Trọng Cúc and A. Terry Rambo. 2001. *Bright Peaks, Dark Valleys: A Comparative Analysis of Environmental and Social Conditions and Development Trends in Five Communities in Vietnam's Northern Mountain Region*. Hanoi: The National Political Publishing House.

Lee, Gary Yia. 2008 [2000]. "The Hmong Rebellion in Laos: Victims of Totalitarianism or Terrorists?" *Indigenous Affairs* 4. Updated version available at www .garyyialee.com/ (accessed January 23, 2011).

———. 1996. "Cultural Identity in Post-Modern Society: Reflection on What Is Hmong." *Hmong Studies Journal* 1(1): 1–14.

———. 1988. "Household and Marriage in a Thai Highland Society." *Journal of the Siam Society* (76): 162–73.

———. 1987. "Ethnic Minorities and National-Building in Laos: the Hmong in the Lao State." *Peninsule* 11/12: 215–32.

Leepreecha, Prasit. 2008. "The Role of Media Technology in Reproducing Hmong Ethnic Identity." In *Living in a Globalized World: Ethnic Minorities in the Greater Mekong Subregion*, ed. Don McCaskill et al., 89–113. Chiang Mai: Mekong Press.

———. 2001. "Kinship and Identity among Hmong in Thailand." PhD diss., University of Washington.

Lemoine, Jacques. 1983. *Kr'ua Ke: Showing the Way*. Trans. Kenneth White. Bangkok: Pandora.

Lenin, Vladimir. 1920. *Our Foreign and Domestic Position and Party Tasks*. Moscow.

Lentz, Christian C. 2014. "Cultivating Subjects: Opium Regimes from Colony to Nation in Vietnam." Paper presented at the Association for Asian Studies Annual Meeting, Philadelphia, March 29, 2014.

———. 2011. "Making the Northwest Vietnamese." *Journal of Vietnamese Studies* 6(2): 68–105.

Leonard, Karen I., Alex Stepick, Manuel A. Vasquez, and Jennifer Holdaway. 2005. *Immigrant Faiths: Transforming Religious Life in America*. New York: Altamira Press.

Levitt, Peggy. 2007. *God Needs No Passport: Immigrants and the Changing American Religious Landscape*. New York: The New Press.

———. 2003. "'You Know Abraham Was Really the First Migrant': Transnational Migration and Religion." *International Migration Review* 37(3): 847–73.

———. 2002. "Migration and Religion in Transnational Perspective." In *Transnational Religion, Migration, and Diversity*. International Migration Program, Social Science Research Council, New York. Accessed October 8, 2010. http:// www.ssrc.org/programs/intmigration/productions/transnational_Religion_ and_Migration_document.pdf.

———. 1999. "Social Remittances: A Local Level, Migration-Driven Form of Cultural Defusion." *International Migration Review* 32(124): 926–49.

Levitt, Peggy and B. Nadya Jaworsky. 2007. "Transnational Migration Studies: Past Developments and Future Trends." *Annual Review of Sociology* 33: 129–56.

Lewis, James. 2002. "The Evangelical Religious Movement among the Hme E of Northern Vietnam and the Government Response to It: 1989–2000." *Crossroads: An Interdisciplinary Journal of Southeast Asian Studies* 16(1): 226–62.

Linton, Ralph. 1943. "Nativistic Movements." *American Anthropologist* 45: 230–40.

Lukens, Carol. 2008. "Conversion or Integration: Religion and Hmong Immigrants." In *Looking Back, Stepping Forward: The Hmong People*. The DC Everest Oral History Project. Weston: DC Everest Area Schools.

Luong, Hy Van. 1993. "Economic Reform and the Intensification of Rituals in Two North Vietnamese Villages, 1980–90." In *The Challenge of Reform in Indochina*, ed. Börje Ljunggren, 259–91. Cambridge: Harvard Institute for International Development.

Lymann, Thomas Amis. 2004. "A Note on the Ethno-Semantics of Proverb Usage in Mong Njua (Green Hmong)." In *The Hmong/Miao in Asia*, ed. Nicholas Tapp et al., 167–78. Chiang Mai: Silkworm Books.

———. 1974. *Dictionary of Mong Njua, a Miao (Meo) Language of Southeast Asia*. The Hague: Mouton.

Ma Văn Kháng. 1983. *Vùng biên ải* [The border region]. Hà Nội: Nhà xuất bản Công an Nhân dân.

Madsen, Richard. 2010. "The Upsurge of Religion in China." *Journal of Democracy*, 21(4): 58–71.

———. 1998. *China's Catholics: Tragedy and Hope in an Emerging Civil Society* Berkeley: University of California Press, 1998.

Malarney, Shaun. 2002. *Culture, Ritual and Revolution in Vietnam*. Honolulu: University of Hawai'i Press.

———. 1996. "The Limits of 'State Functionalism' and the Reconstruction of Funerary Ritual in Contemporary Northern Viet Nam." *American Ethnologist* 23(3): 540–60.

Marx, Karl. 2005 [1852]. *The Eighteenth Brumaire of Louis Bonaparte*. New York: Mondial.

McAlister, John T. Jr. 1967. "Mountain Minorities and the Viet Minh: A Key to the Indochina War." In *Southeast Asian Tribes, Minorities, and Nations*, ed. Peter Kunstadter, 771–844. Princeton: Princeton University Press.

Meyer, Birgit. 2010. "'There Is a Spirit in that Image': 'Mass-Produced Jesus Pictures and Protestant-Pentecostal Animation in Ghana." *Comparative Studies in Society and History* 52(1): 100–30.

———. 2008. "Religious Sensations. Why Media, Aesthetics and Power Matter in the Study of Contemporary Religion." In *Religion: Beyond a Concept*, Hent de Vries, ed. 704–23. New York: Fordham University Press.

———. 2006. "Impossible Representations: Pentecostalism, Vision, and Video Technology in Ghana." In *Religion, Media and the Public Sphere*, ed. Birgit Meyer and Annelies Moors, 290–312. Bloomington: Indiana University Press.

———. 2003. "Visions of Blood, Sex and Money: Fantasy Spaces in Popular Ghanaian Cinema." *Visual Anthropology* 16(1): 15–41.

———. 1999. *Translating the Devil: Religion and Modernity among the Ewe in Ghana*. Edinburgh: Edinburgh University Press.

———. 1998. "'Make a Complete Break with the Past': Memory and Post-colonial

Modernity in Ghanaian Pentecostalist Discourse." *Journal of Religion in Africa* 27(3): 316–49.

———. 1996. "Modernity and Enchantment: The Image of the Devil in Popular African Christianity." In *Conversion to Modernities: The Globalization of Christianity*, ed. Peter van der Veer, 199–230. New York: Routledge.

Meyer, Birgit and Annelies Moors. 2006. *Religion, Media and the Public Sphere*. Bloomington: Indiana University Press.

Merrill, William L. 1993. "Conversion and Colonialism in Northern Mexico: The Tarahumara Response to the Jesuit Mission Program 1601–1767." In *Conversion to Christianity: Historical and Anthropological Perspectives on a Great Transformation*, ed. Robert W. Hefner, 129–63. Berkeley: University of California Press.

Miyazaki, Hirokazu. 2003. "The Temporalities of the Market." *American Anthropologist* 105(2): 255–65.

Michaud, Jean. 2010. "Zomia and Beyond." *Journal of Global History* (5): 187–214.

———. 2006. *Historical Dictionary of the Peoples of the Southeast Asian Massif*. Lanham: Scarecrow Press.

———. 2004. "French Missionary Expansion in Colonial Upper Tonkin." *Journal of Southeast Asian Studies* 35(2): 287–310.

———. 2000. "A Historical Panorama of the Montagnards in Northern Vietnam under French Rule." In *Turbulent Times and Enduring Peoples: Mountain Minorities in the South-East Asian Massif*, ed. Jean Michaud, 51–78. Richmond: Curzon.

———. 1997. "From Southwest China into Upper Indochina: An Overview of Hmong (Miao) Migrations." *Asia Pacific Viewpoint*. 32(2):119–30.

Mottin, Jean. 1980. *History of the Hmong*. Bangkok: Odeon Store.

Moua, Vayong. 1995. "Hmong Christianity: Conversion, Consequence and Conflict." In *Hmong Electronical Resources Project*. Accessed June 5, 2006. http://www.miaoupg.com/hmong.htm.

Ngo, Tam T. T. 2010. "Ethnic and Transnational Dimensions of Recent Protestant Conversion among the Hmong in Northern Vietnam." *Social Compass*. 57(3): 322–44.

———. 2009. "The Short-Waved Faith: Christian Broadcastings and the Transformation of the Spiritual Landscape of the Hmong in Northern Vietnam." In *Mediated Piety: Technology and Religion in Contemporary Asia*, ed. K. G. Francis Lim, 139–58. Leiden: Brill.

Ngo, Tam T. T and Hue Tam Ho-Tai. 2013. "Myth, History and Community in the Cult of Ho Chi Minh." Paper presented at the International Conference on Remaking Communal Festivals and Social Boundaries in Socialist/Post-Socialist Societies, HKUST, December 16–17, 2013.

Nguyễn Anh Ngọc. 1989. "Những vấn đề lý luận và thực tiễn của công tác định canh định cư" [Theoretical and practical issues of fixed cultivation and fixed settlement]. *Tạp chí Dân tộc học* 2(3): 75–95.

Nguyễn Văn Thắng. 2007. *Ambiguity of Identity: The Mieu in North Vietnam*. Chiang Mai: Silkworm Books.

Nguyễn Văn Văn 2008. "Tinh thần chống Pháp của các dân tộc Lào Cai qua một số câu ca" [Anti-French spirits of ethnic minorities in Lào Cai reflected in a number of songs and folk-songs]. Accessed January 24, 2011. http://egov.laocai.gov.vn/timhieulaocai/vanhoathethao/vanhocnghethuat/nghiencuulyluan/Trang/634046198026944190.aspx.

Nguyễn Xuân Yêm. 1991. "Hãy hiểu đúng về người Hmong" [Please understand the Hmong correctly]. *Nhân Dân*, April 21, 1991.

Ong, Aihwa. 2003. *Buddha is Hiding: Refugees, Citizenship, and the New America.* Berkeley: University of California Press.

Ovesen, Jan. 1995. "A Minority Enters the Nation States: A Case Study of a Hmong Community in Vientiane Province, Laos." *Uppsala Research Reports in Cultural Anthropology* 14: 1–95.

Palmer, David. 2007. *Qigong Fever: Body, Science, and Utopia in China.* New York: Columbia University Press.

Peacock, James L. 2001. *The Anthropological Lens: Harsh Light, Soft Focus.* 2nd ed. Cambridge: Cambridge University Press.

Pelkmans, Mathijs. 2009. *Conversion after Socialism: Disruption, Modernisms and Technologies of Faith in the Former Soviet Union.* Oxford: Berghahn Books.

Peel, J. D. Y. 1968. *Aladura: A Religious Movement among the Yoruba:* London: Oxford University Press.

Pelley, Patricia. 1998. "'Barbarians' and 'Younger Brothers': The Remaking of Race in Postcolonial Vietnam." *Journal of Southeast Asian Studies* 29: 374–91.

Pels, P. J. 1997. "The Anthropology of Colonialism: Culture, History and the Emergence of Western Governmentality." *Annual Review of Anthropology* 26: 163–83.

Pels, Peter and Oscar Salemink. 1999. *Colonial Subjects: Essays on the Practical History of Anthropology.* Ann Arbor: University of Michigan Press.

Pham, Quang Hoan. 1995. "The Role of Traditional Social Institutions in Community Management of Resources among the Hmong in Vietnam." East-West Center Indochina Series Working Papers, No. 5.

Phan Hữu Dật. 1998. "Một số ý kiến về việc bảo tồn, làm giàu và phát triển bản sắc văn hóa các dân tộc nước ta" [Some views on preserving, enriching and developing cultural identities of ethnic minorities in our country]. In *Một số vấn đề về dân tộc học Việt Nam* [Some issues on ethnology in Vietnam], ed. Phan Hữu Dật. Hà Nội: Nhà xuất bản Đại học Quốc gia.

Pollard, Samuel. 1921. *Tight Corners in China.* London: Andrew Crombie.

———. 1919. *The Story of the Miao.* London: Henry Books.

Procacci, Giovanna. 1991. "Social Economy and the Government of Poverty." In *The Foucault Effect: Studies in Governmentality with Two Lectures by and an Interview with Michel Foucault,* ed. Graham Burchell, Colin Gordon, and Peter Miller, 151–68. London: Harvester Wheatsheaf.

Quijada, Justine Buck. 2009. "Opening the Roads: History and Religion in Post-Soviet Buryatia." PhD diss., University of Chicago.

Quinn-Judge, Sophie. 2002. *Ho Chi Minh: The Missing Years: 1919–1941*. Berkeley: University of California Press.

Rafael, Vicente L. 1988. *Contracting Colonialism: Translation and Christian Conversion in Tagalog Society under Early Spanish Rule*. Durham: Duke University Press.

Rambo, Lewis R. 1993. *Understanding Religious Conversion*. New Haven: Yale University Press.

Rapin, Ami-Jacques. 2003. *Ethnic Minorities, Drug Uses and Harm in the Highlands of Northern Vietnam: A Contextual Analysis of the Situation in Six Communes from Son La, Lai Chau, and Lao Cai*. United Nation Office on Drugs and Crime. Hà Nội: Nhà xuất bản Thế giới. Accessed on June 12, 2008. http://www.unodc.org/pdf/vietnam/vietnam_ethnic_minorities_report.pdf.

Rappaport, Roy A. 1994. "Disorders of Our Own: A Conclusion." In *Diagnosing America*, ed. Shepard Forman, 235–94. Ann Arbor: University of Michigan Press.

Robbins, Joel. 2007. "Continuity Thinking and the Problem of Christian Culture: Belief, Time, and the Anthropology of Christianity." *Current Anthropology* 48: 5–38.

———. 2004. *Becoming Sinners: Christianity and Moral Torment in a Papua New Guinea Society*. Berkeley: University of California. Press.

Robinson, W. C. 1998. *Terms of Refugees: The Indochinese Exodus and the International Response*. London: Zed Books.

Rosaldo, Renato. 2003. *Cultural Citizenship in Island Southeast Asia; Nation and Belonging in the Hinterlands*. Berkeley: University of California Press.

———. 1989 *Culture and Truth: The Remaking of Social Analysis*. Boston: Beacon Press.

Salemink, Oscar. 2009. "Is Protestant Conversion a Form of Protest? Urban and Upland Protestants in Southeast Asia." In *Christianity and the State in Asia: Complicity and Conflict*, ed. Julius Bautista and Francis Khek Gee Lim. New York: Routledge.

———. 2003a. *The Ethnography of Vietnam's Central Highlanders: A Historical Contextualization, 1850–1990*. London: RoutledgeCurzon.

———. 2003b. "Enclosing the Highlands: Socialist, Capitalist and Protestant Conversions of Vietnamese Highlanders." Accessed September 10, 2006. http://dlc.dlib.indiana.edu/archive/00001142/.

Savina, F. M. 1924. *Histoire des Miao*. Paris: Sociris des Missions Etrangères.

Scannell, Paddy. 1992. *Broadcast Talk*. London: Sage Publications.

Schein, Louisa. 2007. "Souls, Labor, Landscapes and Loves: Hmong American Transnational Quests." Paper presented at conference, "Religion, Ethnicity and Nation-States in a Globalizing World," Vrije Universiteit Amsterdam, June 7–8.

———. 2004a. "Homeland Beauty: Transnational Longing and Hmong American Video." *Journal of Asian Studies* 63(2): 433–63.

———. 2004b. "Hmong/Miao Transnationality: Identity beyond Culture." In *The*

Hmong/Miao in Asia, ed. Nicholas Tapp et al., 273–90. Chiang Mai: Silkworm Books.

———. 2002. "Mapping Hmong Media in Diasporic Space." In *Media Worlds: Anthropology on New Terrain*, ed. Faye Ginsburg, Lila Abu-Lughod, and Brian Larkin, 229–44. Berkeley: University of California Press.

———. 2000. *Minority Rules: The Miao and the Feminine in China's Cultural Politics*. Durham: Duke University Press.

———. 1999a. "Diaspora Politics, Homeland Erotics and the Materializing of Memory." *Positions: East Asia Cultures Critique* 7(3): 697–729.

———. 1999b. "Of Cargo and Satellites: Imagined Cosmopolitanism." *Postcolonial Studies* 2(3): 345–75.

———. 1998. "Importing Miao Brethren to Hmong America: A Not So Stateless Transnationalism." In *Cosmopolitics: Thinking and Feeling Beyond the Nation*, ed. Pheng Cheah and Bruce Robbins, 163–91. Minneapolis: University of Minnesota Press.

———. 1997. "Gender and Internal Orientalism in China." *Modern China* 23(1): 69–98.

Scott, James C. 2009. *The Art of Not Being Governed: An Anarchist History of Upland Southeast Asia*. New Haven: Yale University Press.

Seigel, Taggart and Dwight Conquergood. 1985. *Between Two Worlds: The Hmong Shaman In America*. Documentary. [Portland]: Collective Eye.

Shur, Vang Vangyi. 1986. "Hmong Employment and Welfare Dependency." In *The Hmong in Transition*, ed. Glenn L. Hendricks, Bruce T. Downing, and Amos S. Deinard, 192–96. New York: The Center for Migration Studies of New York.

Smalley, William A., Chia Koua Vang, and Gnia Yee Yang. 1990. *Mother of Writing: The Origin and Development of a Hmong Messianic Script*. Chicago: University of Chicago Press.

Smith-Hefner, Nancy. 1994. "Ethnicity and the Force of Faith: Christian Conversion among Khmer Refugees." *Anthropological Quarterly* 67(1): 24–38.

Spitulnik, Debra. 2002. "Mobile Machines and Fluid Audiences: Rethinking Reception through Zambian Radio Culture." In *Media Worlds: Anthropology on New Terrain*, ed. Faye Ginsburg, Lila Abu-Lughod, and Brian Larkin, 337–54. Berkeley: University of California Press.

———. 2000. "Documenting Radio Culture as Lived Experience: Reception Studies and the Mobile Machine in Zambia." In *African Broadcast Cultures: Radio in Transition*, ed. R. Fardon and G. Furniss, 144–63. Oxford: James Currey.

Spyer, Patricia. 1996. "Serial Conversion/Conversion to Seriality: Religion, State, and Number in Aru, Eastern Indonesia." In *Conversion to Modernities: The Globalization of Christianity*, ed. Peter Van Der Veer, 171–98. New York: Routledge.

Stark, Rodney. 1997. "Bringing Theory Back in." In *Assessing Rational Choice Theories of Religion*, ed. L. A. Young, 3–23. New York: Routledge.

Stark, Rodney and W. S. Bainbridge. 1987. *A Theory of Religion*. New York: Peter Lang.

Steedly, Marry. 1993. *Hanging without a Rope: Narrative Experience in Colonial and Postcolonial Karoland*. Princeton: Princeton University Press.

Sterne, Jonathan. 2003. *The Audible Past: Cultural Origins of Sound Reproduction*. Durham: Duke University Press.

Stout, Daniel, and Judith Buddenbaum. 1996. *Religion and Mass Media: Audiences and Adaptations*. London: Sage Publications.

Streib, H. et al. 2009. *Deconversion: Qualitative and Quantitative Results from Cross-Cultural Research in Germany and the United States of America*. Research in Contemporary Religion, 5. Göttingen: Vandenhoeck & Ruprecht.

Swinkels, Rob and Carrie Turk. 2006. "Explaining Ethnic Minority Poverty in Vietnam: A Summary of Recent Trends and Current Challenges." Paper for CEM/ MPI Meeting on Ethnic Minority Poverty, Hanoi, September 28.

Symonds, Patricia. 2004. *Calling in the Soul: Gender and the Cycle of Life in a Hmong Village*. Seattle: University of Washington Press.

Tapp, Nicholas. 2010. *The Impossibility of Self: An Essay on the Hmong Diaspora*. Berlin: Lit Verlag.

———. 2006. "A Trip to Vietnam." *Thai-Yunnan Project Bulletin* 7: 1–4.

———. 2002. "Hmong Confucian Ethics and Constructions of the Past." In *Cultural Crisis and Social Memory: Modernity and Identity in Thailand and Laos*, ed. Shigeharu Tanabe and Charles F. Keyes, 95–110. New York: RoutledgeCurzon.

———. 2001. *The Hmong of China: Context, Agency, and the Imaginary*. Leiden: Sinica Leidensia.

———. 1989a. "Hmong Religion." *Asian Folklore Studies* 48: 59–94.

———. 1989b. "The Impact of Missionary Christianity Upon Marginalized Ethnic Minorities: The Case of the Hmong." *Journal of Southeast Asian Studies* 20(1): 70–95.

———. 1989c. *Sovereignty and Rebellion: The White Hmong of Northern Thailand*. South-East Asian Social Science Monographs. Singapore: Oxford University Press.

Taylor, Philip. 2008. "Minorities at Large: New Approaches to Minority Ethnicity in Vietnam." *Journal of Vietnamese Studies* 3(3): 3–43.

Ter Haar, Barend J. 1992. *The White Lotus Teachings in Chinese Religious History*. Honolulu: University of Hawai'i Press.

Thoj, Va-Megn. 2002. *Slaughtered in Hugo*. Documentary. St. Paul: Frogtown Media Productions.

Tỉnh ủy Lào Cai [Lào Cai People's Committee]. 2004. "Người Mông Lào Cai và một số giải pháp, kiến nghị, về xây dựng đời sống văn hóa vùng đồng bào Mông hiện nay" [The Hmong of Lào Cai and some solutions and proposals for building socio-cultural life in Hmong areas]. In *Văn hóa các dân tộc Tây Bắc: Thực trạng và những vấn đề đặt ra* [The cultures of ethnic minorities in the Northwest region: Facts and issues], ed. Trần Văn Bình, 310–28. Hà Nội: Nhà xuất bản Chính trị Quốc gia.

Tô Hoài. 1952. *Vợ Chồng A Phủ* [The A Phủs]. Hà Nội: Nhà xuất bản Văn học.

Trần Hữu Sơn. 1996. *Văn hóa Hmong* [Hmong Culture]. Hà Nội: Nhà xuất bản Văn hóa Dân tộc.

Tsing, Anna Lowenhaupt. 1993. *In the Realm of the Diamond Queen: Marginality in an Out-of-the-Way Place*. Princeton: Princeton University Press.

Tuck, Patrick J.N. 1987. *French Catholic Missionaries and the Politics of Imperialism in Vietnam, 1857–1914: A Documentary Survey*. Liverpool: Liverpool University Press.

Turner, Victor. 1969. *The Ritual Process: Structure and Anti-Structure*. The Lewis Henry Morgan Lectures. London: Routledge & K. Paul.

———. 1967. *The Forest of Symbols: Aspects of Ndembu Ritual*. Ithaca: Cornell University Press.

UBND tỉnh Lào Cai (Ban Dân tộc). 2007. *Báo cáo về sắp xếp dân cư, dân di cư tự do và tình hình hoạt động của các tôn giáo trên địa bàn tỉnh Lào Cai* [Report on the task of population settlement, free-migrating populations and the situation and practice of religions in Lào Cai province]. Lào Cai: UBND tỉnh Lào Cai (Ban Dân tộc).

United States Census Bureau. 2009. "Selected Population Profile in the United States: Hmong Alone or in Any Combination. American Community Survey 1-Year Estimates." Accessed January 6, 2011. http://hmongstudies.org/HmongACS2008.pdf.

van der Veer, Peter. 2005. "Afterword: Global Conversions." In *Mixed Messages: Materiality, Textuality, and Missions*, ed. Jamie S. Scott and Gareth Griffiths, 221–33. New York: Palgrave MacMillan.

———. 2002. "Transnational Religion: Hindu and Muslim Movements." *Global Networks* 2(2): 95–109.

———. 2001. *Imperial Encounters: Religion, Nation, and Empire*. Princeton: Princeton University Press.

———. 1996. "Introduction." In *Conversion to Modernities: The Globalization of Christianity*, ed. Peter van der Veer, 1–22. New York: Routledge.

———. 1993. "The Foreign Hand: Orientalist Discourse in Sociology and Communalism." In *Orientalism and The Post-Colonial Predicament: Perspectives on South Asia*, ed. C. Breckenridge and Peter van der Veer. 23–45. Philadelphia: University of Pennsylvania Press.

Vang, C. 2008. *Hmong in Minnesota*. St. Paul: Minnesota Historical Society Press.

Vang, Chia Youyee. 2009. "Hmong Anti-Communism at Home and Abroad." In *Anti-Communist Minorities in the U.S.: Political Activism of Ethnic Refugees*, ed. Ieva Sake, 211–31. New York: Palgrave Macmillan.

Vang, Mayli. 2003. "Art and Religion in our Living Culture." *Paj Ntaub Voice: A Journal Giving Expression to Hmong Voices* 8(2): 11.

Vang, Timothy. 2000. *The History of a People Movement*. Thornton: The Hmong District of the Christian and Missionary Alliance.

———. 1998. "Coming a Full Circle: Historical Analysis of the Hmong Church Growth, 1950–1998." PhD diss., Fuller Theological Seminary.

Vasquez, Manuel A. 1999. "Toward a New Agenda for the Study of Religion in the Americas." *Journal of Interamerican Studies and World Affairs* 41(4): 1–20.

Vũ, Đường Luân. 2014. "The Politics of Frontier Mining: Local Chieftains, Chinese Miners, and Upland Society in the Nông Văn Vân Uprising in the Sino-Vietnamese Border Area (1833–1835)." *Cross-Currents: East Asian History and Culture Review*, no. 11 (June): 31–58.

Vũ Ngọc Kỳ. 1999. "Hoạt động Tiểu Phỉ ở Hà Giang trong khong chiến chống thực dân Pháp [Anti-Phi work in Ha Giang during the resistance against the French colonialists]." In *Quân và dân Tây Bắc với chiến thắng Điện Biên Phủ* [Northwestern soldiers and people and the success of Điện Biên Phủ]. Hà Nội: Nhà xuất bản Quân đội.

Vương, Duy Quang. 2005. *Văn hóa tâm linh của người Hmong ở Việt Nam: Truyền thống và hiện tại* [The spiritual culture of the Hmong in Vietnam: Tradition and modernity]. Hà Nội: Nhà xuất bản Văn hòa-Thông tin and Viện Văn hóa.

———. 2004. "The Hmong and Forest Management in Northern Vietnam." In *The Hmong/Miao in Asia*, ed. Nicholas Tapp, Jean Michaud, Christian Culas, and Gary Yia Lee. Chiang Mai: Silkworm Books.

———. 1998. "Ý kiến của một cán bộ người Hmong về vấn đề người Hmong theo đạo hiện nay" [Opinion among Hmong cadres about the issue of Hmong conversion]. In *Những vấn đề liên quan đến hiện tượng "'Vàng Chứ"* [Issues relating to the "Vàng Chứ" phenomenon], ed. Viện Nghiên cứu Tôn giáo. Hanoi: Viện Nghiên cứu Tôn giáo.

———. 1997. "Traditional Social Relations of the Hmong Ethnic Group and the Questions of Protecting and Developing Forest in Mountainous Areas of North Vietnam." Institute for Religious Studies, Hanoi.

Vương, Xuân Tình. 2002. "Looking for Food: The Difficult Journey of the Hmong in Vietnam (Anthropological Perspectives on Food Security)." Unpublished paper. Accessed June 20, 2006. http://digital.library.wisc.edu/1793/23092.

Vương, Xuân Tình and Peter Hjemdahl. 1996. "A Study of Hmong and Dao Land Management and Land Tenure, Nam Ty Commune, Hoang Su Phi District, Ha Giang Province, Vietnam." Vietnam-Sweden Mountain Rural, Hanoi.

Wagner, Melinda Bollar. 1997. "The Study of Religion in American Society." In *Anthropology of Religion: A Handbook*, ed. Stephen D. Glazier, 85–101. Westport: Greenwood Press.

Walker, Anthony R. 2003. *Merit and the Millennium: Routine and Crisis in the Ritual Lives of the Lahu People.* New Delhi: Hindustan.

Wallace, Anthony F. C. 1956. "Revitalization Movements." *American Anthropologist* 58(2): 264–81.

Warner, R. 1995. *Backfire: The CIA's Secret War in Laos and Its Link to the War in Vietnam.* New York: Simon and Schuster.

Watt, Hilary. 2008. "The Power of the Spoken Word in Defining Religion and Thought: A Case Study." *Hmong Studies Journal* 9: 1–25.

Weber, Marx. 1947. *The Theory of Social and Economic Organization*. Trans. A. M. Henderson and Talcott Parsons. New York: The Free Press.

Weber, Samuel. 2001. "Religion, Repetition, and Media." In *Religion and Media*, ed. Hent De Vries and Samuel Weber, 3–42. Stanford: Stanford University Press.

Winland, Daphne N. 1994. "Christianity and Community: Conversion and Adaptation among Hmong Refugee Women." *Canadian Journal of Sociology* 19(1): 21–41.

———. 1992. "The Role of Religious Affiliation in Refugee Resettlement: The Case of the Hmong." *Canadian Ethnic Studies* 24: 96–119.

Weidman, Amanda J. 2006. *Singing the Classical, Voicing the Modern: The Postcolonial Politics of Music in South India*. Durham: Duke University Press.

Westwood, Sallie and Annie Phizacklea. 2000. "Introduction." In *Trans-nationalism and the Politics of Belonging*, ed. Sallie Westwood and Annie Phizacklea, 1–16. New York: Routledge.

Winrock International. 1996. "Ethnic Minorities in Vietnam: A Country Profile." Development program prepared for the World Bank by Winrock International, Hanoi, October.

Woodside, Alexander. 1971. *Vietnam and the Chinese Model*. Cambridge: Harvard University Press.

World Bank. 2009. *Country Social Analysis: Ethnicity and Development in Vietnam*. Hanoi: The World Bank.

Worsley, Peter. 1968. *The Trumpet Shall Sound: A Study of "Cargo" Cults in Melanesia*. 2nd ed. New York: Schocken Books.

Yang, Kaoly. 2005. "Criticism on Bride Price." Accessed July 20, 2009. http://www.hmongcontemporaryissues.com/archives/CritiqueBridePrice0605.html.

Zake, Ieva. 2009. *Anti-Communist Minorities in the U.S.: Political Activism of Ethnic Refugees*. New York: Palgrave Macmillan.

INDEX

Note: page numbers in *italics* refer to figures, maps, or tables; those followed by "n" indicate endnotes. *"Plate"* refers to photographs following page 20.

nary and, 118–19; post-socialism and, 168–69; shamanism, the New Socialist Person, and, 112–16; shifts in, 103; state anti-superstition campaigns and, 107–8, 115–16; young people's aspirations, experiences of discrimination, and, 116–18

Cooper, Robert, 105

costume of Hmong Leng women, *Plate*

courtship, 148–50. *See also* marriage

cultural campaigns, 107–8, 112–13

cultural preservation and missionary encounters, 77–78

cultural revival, state turn toward encouraging, 135–37

D

dabs (spirits), 46, 47–48, 104–5

Đắc Lắc province, migration to, 117–18

Danai, Dr., 73, 80–81

Đặng Nghiêm Vạn, 93

deconversion: Mr. Gi, story of, 4; state classifications and, 129, 130; transformation of subjectivities and, 13; in United States, 69–71

Democratic Reform (Cải Cách Dân Chủ) program, 31

development programs. *See* Land Reform campaigns and development programs, state

De Vries, Hent, 53

diaspora and US Hmong: bride price and, 110–11; calling as missionaries and, 72–75; common global Miao-Hmong identity, reconstruction of, 63; cultural preservation and, 76–77; deconversions, 69–71; double transnationality and, 62–64; ethnic ties and, 62; FEBC broadcasts and, 45; homeland, desire to reshape, 76; identity politics and, 14; immigrant and diaspora identities, parallel,

73–74; incomplete conversion and cultural assimilation, 66–69; marriage by capture and, 152; modernity desire and, 13; Mường Nhé incident and, 100–101; number of Hmong by country, 171n1(ch1); racism and religious defensiveness, 71–72; sense of marginality in relation to, 14–15; visits to Vietnam in search of separated relatives, 63–64; White Hmong and, 174n13. *See also* missions and missionaries, Protestant

Đổi Mới era, 6, 9, 33, 168

Don't Follow Bad Elements (Đừng Theo Kẻ Xấu) booklet, 127–28

Dubois, Thomas, 167

E

education, 107, 116–18

Eisenlohr, Patrick, 174n11

Eliminating the Bandit/Rebels program (Tiễu Phỉ), 27–29

elopement, 151

endogamy, religious, 155–56

ethics. *See* morality and moral narratives

ethnic groups in Vietnam: Hmong subgroup classification, 21; marginality and, 13–15; number of, in Vietnam, 171n1(intro); Việt Minh classification scheme, 9, 14

Ethnic Liberation Organization of Laos, 90

ethnic ties, Hmong missionaries and, 62

Evangelical Protestantism: comparison of global communism and, 122; the Great Mission and, 54; Hmong millenarianism, resonance with, 7–8; indigenization of, 44–46, 167; millenarianism, relationship with, 95–101; moral narrative of modernity and, 11;

Thailand, 144; in Vietnam (overview), 21–22. *See also specific topics*
Hmong Romanized Phonetic Alphabet (RPA), 20, 118
Hmong Studies Conference, First (Concordia University, 2006), 18, 64
Hmong Traditional Culture Procedural Guide, 111
Hòa Hảo movements, 8, 91, 94
Hồ Chí Minh, 48, 168
Hồ Chí Minh trail, 174n1
holy cow sacrifice ritual (*nyub dab*), 104–5, 177n1
homeland, sense of, 63, 76
homogeneous unit principle, 65
Horton, Robin, 106
house churches: church leaders, education of, 118; easing of state policy toward, 135; Ede house church, 118; leadership in, 116, 118; marriage and, 154, 160; millenarianism, rumors of separatism, and, 97, 98–99, 121; public presence of, 136; raids of, 51; registration of, 130–31, 145–46; sexual behavior, regulation of, 150; Sunday service, *Plate*; Tiên Phong–Tòng Già–Sảng Pả house church, 23
Hua Tra villages, FEBC broadcasts and, 41–42, 46–48
human rights narratives, 78–80, 100–101
Huyền Tâm, 19
hymnal music DVDs, 119

I

identity politics, diasporic, 14, 79–80
indigenization of Christianity, 44–46, 167
internal stress vs. external inducement model of conversion, 126–27

J

Jenks, Robert, 88
Jesus Christ, Vang Tsu as father of, 49

K

Keane, Webb, 10–12, 158
Kendall, Laurel, 106
kevcai ("ways"), 58–59
Keyes, Charles F., 44, 105
"kidnapping" of brides. *See* capture, marriage by
Kinh majority: coevalness of Hmong and, 6, 164; cultural hegemony of, 169; distrust of Kinh traders, 35–37; ethnic marginalism and, 14; millenarianism and, 165, 168; morality and, 144; in Phong Hải, 22
Kinh prejudices and stereotypes: "backwardness," 6–7, 9, 35, 59, 126; "barbarism," 9, 13, 146, 168; development programs, effects on, 37–39; of Hmong as *phi*, 29–30; marginality and, 169; sin conceptions and, 146
kinship connections: convert-nonconvert solidarity and, 137; Hmong missionaries and, 61–62; visits to Vietnam in search of separated relatives, 63–64. *See also* ethnic ties, Hmong missionaries and
Kunreuther, Laura, 173n11

L

Land Reform campaigns and development programs, state: Building New Economic Zones, 172n6; Clearing the Wilderness, 32; Democratic Reform, 31; Fixed Cultivation and Settlement, 31–32, 35, 37–38; Kinh condescension, effects of, 37–39; land law (1993), 33–34; Moving

millenarianism: Chao Fa (Lord of the Sky) millenarian revolts, 19, 87–91; in China, 8, 87–88; communism, relationship with, 91–94, 167–68; continuity and change in regard to, 165–66; evangelicalism, resonance with, 7–8; failed prophecy and, 50, 83; FEBC and, 86, 167; journey from millenarianism to Protestantism, 83–87; Miao groups overassociated with, 88; Mường Nhé incident, 95–97, 100–101, 126; Protestant Christianity, relationship with, 95–101; representation, problem of, 165; routinization of Christian faith, impacts on, 131; rumor of imminent return of Fua Tais/Vang Tsu, 46–47, 84–85; shared history of, between Kinh, Han, and Hmong, 165; in Vietnamese popular religion, 8. *See also* messianism

millennial capitalism, 94

Minh Mạng, Emperor, 125

missionaries, Catholic, 26–27

missions and missionaries, Protestant: as agents of historical change, 6–7; calling among US Hmong, 72–75; colonial vs. contemporary Hmong missionaries, 64–65; communism vs., 6; cultural preservation and, 76–77; double impact of missionary encounters, 75–81; the Great Mission, 54; homogeneous unit principle and, 65; kinship connections and, 61–62; modernity desire and, 13; Northern Evangelical Church, Hanoi, and, 50–51; remittance of faith and modernity, 80–81; shift from expansion to internalization after 2005, 145–46; state fears and blaming of, 15; Vietnamese communist state, negative viw of,

79. *See also* Far East Broadcasting Company

modernity: conversion, subjectivity, and, 10–13; *kevcai* ("ways") and, 58–59; Marxist-Leninist socialism and Evangelical Protestantism as competing paths to, 8–10; media and, 51; mediation of religion, assumptions about, 52; remittance of, 80–81

morality and moral narratives: Christianization of Hmong compared to Urapmin and, 143–44; conversion as transformation of moral consciousness, 140; courtship, 148–50; development program failures and, 34–37; eroticizing gaze of the Other and, 161; finger-pointing at non-Christian "sinful behavior," 159; Foucault on subjectification and technology of the self, 146, 157–58; Foucault's genealogy of ethics, 142; free will and self-control, 158; internalization of Christianity and, 144–45; marriage by capture, 150–54, 159; of modernity, 10–13; New Socialist Person and, 140, 161; "old" vs. "new" morality, 144, 160; *phi* (banditry, counter-revolutionary activity, or ethnic tensions), 27–31, 92–93; polygyny, 156–57; public confessions and, 158–59; religious law and sexuality as sinful, 146–48; Robbins on Urapmin Christianization (Papua New Guinea) and, 142–43; romantic love and freedom to marry, 154–56; sexual freedom vs. regulation, 148, 150; sin, conception of, 139–40, 161, 168; Tapp on traditional and urbanized morality, 141–42; tension between ethnic ties and religious community and, 143–44

No Concessions: The Life of Yap Thiam Hien, Indonesian Human Rights Lawyer, by Daniel S. Lev

The Buddha on Mecca's Verandah: Encounters, Mobilities, and Histories along the Malaysian-Thai Border, by Irving Chan Johnson

Dreaming of Money in Ho Chi Minh City, by Allison Truitt

Mapping Chinese Rangoon: Place and Nation among the Sino-Burmese, by Jayde Lin Roberts

The New Way: Protestantism and the Hmong in Vietnam, by Tâm T. T. Ngô